HISTORY OF INDIA

HISTORY OF INDIA

Edited by

A. V. WILLIAMS JACKSON, Ph. D., LL.D.

VOLUME VIII

From the Close of the Seventeenth Century to the Present Time

BY

Sir Alfred Comyn Lyall, P.C., K.C.B. D.C.L.

GYAN

Published by

GYAN

Gyan Publishing House
5, Ansari Road
Daryaganj, New Delhi-110002
Phone: 011-47034999, 9811692060
E-mail: books@gyanbooks.com

Distribution Network
gyanbooks.com
India, USA, Canada, UK, Australia, France

ISBN : 978-81-212-6772-4 (Set)
978-81-212-6765-6 (PB)

First Published, 1906

2nd Impression 2022

Printed at: Gyan Press, Delhi.

HISTORY OF INDIA (VOL. VIII)
Author: Sir Alfred Comyn Lyall

The Jain Temple, Mount Abu, Dilwara

At Dilwara on Mount Abu in Western India there are two of the oldest and finest specimens of temples consecrated to the Jain religion that are to be found anywhere in Hindustan. They date from the eleventh and twelfth centuries of our era, and fabulous sums of money were spent in erecting and adorning them. They are remarkable not only for their beauty and wonderful carving, but also for the picturesque scenery amid which they stand on a mountain-top five thousand feet above the level of the sea.

History of India

Edited by

A. V. WILLIAMS JACKSON, Ph. D., LL. D.

Professor of Indo-Iranian Languages in Columbia University

VOLUME VIII

From the Close of the Seventeenth Century to the Present Time

By

SIR ALFRED COMYN LYALL, P. C., K.C.B., D. C. L.

Author of "Asiatic Studies" and "Life of Warren Hastings"

INTRODUCTION BY THE EDITOR

A connected account of the principal events of Anglo-Indian history from the seventeenth century to the present time is given in this volume. The presentation, though concise, affords a broad view of the rise of British power in the East and makes clear the causes that led to England's supremacy. The first chapter reviews in a brief manner the main current of events in India's development prior to the seventeenth century and forms a convenient supplement to the two preceding volumes, and the succeeding chapters trace the chief historical movements, era by era, down to the present time.

The chronological sequence has been indicated throughout the work, but care has been taken not to overload the text with unnecessary dates. Lack of space compelled the author to forego treating several historic incidents, though important, because they have a less direct bearing upon the main theme — the expansion of British dominion in India. Considerations of space also forbade elaborating upon the details of certain well-known events, but room was gained in that way for the important chapter which brings the history down from the time of the Mutiny to the Durbar of King Edward, as well as for the concluding chapter on Britain's wider dominion in Asia.

The illustrative matter has been drawn from varied sources, and I am grateful for permission to reproduce one or two somewhat rare pictures. The ready collaboration of the author and the courtesy of his publisher in helping to make this volume a complete outline of India's later history down to the present time, is cordially appreciated.

A. V. WILLIAMS JACKSON.

AUTHOR'S PREFACE

The principal object of this book has been to sketch in outline the Rise of the British Dominion in India, and to relate the circumstances that led to the gradual extension of our territorial possessions up to 1858, when the Crown superseded the East India Company in the direct government of the country. It has also been thought expedient to give, toward the end of the volume, a short dissertation upon the nature and operation of the system of protectorates, by which the independent native states within India have been preserved under the superior control of the imperial government, and the foreign states or outlying tracts adjacent to the British frontiers have been brought under our political influence. But since the main purpose of the work is to present a connected view of the historical events and transactions, in Europe and in Asia, that combined to promote the foundation and to expedite the spread of the Dominion, the later stages of its expansion have been traversed in this narrative more rapidly than the earlier stages, which have perhaps attracted less general attention, and are not so commonly understood. Moreover, several remarkable incidents (as, for example, the famous trial of Nuncomar) have been omitted or barely mentioned, because they seemed to have little bearing upon the larger political issues with which this book is concerned, and also because a detailed account of them can be found in any history of British India.

In a supplementary chapter, now added, the course of Indian affairs, external and internal, from the date when the whole government was assumed by the Crown up to the present time, has been briefly surveyed. The character and important consequences of the foreign policy adopted by the British Government during this period has been explained; and some attempt has been made to review the constitutional changes and legislative measures that have been introduced in the last fifty years for the improvement of our interior administration and for the welfare of our fellow subjects in India.

A. C. LYALL.

June, 1907.

INTRODUCTION

The narrative of the acquisition of British India forms no more than an episode in the annals of the English nation. It is therefore not unnatural that historians, being mainly intent upon European affairs, should usually be satisfied with treating the foundation of a great Oriental empire by an English trading company as a marvellous and almost incomprehensible stroke of national good fortune. To those, however, who carefully follow the course and connection of events that led up to this magnificent result, and who bear in mind that foreign commerce is the life-blood of a maritime people, and that, for two centuries at least, the whole policy of England has been mainly directed toward the increase of her sea-power and the enlargement of her foreign commerce—insomuch that, as Sir H. Parnell has said, almost all our wars during the eighteenth century were virtually waged on behalf of that commerce—the fact that India has been the great prize of continuous success in naval war and trading adventure will not appear astonishing, and certainly not inexplicable. The object of this short treatise is not only to give a concise account of the rise of British dominion in India, but also to explain it by tracing rapidly the causes and convergent influences that brought about so remarkable a conclusion.

It is a matter of general remark that Anglo-Indian history, when related at length, is tedious and confusing. This is partly due to unfamiliarity with outlandish names and places, but chiefly to its essential character. The history, like the annals of almost all Oriental states, is mainly concerned, up to very recent times, with military operations, which in India seldom rise above the level of desultory fighting, and with that class of politics that consists largely of revolts, conspiracies, dynastic contests, and the ordinary incidents of a struggle for existence among rival despots.

In Asia there is no scope for examining the growth of institutions or the development of civil polity or the forming of nations; the famous men are all either able tyrants (in the Greek sense) or successful men of war; the type of civilization is uniform and stationary; the spirit of nationality, where it exists, is in its most elementary stage; the people of the great kingdoms known to history are an immense mixed multitude, broken up into tribal or religious groups, and united under one leadership by force or accident. At the present moment every great country in Asia is governed by an alien race or foreign dynasty that has come in by conquest; there is no general identity of language or of religion between the rulers and the mass of their subjects; they accordingly accept changes of government with indifference; they have no inveterate antipathy to the domination of foreigners. The Indian people were, from the beginning, so far from objecting to the English dominion in India that they co-operated willingly in promoting it.

Nevertheless, the existing relations between India and England constitute a political situation unprecedented in the world's history. The two countries are far distant from each other and in different continents; they present the strongest contrasts of race and religion. There is no previous example of the acquisition and successful government of such a dependency, so immense in extent and population, at such a distance from the central power. A state that is distinctly superior to its neighbours in the arts of war and government has often expanded into a great empire. In Europe the Romans once united under an extensive dominion and still wider ascendency a number of subject provinces, client kingdoms, protected allies, races, and tribes, by a system of conquest and an administrative organization that anticipated in many salient features our methods of governing India. But the Roman dominions were compact and well knit together by solid communications. The Romans were masters of the whole Mediterranean littoral, and their capital, whether at Rome or Constantinople, held a central and commanding position. Then at the present time we see Russia holding down Northern Europe with one foot, and Central Asia with the other. She is the first power that has succeeded so completely in throwing down the barriers which have hitherto divided the East from the West, as to found a colossal dominion in the heart of both continents.

But with the Roman, Russian, and all other historical empires the mass of their territory has been accumulated by advancing step after step along the land from the central starting-point, making one foothold sure before another was taken, firmly placing one arch of the viaduct before another was thrown out, allowing no interruption of territorial coherence from the centre to the circumference. This was not so in the case of the Indian empire. During the time when the English were establishing their predominance in India, and long afterwards, England was separated from India by thousands of miles of sea; the Atlantic and Indian oceans lay between. The government of the English in India may thus be said to present a unique instance of the dominion over an immense alien people in a distant country having been acquired entirely by gradual expansion from a base on the sea.

Of the political changes introduced during the last one hundred and fifty years by the overflow of Europe into Asia, the acquisition of all India and Burma by the English has hitherto been incomparably the greatest; although the steady advance of Russia, pushing forward her steel wedges into the central regions, is fraught with no less momentous import to the destinies of the continent. But while Russia has been laboriously following the well-known and well-worn routes of conquest by land through the central steppes of Asia, the

English have reached South Asia swiftly and securely by the open waterways. And thus it has come to pass that, whereas all previous conquests of India have been made from the mountains southward to the sea, the English have acquired their dominion by an expansion from the sea northward to the mountains. It need hardly be observed that this very remarkable exploit could only have been performed by virtue of great naval strength and superiority.

In the following pages dealing with the rise and expansion of British dominion in India some attempt is made to sketch the preliminary events and predisposing conditions that attracted the maritime nations of Europe into the field of competition for predominance in India, and to explain the combination of direct effort and favourable circumstances to which England in the eighteenth century owed her success.

CONTENTS

CHAPTER		PAGE
I.	Early Competition for Indian Commerce	1
II.	Influence and Connection of Politics in Europe and Asia	35
III.	Consolidation of the English East India Company	56
IV.	The French and English East India Companies	75
V.	The French in India under Dupleix	103
VI.	The Second French War	136
VII.	The Conquest of Bengal	156
VIII.	The Situation in Bengal	176
IX.	The Marathas and Mysore	198
X.	Administrative Organization	216
XI.	The Governor-Generalship of Warren Hastings	237
XII.	The Interval between Hastings and Cornwallis	265
XIII.	The Administration of Lord Cornwallis	281
XIV.	The Governor-Generalship of Lord Wellesley	306
XV.	The Stationary Period	343
XVI.	The Governor-Generalship of Lord Hastings	363
XVII.	Completion of Dominion	385
XVIII.	India under the Crown	427
XIX.	The British Dominion in Asia	469

LIST OF ILLUSTRATIONS

PAGE

The Jain Temple, Mount Abu, Dilwara . . . . *Frontispiece*
An Indian Decorative Design 1
Aden from the Arab Cemetery 2
Constantinople at the End of the Seventeenth Century 7
Queen Elizabeth knighting Sir Francis Drake on board the "Golden Hind" at Deptford, April 4, 1581 9
The Moghul Mosque at Fathpur-Sikri 16
Boats on the Persian Gulf 20
The Hugli River at Barrackpur 24
The Old East India House (1726–1796) 28
Bombay in 1773 31
Bird's-eye View of Trincomali 37
Mountain Scenery in the Himalayas 40
Sivaji on the March 43
The Lake of Utakamand in the Nilgiri Hills, Southern India 49
Peasants drawing Water 54
A Cart at Madras 56
Matharan, a Hill-station near Bombay in Western India 58
The Great Temple of Boro-Budur in Java 64
The Old East India House (1796–1858) 67
The Nizam's Capital, Haidarabad 71
A Corner of the Divan-i-Khas at Amber 76
Arms of the New East India Company 81
A Water Scene near Garrett, Java 87
A Pagoda at Pondicherri 92
Mandhata Island in the Narbada River 97
The Colombo Breakwater, Ceylon 105
A Scene in Pondicherri 110
The Main Gateway of the Temple at Tanjore 115
The Rock of Trichinopoli 119
A Monolithic Temple at Mahabalipur on the Southeast Coast . . . 122
A Raja of India Receiving a Representative of France 127
Body-guard of a Native Prince 132

PAGE

The Temple Tank at Tirupati 138
Brahmans of Bengal 141
Military Practice at Old Fort Jhansi 146
An Indian Native Ruler 149
The Sacred Bull at Mysore 154
Shah Sutlaj Mosque at Multan in Sind 157
A Sikh Warrior 161
The Government House and Treasury, Calcutta, from the Old Course . 165
The Black Hole of Calcutta 166
An Indian Mohammedan Helmet 169
Shivary Hills near Salem in Southern India 173
A Native Boat of Bengal 177
The Great Mosque at Kalbargah in Haidarabad 181
Lord Clive 185
The Jami' Masjid at Lucknow 189
A Mohammedan Tomb at Lahore 193
The Residency at Lucknow 201
Mountain Tribes of the Afghan Border 205
The Old Palace at Bhartpur 209
A Temple near Tinnevelli in the Madras Presidency 213
A Native Indian Prince and His Court, with Two Europeans . . . 217
The Fort of Chengalpat 223
A Mountain Road at Mahableshwar, in the Bombay Presidency . . . 227
Simla, the Summer Seat of the British Government 230
Victoria Station, Bombay 232
Katkari Natives on the Western Ghats 235
Warren Hastings, Governor-General of Bengal 239
Raghunath Rao 245
The Great Cave at Elephanta, near Bombay 248
A Castle on the Barwa Sagar, Gwalior 253
Hilt of Tippu's Sword 256
Some of Tippu's Forces 258
Umbrella Tree and Granite Boulder at Bellary in the Madras Presidency . 263
Cenotaph of a Native Ruler at Jaipur 268
Lord Cornwallis 273
A Village God in the Bombay Presidency 277
The Ghat Temple, Cawnpur 278
Tippu's Tomb at Seringapatam 284
An Action at Seringapatam 287
Tomb of the Sindhias, at Lashkar 290
A Street-corner in Bhopal 294
The Attack on the Sialkot Mutineers by Gen. Nicholson's Irregular Cavalry, July 12, 1857 300
The Jami' Masjid, or Great Mosque, at Delhi 308
The Atal Tower at Amritsar 315
The Residency at Lucknow 322
A Mosque at Aligarh 328
Gen. Havelock's Attack on Nana Sahib at Fathpur 334

PAGE

The Royal Palace at Baroda 337
The Kali Ghat, Calcutta 344
The Hugli River at Calcutta 347
Ranjit Singh's Samadh at Lahore 353
Site of Ranjit Singh's Encampment near Rupur, on the Sutlaj 356
A Temple at Gwalior 360
Bakhlawar Singh's Cenotaph at Ulwar in Rajputana 365
Ruins of Tyre, the Ancient Phœnician City on the Mediterranean 369
A Nepalese Shield 376
Peasants of Mahableshwar, near Satara, in the Bombay Presidency 381
An Indian Rupee of Queen Victoria's Reign 385
Burmese Warriors 387
The Golden Throne of Ranjit Singh 391
Lord William Bentinck 393
On the Northern Indian Border 396
The Relief of Lucknow by Sir Henry Havelock 400
Sir Charles Napier 405
The Battle of Miani, at which Napier defeated the Amirs 407
The Battle of Mudki, at which Hardinge defeated the Sikhs 411
The Battle of Aliwal, in which Smith was Victorious over the Sikhs . . 415
Finding the Colours of the 24th Regiment after the Battle of Chilianwala 418
The Fort and Harbour of Karachi 420
The Charge of the Highlanders before Cawnpur, under General Havelock . 424
Sir John Lawrence 427
Mountain Passes near Quetta in Baluchistan 435
Abd-ar-Rahman, Amir of Afghanistan 442
The Golden Monastery, Mandalay, Burma 446
The Massacre at Cawnpur 451
The "Slaughter-House," where the Cawnpur Massacre took place . . 454
Detail from the Hall of a Hundred Columns at Conjevaram 462
The Durbar of 1902 465
George Frederick, Prince of Wales, etc. 468
Submission of the Maharaja Dhulip Singh to Sir Henry Hardinge, at Kanha Cushwa 470
View of Muscat from the Housetops 474
Reception of General Outram and Staff at the Durbar of the Raja of Travancore 478
Major-General Sir Henry Havelock 481
A Pillar at Tirumala Nayaka, Madura 484
The Tilo-Milo Pagoda at Pagan, Burma 487
A Sacred Pool at Tiruparankundram near Madura 491
The Ganesa Temple at Tiruvenamalai in South Arkot 495

AN INDIAN DECORATIVE DESIGN.

CHAPTER I

EARLY COMPETITION FOR INDIAN COMMERCE

FROM time immemorial the trade of Europe with the rich and productive countries of Southeastern Asia, particularly with India and the islands of the Malay Archipelago, has been the most lucrative branch of the world's commerce. It has been the object of fierce and persistent competition by sea and land among the more enterprising and civilized European states, of a contest that increased with the spirit of adventure and the desire for wealth; and it has made the fortune of every city or nation that has successively obtained the largest share of it. For nearly eighteen centuries, from the days of the Ptolemies almost until the Portuguese rounded the Cape of Good Hope, Alexandria was an emporium and half-way station of the sea-borne trade.

The Roman emperors, who were deeply interested

in developing the prosperity of Egypt, spared no pains to monopolize the commercial navigation of the Red Sea. They sent more than one naval expedition against the southwest coast of Arabia with the object of seizing Aden (then, as now, a most important station) and

ADEN FROM THE ARAB CEMETERY.

of wresting the Indian trade from the hands of the Arabs. In fact, they attempted, though unsuccessfully, to acquire very much the same position in those waters as that which the English have at last succeeded in establishing after an interval of sixteen centuries. Although the Roman navy was not strong enough to dislodge the Arabs, yet the direct European maritime traffic with the East in the time of the Flavian emperors took almost exactly the route into which, after some wide aberrations, it seems at length again to have settled down—that is, the route by Egypt, Suez, and Aden across the Indian Ocean to the ports on the Western coast of India.

The jealousy that was excited in Rome by the rich and enterprising merchants of Palmyra, who were diverting the stream of Eastern traffic into an overland route from the Persian Gulf up the Euphrates to Syria, is said to have been one reason for the destruction of that flourishing city. In this manner the Roman empire, while at its zenith, obtained a wider command over the main channels of Asiatic trade than has ever since been held by any European power except England; and England has also the great advantage that she not only commands the channels but, by her dominion in India, possesses the largest source of this mighty commercial stream.

The outpouring of the Arab tribes under Mohammed's successors upset the civilized government to which the routes by the Red Sea and the Persian Gulf owed their security. When the conquests of Islam had overflowed Egypt and Syria, Constantinople became for a time the chief storehouse of the Levant, and the main current of trade with India and China took the line across Central Asia to the Black Sea, avoiding the countries recently overrun by the Mohammedans. "The commerce of Europe," as Professor Finlay remarks, "centred at Constantinople in the eighth and ninth centuries more completely than it has ever done since in any one city"; the Greek navy was the largest then in existence.

But misrule, fiscal oppression, and foreign invasions ruined the Byzantine empire. As Constantinople declined, Venice and Genoa, the cities of the inland sea which lay beyond the desolating range of Asiatic conquest, rose into splendid prominence. It was the spirit of very short-sighted commercial jealousy that actuated the Venetians when, having contracted to convey the armies of the Fourth Crusade across the Mediterranean to Egypt, they insisted on an expedition against Constantinople, which was taken by the Latins in 1204. The blow fatally weakened the Greek power in the East, which henceforward opposed less and less resistance to the invading Turkish hordes. In the meantime the Italian cities had become the principal agents for the importation into Europe of the precious commodities of Asia; insomuch that in the fifteenth century the Venetians appeared literally to "hold the gorgeous East in fee," for they were not far from possessing the whole of this enormously profitable business.

At the end of that century two capital events in the annals of the world's commerce occurred suddenly and almost simultaneously—the discovery of America and the doubling of the Cape of Good Hope. Their effect was to give vast extension to the sea-borne trade with Asia, to turn its main volume into new channels by opening out direct communication by ships between South Asia and the countries bordering on the Atlantic, and to augment very greatly the supply of gold and silver for exchange against Asiatic products. The exploration of the globe, eastward and westward, produced navigation on a grand scale; and the superior skill, audacity, and capital of Europeans have ever since secured them a monopoly of the carrying trade on all the high seas.

The contest among the nations of Europe for superiority in this new field of enterprise soon began in earnest. When Pope Alexander Borgia issued his Bull dividing the whole undiscovered non-Christian world between Spain and Portugal, he awarded India to the latter power, so that the Portuguese, who had been pushing their dominion southward along the West African coast throughout the fifteenth century, at once took a much wider flight. They proceeded with ruthless energy to establish their fortified settlements on the Indian coast, to seize points of vantage in the Indian Ocean, and to beat off all attempts of the Mohammedan sovereigns at Alexandria and Constantinople to resist European predominance in those waters.

It is doubtless fortunate that even Solyman the Magnificent, in the height of his glory, failed in his efforts to expel the Portuguese from the Indian Ocean; for his success might have been disastrous to Eastern Christendom. If the Turkish Sultan, who at the opening of the sixteenth century was supreme in the Red Sea and the Persian Gulf, and whose fleets swept the Mediterranean, could have kept the Indian trade to its ancient and direct course through Egypt and Syria, the wealth that he might thus have secured must have added prodigiously to the force of his arms by sea and land. A colossal military empire upon the Bosphorus, commanding the avenues of Asiatic trade, might even in our own days overawe half Europe, and would have been irresistible three hundred years ago.

Yet Venice foresaw so clearly that the diversion of trade to the ocean route would be her death-blow, that she vigorously supported the Turkish Sultan, though in vain. When Benbo, the Venetian envoy at Lisbon, wrote that he had seen vessels return to that port from Asia loaded with Indian goods, his government became aware that the most important branch of their commerce was in danger of being cut off. By the end of the sixteenth century that inestimable privilege, the chief control of Eastern commerce in European waters, had passed for ever out of the hands of the Italian cities, whose gradual commercial decay from that epoch showed plainly where lay the mainspring of their prosperity and political expansion.

From the shores of the Mediterranean and the Black Sea, from Alexandria and Constantinople, from Venice and Genoa, the rich trade of India with Europe was now transferred to the ocean-going peoples of Western Europe. It was cut off in the Indian seas and almost monopolized for a time by Portugal, whose sovereigns improved their opportunity with remarkable activity, sending out fleets to range over the whole coast of South Asia from the Persian Gulf to Ceylon. Nevertheless their period of triumphant prosperity was short, for in 1580 all the strength and soul of Portuguese enterprise were crushed out of her by annexation to Spain. The Spaniards threw away their opportunity; they found it easier to mine the precious metals in America than to make long voyages to India; and instead of using their treasure they tried to hoard it.

From the days of the Romans up to our own time, the Indian trade has drained the gold and silver of

CONSTANTINOPLE AT THE END OF THE SEVENTEENTH CENTURY.

Europe; but the Spaniards were under the delusion, so long prevalent in Europe, that to export bullion is to exhaust a country's wealth; so that their commerce with Asia was fatally hampered by strict prohibitions against sending the precious metals abroad. This false mercantile theory must have materially retarded the expansion of the foreign trade of Europe; for we find the East India Company in the seventeenth century constantly accused of impoverishing England by their despatches of bullion. It was indeed long before any but the maritime trading classes, to whom the needs and practice of distant commerce brought real experience, understood that the precious metals, no less than quicksilver, must find their own natural level, or must fall in value.

By the end of the sixteenth century, therefore, the sea-borne trade of Asia with Europe had passed away from the Mediterranean cities, from Alexandria and Constantinople, from Venice and Genoa, and was being rapidly taken up by the maritime populations of the Atlantic and the North Sea. The direct waterway had been discovered; commercial competition among the Western nations was beginning; and the opening of sea communication established new points of contact between Europe and Asia, slowly but surely growing into a close connection that has affected the subsequent history of both continents, has largely influenced the politics of the maritime powers, and has determined the whole destiny of India.

When Queen Elizabeth recognized the independence of the Dutch republic (declared in 1578) and thus became committed to war with Spain, the united naval forces of England and Holland were directed against the Asiatic settlements of Portugal, which were then, as has been said, under the Spanish crown. The desperate struggle of the United Provinces against Philip II exposed Spanish vessels to the vindictive hostility of the Protestant traders in Eastern waters; and the great victory over the Spanish Armada in 1588 gave confidence to England. In a memorial addressed to the queen in the following year, the English merchants ask for license and encouragement to their project of pushing forward adventures in the East Indies. Such a trade, they say, " would by degrees add to the shipping, seamen, and naval force of the kingdom, in the same manner as it has increased the Portuguese fleets."

The Spaniards, however, took such grave umbrage

QUEEN ELIZABETH KNIGHTING SIR FRANCIS DRAKE ON BOARD THE "GOLDEN HIND" AT DEPTFORD, APRIL 4, 1581.

at the preparations made in England to interfere with their East Indian monopoly, that in 1599 the granting of a charter to the English Company was postponed for eighteen months by Elizabeth's Privy Council, who were at the moment negotiating peace with Spain. In 1600, however, upon renewed solicitations from the Adventurers for the East Indian voyage, a charter was given by the Crown to the London Company for fifteen years. This deed of incorporation stands as a historic monument, commemorating the inception of a great enterprise; it records the origin and indicates the direction of that great current of Asiatic trade whose ever rising flow during three centuries has brought wealth and power to the English nation.

At this period, moreover, the common right of all nations to trade freely and peacefully with Asia, though it was asserted by the Dutch as against the Spanish monopoly, was in fact no more recognized than a common international right to cultivate or colonize. Each country was striving to seize and appropriate the largest possible share of this profitable commerce, to the forcible exclusion of all interlopers; they were all contending for complete and masterful possession; they were conquering by water as they might be conquering by land, and fiercely attacking any intruder upon their trading ground as if he were an invader of their territory.

At the end of the sixteenth century the Spaniards claimed the whole right of trade with the East Indies as part of their sovereignty; the Indian seas were their territorial waters; they permitted no European port except their own to exist upon the Indian seaboard. "The Indies," they declared, "East and West, are our house, privately possessed by us for more than a hundred years; and no one has a right to enter without our permission;" they claimed over these vast regions the same sovereign jurisdiction that England affirms over her Indian empire. The Spanish President of the Council of the Indies told the British ambassador plainly "that in coercions and punishments to restrain access to these countries, he had an inclination rather to cruelty than to clemency," and that the case for free trade was far different there from elsewhere, because these dominions were Spanish by the rule of nations. In 1605 the Spaniards threatened with the severest penalties any Hollander presuming to trade in the East Indies; but the war between Spain and her revolted provinces was carried on in Asia as bitterly as in Europe, and largely accelerated the downfall of the old Portuguese domination on the Indian seaboard. There was some desperate fighting in the Malacca Straits, and in the China Sea, with merciless slaughter after a defeat.

The question of the Eastern trade was the most difficult and obstinately disputed point in the negotiations which ended with Spain's recognition of Holland's independence. In 1607, the Spanish king offered to renounce his claim of sovereignty over the United Provinces if the Dutch would abandon their navigation to the East Indies. But the Dutch treated this as the most valuable property of their own State; they knew the Indian commerce to be the chief stay and subsistence of naval dominion in either country; they saw that while they would be ruined by resigning it, by retaining it they should keep the power of retaliating upon Spain in Asia for oppression or injuries in Europe. They insisted so firmly on their right to trade freely in the East Indies that the Spaniards at last gave way upon the point, though it was never conceded openly.

But although the Dutch asserted trade liberties against Spain, their own policy was to establish the strictest monopoly. Between 1597 and 1600, the Dutch ships had first rounded the Cape of Good Hope into Asiatic waters, where they were very fiercely handled by the Spanish forces in that quarter. In 1602, the Universal East India Company had been founded in Holland, with exclusive privilege of trading east of the Cape and west of the Magellan Straits, with a great capital subscribed by all the provinces, with full power to make peace and war in the name of the United Provinces, to levy troops, and to appoint generals. Strong fleets were sent out with orders to expel the Spanish and Portuguese from the Spice Islands and the Indian coasts, to found settlements, and in fact to annex the trade to Holland precisely as they might annex an enemy's province.

In the beginning these proceedings were taken in co-operation with the English, who now make their first substantial appearance, as represented by a Company, in the field of Asiatic commerce. But the two nations soon began to quarrel in Asia, though in Europe they preserved amity, and in 1611 the London merchants prayed for protection and redress, representing that the Hollanders were driving them out of all places of traffic in the East Indies. When a joint commission was appointed to settle matters, the Dutch challenged the sole trade in spices, nor could any arrangement be mediated. It is worth noticing, as showing the value of the trade even at that early time, that in 1615 the Dutch were reported to have fifty-one ships in the East Indies, with a stock of £900,000 sterling, and £400,000 taken up at interest. The English Company paid £14,000 customs in 1615 for the cargo of two ships, and in 1616 one ship alone was valued at more than £140,000. A proposal by Holland that the Dutch and English should form one Joint Stock Company, divide their spheres of traffic, and combine forces in order wholly to drive Spain out of the East Indies was rejected, partly because James I still leaned toward a Spanish alliance. Thus all attempts to arrest or adjust the earliest disputes of England and Holland over their respective limits and shares in such an enormously lucrative trade naturally failed; indeed they served only to complicate the impending quarrel.

Upon only one point the two Protestant nations agreed cordially—in their inveterate hostility to the Spanish and Portuguese. They spared no pains to beat off and expel from the coast of India the Portuguese, who were, in 1613-1615, in very bad odour with the Moghul government for having seized a great ship in which the emperor's mother was the principal shareholder. The correspondence of the English Company at this period is filled with reports of fierce battles with the Portuguese, in one of which, at Surat, for example, between four and five hundred "Portugals" were slain, burned, and drowned. This rather sanguinary business is mentioned in an ordinary letter, which, without change of tone, goes on to give the prices of commodities and the colours of cloths that will not keep fast in an Indian climate.

By 1615 the trade of Portugal had, we are told, infinitely decayed; and the Spanish government showed very little concern at the rapid impoverishment of that kingdom. In Holland, on the contrary, the Republic looked upon its East India trade as "a high point of state," and assisted the Company with great sums of money. But the substitution of Dutchmen for Portuguese as our rivals in this part of the world was by no means an advantage to us. Their estrangement from England, originally caused by the wavering policy of the first two Stuarts, who leaned first toward Spain and afterwards toward France, was undoubtedly fostered by growing commercial jealousies. Thenceforward, throughout the seventeenth century, the annals of East Indian affairs record a continuous persevering contest between the English and Dutch for advantage in the Indian trade, and for possession of the settlements that were necessary to its existence. The Dutch had gradually annexed most of the principal Portuguese settlements; they asserted paramount European power in all those seas and islands; so that they constantly came into sharp collision with the English, who were still weak in those regions, and whose merchant adventurers were ill supported by the vacillating and unpopular government of James I and his son Charles.

It should be understood that the term "East Indies," according to the nomenclature of those days, comprised not only India proper, but also the countries on the east side of the Bay of Bengal, the Straits of Malacca, Java, Siam, and all the Spice Islands further eastward in the Java and Chinese seas, such as the Celebes and the Moluccas. With China and Japan also a very active commercial intercourse had been established by the English Company, something under 100 per cent. being reckoned a reasonable rate of profit on sales.

In the first half of the seventeenth century the traffic with the Spice Islands was by far the most important and profitable; and from this branch of the general East India trade the Dutch were determined to exclude us; for indeed upon this commerce the prosperity of their state and people largely depended. They did, in fact, so thwart and embarrass the operations of the English Company in the waters of Eastern Asia, beyond the Malacca Straits, that the English gradually withdrew from many of their stations in that region, and shifted their trade more and more, as time went on, toward the coasts of India and the countries adjacent. From this tendency of the English to concentrate their business upon the ports and factories of the Indian mainland, and to cultivate relations with the Moghul Empire, we may deduce some ulterior consequences of much importance in regard to the course and character of their subsequent expansion.

In this manner began the contest for valuable markets that gave so strong an impulse, at this period, to the system of chartered companies; for the early traders in Asiatic waters had to fight their own way and hold their own ground; they could expect little or no help in Asia from their own governments, and nothing but merciless hostility from their European rivals. Trade was more valuable, to the maritime folk, than

THE MOGHUL MOSQUE AT FATHPUR-SIKRI.

territory, and commerce than conquest. But traffic with distant lands could not be carried on without taking up stations and arming ships, since the understanding among European nations was that regular diplomatic relations practically did not extend beyond certain well-known lines of longitude.

According to a treaty made between France and

Spain in 1598, in the regions westward of the Canary Islands *tout serait à la force*; and although Spain and Portugal claimed immense jurisdictions, political and ecclesiastic, in the East, yet these were of a nature too impalpable and fluctuating to be acknowledged distinctly by international law. The Chartered Companies therefore represented a device, invented to suit these conditions of existence, for extending commerce and for securing it by territorial appropriations, without directly pledging a government to answer for the acts of its subjects. The charter expressed the delegation of certain sovereign powers for distinct purposes; it amounted from one point of view to a license for private war; and the system has since had a long, eventful, and curious history, which is even yet by no means ended.

The point to be observed is that this system, under which the foundations of the British Empire of India were laid, was something very different from the kind of scrambling haphazard adventure to which the establishment of that empire is by common imagination so often ascribed. On the contrary, it provided, in the hands of a free and wealthy people, a very powerful instrument of colonial and commercial expansion. The prize in dispute was a share or, if possible, the monopoly of the commerce between Western Europe and all the ports of Asia from the Red Sea to China and Japan. The early records of the East India Company show that along the whole accessible coast line of the Asiatic continent and among the islands, at every point where trading could be done—on the Arabian seaboard, in the Persian Gulf, from the western side of India to Northeastern China—the European nations were now contending vigorously for commercial profits and privileges.

The value of the prize for which they were competing was even then perfectly well known; and subsequent history has proved that the wealth, liberties, and political predominance at home of the contending nations depended considerably on their failure or success. It was the foreign imports that brought the revenue which maintained the great fleets and armies of Spain; it was maritime trade that fed the stubborn power of resistance displayed by the Dutch Republic; and the greatness of England has been manifestly founded upon her world-ranging commerce. By far the most important branch of sea-borne traffic was, in the seventeenth century, the exchange of goods with Asia, and each national government took part, directly or indirectly, in the struggle for it. The first maritime explorers from the despotically governed states of Spain and Portugal seized lands and claimed navigation rights in the name of their Crown, which at once treated all these captures as increments to its complete sovereignty.

Between the Dutch Republic and its East India Company the connection was exceedingly close; although a formal distinction was always maintained. In 1618 this Company, as we learn from an English report, was composed of the great majority of the Privy

Council, the nobility, judges, and gentry, and was furnished with an assured stock of £1,600,000. When, in 1617, the English East India Company raised its second Joint Stock, the sum of £1,620,040 was at once subscribed in London; and the records of 1622 state that goods bought in India for £356,288 had produced £1,914,600 in England. Here were two great commercial associations with power and resources quite equal to those of the minor states at that period.

But while the state of Holland was, so to speak, incorporate in its Company, the English adopted from the beginning, and preserved up to the end of the eighteenth century, a system under which the state held a position not unlike that of partner *en commandite*, taking no risks, acknowledging very slight responsibility, interfering occasionally to demand a share of profits or to lay a heavy fine upon charter renewals, and assisting the Company only when such a course accorded with the general political interests of the nation. Armed with a valuable monopoly, and left to their own devices, the English Company relied not so much upon state aid as upon their own wealth and energy; they underwent some perilous vicissitudes and performed some remarkable exploits.

The extent to which unofficial war was practised, from the sixteenth to the eighteenth century, by the roving nations of Europe, is perhaps hardly appreciated in this age of international law and ubiquitous diplomacy. If English merchants in India or the Persian Gulf had been obliged to refer home for remedy of grievances or settlement of disputes with Dutch, French, or Portuguese, they would have been very soon exterminated. They did no such thing; they took to their own weapons, and their military operations were often upon a considerable scale. In 1622 there was formal peace between Portugal (which then belonged

BOATS ON THE PERSIAN GULF.
From Edwin Lord Weeks's Through Persia and India.
(Copyright, 1895, by Harper & Brothers.)

to Spain) and England; but the English East India Company was at bitter war in the Indian Ocean with the Portuguese, who had disturbed its trade and molested the Honourable Company's ships. So the English Company fitted out a small fleet at Surat, and sent it up the Persian Gulf with orders to assist Shah Abbas, the Persian king, in turning the Portuguese out of the island of Ormuz, which they had held for a century, and which gave them exclusive command of the

Gulf. The business was done, with the aid of the Persians, very thoroughly; there was a regular bombardment of the fortress, and a naval action with the Portuguese royal fleet, until the island was surrendered, the fortifications razed, and the Portuguese garrison transported to Goa.

We do not hear that Portugal made any serious remonstrance against these proceedings, which would certainly startle modern diplomacy; but it stands on record that James I and the Lord High Admiral (the Duke of Buckingham) exacted large sums of money from the Company as the royal share of the profits. Another heavy fine was again demanded by Buckingham from the Company before he would permit them to despatch a fleet for the protection of their commerce against Portuguese reprisals. Probably the English might have claimed to set off against the affair at Ormuz other similar irregularities on the part of the Portuguese; for among the nations then engaged in the East India trade there was little scruple about ways and means of dealing with rivals.

But the Dutch, though formally friends and allies of England, soon became much more dangerous enemies in Asia than the Portuguese, and were now inflicting heavy damage on the British East Indian trade which the English Company was by no means disposed to endure. The two Companies were rapidly drifting into a rather ferocious war, quite uncontrolled by international law or military usage, in which little quarter was given and nothing spared that might extirpate the enemy. Both sides possessed armed ships and fortified stations; but although the Dutch had many more forts and a much larger territory than the English, their policy of seizing all the points of vantage had the drawback that it involved them in quarrels with the native chiefs and crippled their capital by heavy military charges. After protracted negotiations, however, a treaty was at last arranged between Holland and England in 1619 on the basis of mutual restitutions and compensations. The news, we learn from the correspondence, reached India just in time to prevent "a bloody encounter between eleven of our best ships and seventeen of the Dutch."

This treaty, which was made for twenty years, actually lasted less than twenty months, and seems to have been little regarded in the East Indies, where the necessities of commercial competition went on multiplying disputes and reciprocal violence, until one particularly atrocious outrage brought matters to a climax. The massacre by the Dutch of almost all the English at Amboyna in the Moluccas in 1623 was a piece of cruel iniquity that bred long and fierce resentment against Holland among the English merchants and mariners of that generation, and heated the animosities that broke out later between the two nations in Europe.

The preponderance of the Dutch in the Spice Islands, and their dangerous enmity, had undoubtedly much weight in diverting English trade toward the Asiatic continent, and thus in making the factories on the Indian seacoast the principal object of our attention. On the western side of India the English had settled first at Surat, in 1612, under a *farmān* of the Moghul government, with special privileges procured by Sir Thomas Roe's embassy from James I to the Emperor Jahangir in 1615 - 1618. In 1630 the English and Portuguese fleets fought a respectable battle in that roadstead, without prejudice to international relations at home. And as the Dutch were now making virulent attacks upon the possessions of Portugal in India and Ceylon, her power had by this time fallen into a rapid decline. When, in 1640, she recovered her independence as a kingdom, she made some feeble attempts to hold her ground in Asia; but after the Treaty of Münster in 1648, which limited her Indian possessions, Portugal fell irremediably into the background.

In 1638 Surat became the English Company's chief establishment; and by 1643 it was established on the east coast at Masulipatam and Madras, with a factory up the Hugli River for the Bengal traffic. Their influence at the Moghul's court was substantially promoted by the deputation of Mr. Boughton, a surgeon in the East India Company's service, to Agra for the purpose of professionally treating the emperor, who afterwards appointed him physician to the household. By the middle of the seventeenth century, the Company was trading all along the southern seaboard of Asia from the Persian Gulf eastward to the borders of China; and as the commercial operations of the Dutch took the same geographical range, the two nations were in close competition and incessant collision throughout this extensive line. But the quarrel at home between king and Parliament checked English enterprise at the fountainhead, for our government could lend only a weak and fluctuating support in disputes with foreign rivals; while Holland and even Portugal were actively backed by their respective governments, who gave the

THE HUGLI RIVER AT BARRACKPUR.

direct weight of national authority to all expeditions and annexations in the East.

As the English Company was thus virtually in the position of a private association contending against two sovereign powers, it is not surprising that toward the end of the civil war they were in very low water, while the Dutch had gained superiority over the English on the Indian coasts, were cutting off their trade with the Spice Islands, and treating them with the greatest arrogance everywhere. The State Papers of this time record incessant complaints of the "intolerable injuries, cruelty, insolency, and cunning circumventing projects" of the Dutch in the East Indies, who made no scruple about sending fleets with large bodies of soldiers to seize or expel foreign merchants and to occupy stations whenever it was their interest to do so.

The English Company was also much troubled by the encroachments of interlopers, or private independent traders, some of whom were little better than pirates, but for whose misconduct in Asiatic waters the Company was often called to account by the local authorities. In default of any diplomatic or consular relations between Europe and Asia, a responsible trading association, holding regular grants and licenses from the Moghul or his governors, was naturally regarded as representing the nationality to which it belonged, and had to suffer reprisals or pay indemnities for the misdeeds of its compatriots. Still graver consequences might follow offence given by the independent English merchantmen to the Portuguese or the Dutch, who thought little of sinking an intruding vessel, deliberately drowning the whole crew, or levelling an obnoxious factory.

Only a company supported by the state, with an exclusive trading charter, could command the capital, exert the strength, and maintain the consistent organization that was indispensable in those days, when English commerce had to fight its own battle against enemies who would have entirely expelled it from the great markets of the East. In these essential qualifications for success the Dutch excelled all other nations during the greater part of the seventeenth century. The whole Republic, as is observed by an English writer of the time, was virtually an association for the purposes of navigation and trade; the Dutch companies were connected organically with the constitution of the States-General. And since in Holland the people at large were merchants and mariners, their commercial policy was stronger, more stiffly resolute, and better supported than that of states ruled by a court and a landed aristocracy, whose aims and interests were diverse and conflicting.

It has been thought worth while to relate and explain, in some detail, the history of the East Indian trade during the first half of the seventeenth century, because the importance and magnitude of the public interests involved in it at that early stage have not been generally apprehended. In these transactions we may observe the precursory signs of that connection between European and Asiatic politics that has grown closer and has multiplied its points of contact during the last three hundred years. If it had been possible for one great seafaring nation to draw to itself all the sea-borne Asiatic commerce—as the Phœnicians seem to have once almost monopolized the Mediterranean trade—that commerce might have been carried on for a long time peaceably, with as little disturbance as was given by the overland trade to the countries through which it passed. But while the land routes traversed recognizable territorial jurisdictions, the waterways lay open to all, and when the various traders began to jostle each other in the Asiatic ports, the Dutch, English, and Portuguese fell out among themselves in the Eastern seas as naturally as Greeks, Italians, and Arabs quarrelled, two centuries earlier, over the same prize in the Mediterranean.

These quarrels affected, and were affected by, the changing course of politics during an age of incessant war in Europe; for while kings and ministers were already influenced by the interests of a trade that constantly aided their treasuries, the acts and relations of European rulers bore directly, then as now, on their foreign commerce. The persecution of the Reformers in Holland by Spain led to the foundation of the Dutch East India Company; the success of the Dutch stimulated English enterprise; and the long quarrel in the East Indies between these two Protestant nations not only diminished and for a time dissolved their natural connection, but also gave to early English enterprise in Asia its warlike character, its taste for armed independence, and latterly its policy of territorial acquisition imitated from the Dutch. Never before or since in the world's history has there been so much bloodshed over commerce as distinguished from colonization, for a very brief experience of the perils of East Indian adventure seems to have convinced the English that they must abandon the hope of peaceful trading in that part of the world. They are, however, justly entitled to the credit of having done their best to confine themselves to commerce throughout the seventeenth century, whereas Portugal and Holland began at once to seize territory. But the inevitable consequence of uncontrolled self-reliant competition among the European nations was to convert all their East Indian Companies into armed associations. How these armed associations were subsequently converted into political powers will be seen hereafter.

In the meantime, as the strength and stability of

THE OLD EAST INDIA HOUSE (1726-1796).

the Dutch Republic increased in Europe from the beginning of this century, their enterprise in Asia became bolder and more high-handed. During the Thirty Years' War, Holland was supported on the Continent by the Protestant States of Germany and by France against Austria and Spain, the two countries that menaced all Europe. Such an alliance, being peculiarly favourable to the security of Holland on the land, rendered her a very serious rival to England on the sea. The Dutch were throwing the English into the shade; they had founded their East Indian empire; they had made good a footing in Brazil; they had captured in West Indian waters the Spanish ships that carried a rich cargo from Mexico to Havana; they had annihilated the fleet of the Infanta Isabella. They were becoming masters of the narrow seas at home; they were threatening, with the aid of France, the Spanish Netherlands; and the English were feeling much alarm lest Holland and France together should possess themselves of the whole coast line over against England across the Channel.

These were the advantages that gave Holland pre-eminence in Asiatic commerce during the greater part of the seventeenth century. She had stripped Portugal of some of her most important possessions in the East and had fixed her trading-posts firmly in well-chosen places. Under Cromwell's vigorous rule, however, the English began to recover their position in the East Indies.

The jealousies, political and commercial, between the two Republics culminated in the war of 1651 - 1654, when East India merchants, whose grievances had formed one of the chief grounds of hostility, prayed for permission to fit out an armed fleet against the Dutch in Asia, who had been making depredations on the English shipping in Indian waters. In 1654 a peace was patched up upon payment of compensation for injuries, especially for the "bloodie business of Amboyna," and with the effect of defining the situation of the English on the Indian littoral.

Nevertheless, although the enmity and the encroachments of the Dutch in Asia by no means ceased, the proposals made to Cromwell for dissolving the Company's monopoly and throwing open the whole Asiatic trade were so tempting to a ruler who was in sore need of ready money that he was hardly dissuaded from it by the combined weight of the arguments and liberal subsidies of the London Company. Yet it was absolutely clear that free-traders in Asia would have fallen an easy prey to the common enemy, for the power of the Dutch was again on the increase. They now maintained large military and naval forces in the East Indies, obstructed our trade, harassed our agencies, and disregarded all treaties. They drove the English off the coast of Eastern Asia, seized Ceylon, blockaded Bantam—the Company's headquarters in Java—and once more tried to exterminate the English factories in the Spice Islands.

Meanwhile, trade was much disturbed, and the Company's settlements were put in jeopardy by the civil war that broke out in India among the sons of Shah Jahan in 1658 during that emperor's life. By 1660, however, Aurangzib's triumph over his brothers had restored tranquillity. The beginning of his long reign, full of importance to Anglo-Indian history, synchronizes with the Restoration of Charles II, an event which changed the political connections of England and materially affected our commercial system. The Company wanted more extensive powers, and Charles II wanted to obliterate from their existing charter the name of Cromwell; so he gave them a new charter, authorizing them to make peace and war with any non-Christian people, although in fact their only troublesome enemies belonged to Christendom.

Portugal now sought the English alliance in the hope of recovering some of her Eastern possessions that

BOMBAY IN 1773.
From an old print.

she had lost while under the Spanish yoke, or at least of defending against the Dutch what she had been able to retain. These negotiations brought us the valuable acquisition of the island of Bombay, which was ceded to England in 1661 as the pledge of an arrangement for a kind of defensive war against the Dutch in Asia. But since the Portuguese were as jealous of the English as they were afraid of the Dutch, some years passed before the English found themselves in quiet possession of the island; nor was it until 1669 that Bombay and St. Helena were granted in full property to the London Company.

In 1661 Charles II had granted to this Company by charter the entire English traffic in the East Indies, with license to coin money, administer justice, and punish interlopers; and he confirmed their authority to make war and peace with non-Christian states in those parts. He also adopted Cromwell's famous Navigation Law, which was devised to give British sailors and shipping a monopoly of the transport of goods interchanged with England, and was aimed chiefly at the Dutch, who were then the principal carriers of the sea-borne trade of Europe.

In this manner the commercial resources of England were formed, organized, and directed toward maintaining an equal contest against inveterate foes; nor can there be any doubt that trade monopolies were in those days essential to the existence of British commercial settlements in Asia. England then had no diplomatic representatives in non-Christian countries; the home governments paid no attention to the grievances of any single merchant or ship-master; and the Amboyna massacre is only one example of the reckless methods in use among commercial rivals in distant countries. Without large capital, an armament, and authority to use it, without some kind of rough jurisdiction over their countrymen in distant settlements, no mercantile association could preserve sufficient influence at home or security for their foreign stations and their ships at sea.

All these measures for strengthening the East India trade angered the Dutch, who were also alarmed by the sale of Dunkirk to France, which let the French into the narrow seas, and by the weakening of the Spanish barrier of the Netherlands between France and Holland. The quarrel with England over Eastern affairs became sharper and more virulent; for the Dutch were resolved to check and beat back the encroachment of the English on their Asiatic trade; and the English, on their side, were continually exasperated by the acts of violence committed against their traders in the East. In 1664 the French ambassador reported from London that England was ready to come to blows with the Hollanders, but it was then the policy of Louis XIV, who had just been induced by Colbert to launch the French East India Company, to preserve peace. He feared that if war broke out it would end by giving irresistible naval superiority to the nation that won, and as his navy was not ready, he was anxious to maintain a balance of naval power on the French coast. Nevertheless, the quarrel grew so bitter that war did begin in 1665, when the French king was reluctantly obliged to join the Dutch, being under treaty obligation to do so.

In short, at the beginning of the seventeenth century the desire to destroy the colonies and commerce of Spain and Portugal united against them the Dutch and English in the East Indies. Then, as the power of the Spanish empire waned, the two Northern nations, having the Asiatic field to themselves for a time, turned savagely on each other. But the fierce naval fighting that ensued between the Dutch and English enfeebled both nations; and they soon became equally distrustful of the designs of the French not only in Europe, but also in Asia; for France was now entering the arena, although many years were still to pass before she could establish herself substantially upon the coast of India.

CHAPTER II

INFLUENCE AND CONNECTION OF POLITICS IN EUROPE AND ASIA

1660 - 1700

IN the last quarter of the seventeenth century, the three maritime peoples of the West—the English, Dutch, and French—had manifestly entered the lists of competition for commercial ascendency in Asiatic waters, Spain and Portugal having already fallen far into the rear. The English Company's establishments in the East Indies consisted at this time of the presidency of Bantam, with Macassar and other places in the Indian Archipelago; Fort St. George and its dependent factories on the Coromandel Coast and in the Bay of Bengal; and Surat on the west coast of Bombay, with other subordinate posts on that side of India; as well as some places on the Persian Gulf.

It is of primary importance, in order to set in clear light the earlier subsequent stages of the rise of British dominion, and to explain why England finally distanced other competitors in this long and eventful race, that the vicissitudes of European politics in the latter part of this century should be briefly touched upon; because the success of England in the East is largely due to the mistakes of France and the misfortunes of Holland in the West. From the beginning of the century the Eastern trade had been a make-weight and a perceptible element in the regulation of English policy abroad, for the London merchants had never been without means of influencing the court or the Parliament; but the adjustment of this important national interest to the varying exigencies of the general situation in Europe had about this time become peculiarly difficult.

During the interval between the Restoration of 1660 and the Revolution of 1688, when our commerce increased and throve mightily, we had to make head in Asia against the jealous antagonism of the Dutch; while in Europe the Dutch were our natural allies against the arbitrary aggressiveness of France. In the East it was of vital importance to our commerce that the power of Holland should be repressed, in the West we were vitally interested in upholding it; the balance of trade in Asia was inconsistent with the balance of politics in Europe. It was remarked by a contemporary diplomatist that England's problem was to keep the peace with Holland without losing our East India trade; for if we supported the Dutch against France, they went on elbowing us out of Asia; while in joining France against Holland, we were breaking down one maritime power only to make room for another that might become much more formidable.

The organization of the French navy had now been seriously taken up; and in 1664 was founded the French

East India Company, which fitted out a squadron for the East Indies in the following year. In 1672, when England and France were allied against Holland, a French armament under De la Haye sailed for India, occupied the excellent harbour of Trincomali in Ceylon, and took possession of St. Thomé, close to Madras. The English could not decently oppose the emissaries

BIRD'S-EYE VIEW OF TRINCOMALI.

of a friendly nation, although this first appearance of the French on the Coromandel Coast—where in the next century our contest with them was fought out—could not but excite considerable uneasiness. Nor was the situation much improved in our favour when both places were subsequently captured from the French by the Dutch.

The foreign relations of England at this period were unsettled and curiously complicated. In 1665 Holland and England were at war; in 1666 France joined Holland against us; but in 1668 England, Holland, and

Sweden had formed the Triple Alliance against France; while in 1672 France and England combined to attack Holland; and in 1678 the English again made a defensive league with Holland against France, when the English Company were required by the government to send out a large body of men to defend Bombay, and also employed an armed fleet of some thirty-five vessels. The motives for these rapid changes of attitude were largely connected with Asiatic commerce.

The three wars against Holland into which England drifted between 1652 and 1672 were all prompted, more or less, by commercial and colonial animosities. For the quarrel in Cromwell's time had arisen directly out of grievances against the Dutch in Asia; and we have seen that their determined attempts to thwart and repel the expansion of English commerce in the East Indies produced the rupture of 1665. France joined Holland in 1666, and some desperate naval engagements ensued, until the invasion of Spanish Flanders by Louis XIV so alarmed the Dutch that they consented to pacific proposals from the English and signed the Treaty of Breda in 1667 upon the basis of *Uti possidetis* as to territory, and the amicable adjustment of all commercial disputes.

England also made peace with France, but as Louis XIV nevertheless pushed on his invasion of Spanish Flanders, the Triple Alliance was formed to stop him by insisting on France and Spain coming to some arrangement. Then followed a fresh shuffle of the cards, for in 1670 the French and English kings agreed, by their secret treaty of Dover, to make a joint attack upon the Dutch. It is a mistake to suppose, as is commonly thought, that Charles II was induced to join France in 1672 merely by French bribes and his sympathy with Roman Catholicism. His alliance with France was undoubtedly aimed against civil and religious liberty at home; but abroad one of its objects was to cut down the naval and commercial growth of Holland, with whom the English had many unsettled quarrels both in America and in Asia.

By a secret treaty projected between France, England, and Portugal in 1673, the three powers were to send a joint naval expedition against the Dutch possessions in Asia, which were to be seized and divided among the allies. It is thus clear that there were strong and recurrent motives for hostility between the two nations, closely connected with Asiatic affairs. Even Sir William Temple, the negotiator of the Triple Alliance, discusses in one of his essays the question whether England would derive greater advantage than France from the ruin of Holland. Whether in that case it would be possible to bring over to England the Dutch trade and shipping, seemed doubtful to him; yet he feared that, unless England joined France against Holland, the two Continental states might combine against England.

In 1671, accordingly, England did join France in a war which ended, so far as we were concerned, in 1674, when the Dutch agreed to salute the English flag in the narrow seas and to refer all commercial differences to arbitration. Louis XIV, on the other hand, went on capturing town after town on the Flemish border; his great armies were overrunning Holland; and the Prince of Orange had declared that he would die in the last ditch. Finally, when the English had made a defensive treaty with Holland to save her from ruin, a general peace was ratified at Nimeguen in 1678, on terms very favourable to France, who retained many of the barrier towns in the Netherlands.

The upshot of these long continental wars was manifestly to strengthen England and to weaken Holland. In 1677, when the French invasion had thrown the Dutch into peril and distress, the commerce of England was prospering wonderfully. Moreover, the truce of 1678 was soon broken by fresh hostilities; and from that time up to the end of the century the French king was entirely engrossed in his ambitious and extravagant wars, while the Dutch were fighting desperately for their existence; so that the only two maritime powers from which England had anything to fear in the East were entangled in a great struggle on the European Continent. From these contests Holland emerged, at the Peace of Ryswick in 1697, with enfeebled strength, with her commerce severely damaged, and with her resources for distant expeditions materially reduced.

But the Dutch had done much injury to the earliest French settlements planted under Colbert's auspices in the East Indies; and France had been so much occupied on the land, particularly when the fortune of war began to turn against her, that she was now incapaci-

Mountain Scenery in the Himalayas.
From a Photograph.

tated from pursuing Colbert's wise and far-reaching schemes of commercial and colonial expansion. Her naval development was checked and her maritime enterprise took no fresh flight until after the Peace of Utrecht in 1713. In short, the French and Dutch had mutually disabled each other, to the great advantage, for operations beyond sea, of the English, who thenceforward begin to draw slowly but continuously to the foremost place in Asiatic conquest and commerce.

From this period of great Continental wars in Europe we may date the beginning of substantial prosperity for our East Indian trade; for it was then that the English made good their footing on the Indian coasts. We learn from Macaulay's History that during the twenty years succeeding the Restoration, the value of the annual imports from Bengal alone rose from £8000 to £300,000, and that the gains of the Company from their monopoly of the import of East Indian produce were almost incredible. In 1685 the headquarters of their business on the Western side was transferred from Surat to Bombay; in 1687 the chief Bengal agency was removed from Hugli to Calcutta; and Madras had become their central post on the eastern shores of the Indian peninsula.

The Company were liberally encouraged by the government of the last two Stuarts, who granted ample charters, and even despatched armed reinforcements to their settlements. After the establishment of these three principal stations—which became afterwards, as Presidency towns, the cardinal points where the British dominion was first fixed and whence it issued out into spacious radiation—the East India Company resolved, in 1687, to assume independent jurisdiction within their own settlements, to fortify them, to coin money, to collect customs, and to act, in short, as a self-governing body within their own limits. They now began to enlist a native militia for the purpose of using their chartered right of protecting themselves by reprisals against oppression or direct attack, and of fighting for their own hand in quarrels with the local governors or petty chiefs. The new system thus introduced contained the germ out of which these scattered trading settlements eventually expanded into wide territorial dominion; and the incipient weakness of the Moghul Empire furnished both the motives and the opportunity for the change.

So long as the imperial administration prevailed up to the limits of its farthest Indian provinces and was effectively felt on either seaboard, the English merchants were quite satisfied with licenses allowing them to compound for the export duties, with grants of land for building their factories, and with other privileges for which they paid readily while they got their money's worth. But the outlying possessions of the empire were now no longer peacefully subordinate. The Maratha chief Sivaji was ranging about the Deccan, invading the Karnatic, and dominating the whole upper line of the west coast, not excluding the seaports and settlements held by Europeans. In 1664 he had pillaged Surat, where the English factory was bravely and successfully defended by Sir George Oxenden; and in 1671 he had levied heavy contributions on Surat and the Portuguese colony. Nor could the Moghul governors give any trustworthy protection, for Aurangzib's attention was distracted by a revolt in Afghanistan, which he was totally unable to put down, despite a

SIVAJI ON THE MARCH.

long and arduous campaign. When he returned to the Deccan, he found his enemies stronger than before in the field.

After Sivaji's death in 1680, his son Sambaji continued the revolt; the imperial armies were gradually worn out by incessant warfare, by futile pursuits of an enemy that always avoided a decisive blow, and by the disorganization of the central government caused by the emperor's long absence from his capital upon distant campaigns. Aurangzib had destroyed the Mohammedan kingdoms of Golkonda and Bijapur in Southern India, which might at any rate have served as breakwaters against the spread of the Maratha insurrection; and the war was now becoming epidemic. The dislocation of the native administration led to the consolidation of the foreign settlements, since the Companies were compelled for their self-preservation to act upon this opportunity of taking up a more independent position in the country. The relaxation of the supreme legitimate authority loosened its hold on the more distant governorships, and with local irresponsibility came local oppression. The merchants became exposed to irregular extortion and capricious ransoming by subordinate officials who could give them no valid guarantees or regular safeguard; while their immunities and privileges, even when obtained at the capital from the emperor's ministers, were often disregarded with impunity at the seaports.

Under these circumstances, the English Company convinced themselves, after much anxious discussion, that the success and comparative security of the Dutch, as formerly of the Portuguese, had been founded on their practice of seizing and openly fortifying posts strong enough to render the holders independent of the imperial pleasure, and to resist the arbitrary exactions of neighbouring officials or potentates. Their assumed jurisdiction was still to be confined entirely to the seacoast, and its object went no further than the security of their trade. But the English soon discovered that the time had not yet come when a foreign flag could be safely set up on the Indian mainland. The Portuguese had established themselves at Goa before the Moghul Empire had extended to the west coast; the Dutch had fixed their independent settlements for the most part upon islands.

In the seventeenth century the power of the Moghul emperor, although undermined, was not yet so far reduced that he could be defied with impunity on his own seaboard. When, in 1687, the East India Company ventured to declare war against the Emperor Aurangzib, all the English settlements soon found themselves placed in great jeopardy by this rashness. It was lucky for the foreigners that the capture and execution of Sambaji, the Maratha leader, roused the Hindus of the southwest country to unite in strenuous revolt against the Mohammedan sovereign, who thereafter became too deeply entangled in the meshes of guerilla warfare and sporadic insurrections to find leisure for dealing thoroughly with comparatively insignificant mercantile intruders. Moreover, since the Moghul government maintained no regular navy, it could not keep up a blockade of the harbours and river estuaries or bar the entry of foreign ships; while on the other hand the imperial customs revenue suffered heavily from their hostility.

The Emperor Aurangzib (better known in India by his title of Alamgir) was the last able representative of a dynasty that had conquered and ruled in India from the middle of the sixteenth century. The Moghul Empire was founded by the brilliant audacity and warlike skill of Babar, a Chagatai Tartar, who, with an army of twelve thousand men, overthrew the dominion of the Pathan kings at Delhi and subdued all the northern provinces of India. It had been consolidated and raised to its full height of splendour and power by Akbar, a contemporary of Queen Elizabeth. Four successive emperors reigned one hundred and fifty-one years, from Akbar's accession in 1556 to Aurangzib's death in 1707; and as in Asia a long reign is always a strong reign, for a century and a half the Moghul was fairly India's master.

The dynasty was foreign by descent and habits; the strength of the government was sustained by constant importation of fresh blood from abroad; the military and civil chiefs were mainly vigorous recruits from Central Asia who took service under the Indian sovereigns of their own race and religion. Akbar and his two successors were politic rulers who allied themselves with the princely families of the Hindus, respected up to a certain point the prejudices of the population, and kept both civil and religious despotism within reasonable bounds. The Emperors Jahangir and Shah Jahan were both sons of Hindu mothers; but Aurangzib, the son of Shah Jahan, and the fourth in descent from Akbar, was a Mohammedan by full parentage, and an ardent Islamite by temperament; and after his triumph in the great civil war that broke out among the sons of Shah Jahan, he launched out into a career of persecution and ambitious territorial aggrandizement. In the writings of François Bernier, a Frenchman who was court physician to the Moghul emperor toward the beginning of Aurangzib's long reign, may be found an excellent picture of the condition of the empire at that period. His book contains a lively sketch of contemporary history, and is full of striking observations upon the system of government, the composition of the army, and the more prominent features of Indian society and administration. Perhaps the most valuable part of it is the letter "Concerning Hindustan," which Bernier wrote, after his return to France, to Colbert, the celebrated minister of Louis XIV, who had just set on foot the French East India Company that became the formidable rival of the English in the eighteenth century. His description of the military and official classes is instructive:—

"The great Moghul," he says, "is a foreigner in Hindustan; consequently he finds himself in a hostile country, or nearly so, containing hundreds of Gentiles (Hindus) to one Moghul, or even to one Mohammedan. . . . The court itself does not now consist, as originally, of real Moghuls, but is a medley of Uzbeks, Persians, Arabs, and Turks, or descendants from all these people."

"It must not be imagined," he elsewhere observes, "that the Omrah, or Lords, of the Moghul's court are members of ancient families, as our nobility in France . . . they mostly consist of adventurers from different nations, who entice one another to the court, and are generally persons of low descent, some having been originally slaves. The Moghul raises them to dignity or degrades them to obscurity according to his own pleasure and caprice."

Bernier goes on to show that the total insecurity of all private property, land revenue exactions, instability of government, the denial of justice, the tyranny and cupidity of the sovereign and his subordinates, "a tyranny often so excessive as to deprive the peasant and artisan of the necessaries of life, that drives the cultivator of the soil from his wretched home"—and that was ruining agriculture—accounted abundantly for the rapid decadence of all Asiatic states. "The country is ruined," he says, "by the necessity of defraying the enormous charges required to maintain the splendour of a numerous court, and to pay a large army maintained for the purpose of keeping the people in subjection. No adequate idea can be conveyed of the sufferings of that people"; and he continues: "It is owing to this miserable system that most towns in Hindustan are made up of earth, mud, and other wretched materials; that there is no city or town which, if it be not already ruined or deserted, does not bear evident marks of approaching decay." He thus touches upon the symptoms, already perceptible to a close observer, of the empire's political and economical decline.

Soon after the date at which Bernier wrote, Aurangzib entered upon the interminable wars in South India which gradually involved him in the misfortunes and difficulties that darkened the last years of his reign. He succeeded in upsetting the minor Mohammedan kingdoms which had been strong enough to hold down

THE LAKE OF UTAKAMAND IN THE NILGIRI HILLS, SOUTHERN INDIA.

the Hindu population; but he had, in fact, weakened his empire by extending it; for the new southern provinces could not be effectively managed at a distance from the central authority, and the Hindus were not only provoked by his aggressive Mohammedan orthodoxy, but encouraged by his utter inability to control them.

The Moghul government, moreover, had never paid much attention to its sea frontier, being quite unaccustomed to expect foreign enemies or intruders from any other quarter than the northwest, through the Afghan passes. The only naval force on the Indian coast belonged to the Siddhis, an independent Abyssinian colony, whose chiefs occasionally placed their fleet at the disposal of Aurangzib for employment on the west side of the Indian peninsula.

To these causes and favouring circumstances, therefore, to the incipient decline of the central sovereignty, to the relaxation of imperial authority on the outskirts of the dominion, and especially to the commotion caused by the spread of the Hindu rebellion under energetic Maratha leaders, we may attribute the facility with which the English made good their foothold on the shores of India toward the close of the seventeenth century.

It is important, moreover, to remember that at the time when the mistakes and troubles of the Moghul empire were opening the gates of India to access from the sea, there set in an era of war in Europe which for many years disabled or diverted the resources of England's two maritime rivals, France and Holland. The reigns of the two autocratic monarchs who ruled France and India throughout the second half of the seventeenth century tally very nearly in point of time, for the dates of their respective accessions very nearly coincide; and they died early in the eighteenth century within a few years of each other. In the policy to which each of these celebrated rulers personally attached himself, and in its unfortunate consequences, there is also much more than a fanciful resemblance.

The accession of both Aurangzib and Louis XIV took place at a moment when the splendour and fame of their dynasties were in full lustre; they both inaugurated a career of conquest and unscrupulous attacks upon weaker neighbours that was at first triumphant; they both gradually undermined the prosperity of their kingdoms and the stability of their houses by wasteful and impolitic wars. Religious persecution of their own subjects, unwieldy centralization of all governmental authority by the levelling of local institutions, widespread corruption and a magnificent court under the influence of bigots, lackeys, and panders, were characteristics of the reign of the Bourbon as well as of the Moghul. And in each instance half a century's autocratic misrule, complicated by unfortunate foreign wars, sectarian revolts, and grinding fiscal oppression, brought great misery on the people, and fatally enervated the monarchy.

Toward the end of the seventeenth century, the clouds began to gather, and from the beginning of the eighteenth century the fortunes of both sovereigns were perceptibly on the wane. It so happened that the decline, or eclipse, of each power was eminently favourable to the rising commercial ascendency of the English nation.

In 1691, King William formed the grand alliance of the Germanic States and of the maritime powers, England, Holland, and Spain, against France; whereby the preponderance of the French was checked and their schemes of colonial and commercial expansion were thrown aside or trampled down in a great European war. For although the Peace of Ryswick suspended hostilities for a few years, it may be said that during practically the whole period from 1690 to 1713, the French monarchy was engaged in conflicts with all its European neighbours on a vast scale of ruinous expenditure.

The condition of the Moghul Empire was even worse. We have seen that during the seventeenth century, so long as the Moghul Empire retained its vigour, it was found impossible for any foreign adventurers to obtain more than a precarious footing, by sufferance, on the mainland of India. But when the eighteenth century opened, the disorder of the imperial government was manifestly culminating to a climax. The old age of Aurangzib; the persistence and contagious spread of the Hindu revolt against his oppression; the certainty that his death would be the signal for civil war among his sons, and that the succession must abide the chance of battle; financial distress and the visible loosening of his administration everywhere—these were the ordinary symptoms of debility, decay, and approximate dissolution in an Oriental dynasty.

In the northwest, the Persians and the rebellious Afghan tribes had now wrested from Aurangzib his border strongholds, and thus his grasp on that all-

PEASANTS DRAWING WATER.

important frontier had become insecure, and the high-roads from Central Asia were again open to invaders. In the southwest, the Moghul, after putting down the kingdoms of Bijapur and Golkonda, had been unable to reconstruct an administration strong enough to repress the turbulent elements that his impolitic demolitions had set free. The disbanded soldiery, the plundered peasants, and the disaffected Hindu landholders all rallied round the standard of the Maratha captains, who bribed or daunted the imperial officials, harried the districts, cut off the revenue, and defeated the Moghul forces in detail. All these internal troubles were evident symptoms of the empire's impending disruption, and the precursors of a great political change.

A CART AT MADRAS.

CHAPTER III

CONSOLIDATION OF THE ENGLISH EAST INDIA COMPANY

1690-1702

IN India the last years of the seventeenth century had been for the English East India Company a period of not untroubled transition from a purely commercial system into a kind of elementary local self-government. The increasing weakness of the Moghul Empire doubled the risks and uncertainty of their trade; producing constant alarms from the fighting that went on near their settlements, liability to plunder and incessant exactions, exposure to interference from interlopers, and danger of encroachment or attack from European rivals. They had now deliberately adopted the plan of endeavouring to rid themselves of dependence on the native authorities; and their agents were enjoined to spare no pains for improving their revenue. "The increase of our revenue," they wrote in 1690, "is the subject of our care as much as our trade; 'tis that must maintain our force when twenty accidents may interrupt our trade; 'tis that must make us a nation in India . . . and upon this account it is that the wise Dutch, in all their general advices that we have seen, write ten paragraphs concerning their government, their civil and military policy, warfare, and the increase of their revenue, for one paragraph they write concerning trade." Their purpose was now, to quote a letter to Fort St. George, dated December 12, 1687, to establish "such a Politie of civil and military power, and create and secure such a large revenue, as may be the foundation of a large, well grounded, sure English dominion in India for all time to come."

These instructions show that, to use an Oriental metaphor, the scent of dominion was already in the nostrils of the English Company, that they were by this time on the track of higher game than the profits of trade, and that they were gradually concentrating their operations upon the Indian mainland. At Madras and Bombay, their fortifications were in fair condition, although their troops, besides a few Europeans, were chiefly a rabble of Armenians, Arabs, negroes, and half-breed Portuguese. In Bengal, the imperial viceroy, being himself hard pressed, had permitted their agent to fortify Calcutta, where Fort William was named after the reigning King of England.

In 1687, having resolved to bring all their settlements under a regulated administration, the Company had fitted out a large armament at home, had obtained King James's authority for their governor to make peace and war in India, and had sent out Sir John Child with orders to levy against the Moghul government a war of reprisals for damages and insults suffered from the native officials. That government, however, though it was in a bad plight, had still power and pride sufficient to turn fiercely upon such assailants. In Western India, the Company's attempt to defy the imperial authority brought them to considerable dis-

MATHARAN, A HILL-STATION NEAR BOMBAY IN WESTERN INDIA.

comfiture, for Aurangzib himself was encamped at no great distance with his main army. At Bombay, where the force is reported to have consisted of fifteen European soldiers in addition to a raw native militia, the governor was actually besieged in his own town and castle, and the place was reduced to awkward straits by the fleet of the Abyssinian Siddhi.

The expedition against Bengal and the northeastern coast totally failed; the factories were attacked and had to be temporarily abandoned. Orders were issued by the emperor to expel the English from Madras, where the president, having only a few English soldiers in garrison with some half-caste Portuguese, lost heart on hearing that a Moghul force was moving southward. Sir John Child, who impersonated the war policy of the Company, died in 1690; and the business ended rather ignominiously with the issue by Aurangzib of a lofty order reciting that, on receipt of a humble submissive petition by the English, his Majesty had mercifully pardoned their transgressions. At this message the Company's directors at home professed high indignation, for no petition of that kind had been sent; but the moment was not opportune for prosecuting the quarrel.

During the next ten years, however, the difficulties and decadence of the Moghul empire were manifestly on the increase. One of Aurangzib's sons invaded India from Persia with a foreign army; and the important provinces or kingdoms of South India—the Deccan, Mysore, and the Karnatic—were barely kept in obedience by large forces; for the old age of Aurangzib held all India in fear and expectation of imminent change. All this instability of affairs compelled the foreign settlements to rely more and more upon their own resources for self-defence against arbitrary officials, rebel leaders, marauding banditti, and, finally, against each other. For war had been raging in Europe from 1690 to 1697; the French had been doing enormous damage to the homeward bound ships of the East India Company, having on one occasion captured a whole fleet of merchantmen; nor did the Dutch, though our faithful allies in Europe, relax their inveterate jealousy of our progress in Asia.

That the vast importance of our Eastern trade was already realized to its full extent at the end of the seventeenth century, is abundantly shown by the writings of Sir Charles Davenant, the chief commercial authority of his day. He observes that under the Tudor dynasty England had enjoyed great internal prosperity for a hundred years, and that the Dutch had soon found themselves too many for the narrow territory of their republic; whereby both nations were driven into foreign trade by an increasing population. On the other hand, he says, the French people had diminished during the long religious wars of the sixteenth century; so that the two Protestant nations could push on vigorously to their forward place in the commerce beyond seas.

In his essay on the East Indian Trade, Davenant enlarges further upon the great profits and political advantages that accrued to England from her position in the East Indies, upon the strength of Holland in that quarter, and upon the extreme impolicy of allowing the Dutch to acquire such predominance as would enable them to put down all rivalry. Of the East India trade he says that whatever country can be in the full possession of it will give law to all the commercial world. He declares that if we should lose our hold in India, we would let go half our foreign business; and he insists on the point that by losing this trade we would be entirely deprived of the dominion of the sea, "for only foreign trade can maintain a great fleet." He describes the "formidable power" of Holland in the East Indies; the immense capital that they had spent in raising and consolidating it; the forts and castles well provided and garrisoned; their large fleet; their good harbours; and the energy, wealth, and unity of the Dutch Company, which was an incorporation of the seven chambers of the seven provinces, almost coeval in origin with the state itself, counting among its numbers all the ablest and best heads in the country. He shows that if the English should abandon the traffic, the Dutch would undoubtedly enjoy the whole, while England must be content thereafter to trade under their protection and flag.

In such an event Davenant calculates that an entire monopoly of East Indian goods would bring Holland more treasure yearly than could be got from Peru and Mexico; that they might earn a revenue of six million sterling; and that this great increase of wealth would entirely turn the balance of naval preponderance against the English, which would certainly prove their ruin if (as was not impossible at the time) the Dutch provinces should fall under the ascendency of France. If, on the other hand, the English bestirred themselves and prevailed over Holland, "if our foreign business were enlarged to the utmost extent of which it is capable, we should thereby acquire such wealth and power as that England with its proper forces might be able to deal with any nation whatsoever;" she might even become, like Rome, the head of a vast dominion, the fountain of law, and the source of power, honours, and offices throughout an immense territory.

Let us take, again, another and much more celebrated contemporary authority, Leibnitz, who in 1672 presented to Louis XIV his *Consilium Aegyptiacum*, which was a long state paper urgently advising the king to seize and annex Egypt. His main argument was that the possession of Egypt would secure to France the command of the invaluable Eastern trade, whereby she could easily ruin Holland by cutting off the sources of her wealth and naval power, and would be enabled to build up a maritime empire for herself. As Louis XIV was at that time preparing to attack the Dutch, Leibnitz pointed out that to break down their preponderance in the East Indies would be a far surer way toward subduing them than an invasion of Holland, and he proceeded to throw out some very remarkable suggestions in regard to the facility of establishing a great Asiatic dominion. No one can doubt, he says, that if the Portuguese could have employed larger forces in their earlier expeditions, they would have brought all India under their sway, for the whole of Asia is more easily conquerable than Germany; and the French king needs only the strength and riches that can be drawn from Asiatic commerce to become the supreme arbiter of European affairs.

Such views and arguments as these, emanating from men of the highest reputation and experience in commerce and politics, serve to explain what kind of prize it was over which the maritime nations of the world had been so long contending, and for which the English were now entering the list as competitors. This prize, they insist, is of inestimable value, and, what is more, can be won by the European power that strikes boldly and skilfully for Asiatic dominion. The writings of Leibnitz and Davenant may be read as a useful corrective of the inveterate habit, from which even English historians are not always free, of regarding the development of our Indian empire out of a few scattered trading ports as a marvellous phenomenon, quite unforeseen and almost inexplicable. It is worth while to point out the superficiality of this commonplace view, and to lay stress on the evidence available to prove that the success of the English in India could be naturally explained, could indeed have been predicted to a large degree.

The British dominion in the East grew out of much stronger and deeper roots than is usually supposed. To understand its true origin, we must remember that the English settlements on the Indian mainland were valuable not only as emporia for the very profitable trade in the exchange of goods between India and Europe, but also because they were the fixed points upon which the whole commerce of England with South Asia, from the Persian Gulf eastward to Sumatra, Java, and the Spice Islands as far as the China seas, may be said to have pivoted; they kept open and were indeed indispensable for the communications along the line of what was then the richest sea-borne traffic in the world. For the nation that could engross that traffic held the whole carrying trade between Asia and Western Europe, and supplied all the adjacent European countries. Upon the wealth and multiplied force acquired in extending, step by step, their influence over this wide range of operations, upon the gradual strengthening in English hands of the foundations that supported this command-

THE GREAT TEMPLE OF BORO-BUDUR IN JAVA.

ing position, were built up the first stages of English ascendency in the East.

The constitution of these great commercial associations resembled in many respects that of the proprietary colonies which laid the foundation of such states as Maryland and Pennsylvania in North America. The proprietary bodies appointed the governor and council, and were in fact invested with a kind of autonomy under the general authority of the sovereign; they had many of the attributes, without much of the responsibility, of dependent states. It had become abundantly clear that this organization of a Chartered Company, with powers of internal control and self-defence, possessing in some degree the resources and administrative traditions, the unity of plan and purpose, and the larger interests and relative responsibilities of a local government, was necessary to the existence of British commerce in Asia, where England then had no diplomatic representatives and many dangerous rivals. The long contest throughout the seventeenth century between England and Holland in the East Indies was destined to terminate in a kind of partition of that vast commercial domain.

Not until the nineteenth century was a final political settlement accomplished; yet the first approaches toward this end were already perceptible in the tendency of English enterprise to converge, as we have said, upon India itself, while the Dutch were visibly drawing off and collecting their strength toward Java and Sumatra. Beyond the Straits of Malacca they were still predominant; the headquarters of their administration were at Batavia; and they had seized, in 1683, the valuable position of Bantam in Java, which gave them a virtual monopoly of the trade in pepper, the most valuable commodity from those regions. The English Company had before them the example of the Dutch, who had adopted from the Portuguese the policy of making their settlements self-protective by fortifications and strong garrisons, of acquiring territory, and of treating their acquisitions, not as grants held by traders on sufferance from the nearest Oriental potentate, but as possessions held under direct or delegated authority from the sovereign European power. They saw that they could only maintain their ground by imitating this example; and henceforward their establishments were more and more framed and directed upon this model.

But in London the enormous profits of the Company were exciting jealousy and stimulating energetic attempts to break in upon such a magnificent treasure-house. Sir Josiah Child, who then ruled their affairs autocratically, had enlisted the favour and support of the court by presents to King James II and to all who had influence at Whitehall. Unluckily, the India House had just set its sails upon the Tory tack when a Protestant wind brought over William III, and after the Revolution of 1688 a new Company was formed to compete for the next charter upon a remodelled system. In 1693, the old Company's charter was declared void for non-payment of a five per cent. duty laid by the Crown on their capital stock; and it was renewed only upon condition of its being terminable at three years' notice. Then in 1698 Montague, the Chancellor of the Exchequer, being hard pressed for money, passed an Act of Parliament granting a Royal Charter to the new Company, who undertook to lend two millions to the government at eight per cent. The money was subscribed with an eagerness that proved the country's wealth, as well as its confidence in the strength and expansive power of this great branch of the national trade.

The appearance in India of a second and rival Company created serious internal complications. Each association did its utmost to ruin the other; each hoisted

THE OLD EAST INDIA HOUSE (1796-1858).

the English flag and sent an embassy to contend for the Moghul emperor's patronage at his court; while the local governors played off one against the other, favouring each Company alternately, and taking bribes impartially from both. This discreditable and damaging contest was at last closed by the union of the two Companies, which was effected through Godolphin's intervention in 1702, just before the great war of the Spanish succession began, and immediately after the accession of Queen Anne. The effect of this measure was to concentrate all the enterprise, capital, and maritime experience of one powerful corporation upon the consolidation of the English position in South Asia.

The East India Company, by whom our Indian affairs were administered for the next one hundred fifty-five years, were now backed by the most opulent city and the largest seafaring population in the world, by the favour of the English government, to whom they made liberal advances, and by the increasing influence of the commercial classes upon the politics of the country. With these advantages, with a secure base and headquarters at home, with fortified settlements and armed shipping abroad, with a charter authorizing them to raise troops and to make war and peace in India, the Company were already capable of defending themselves, and even of pushing forward their outposts against any opposition that could be made by the viceroys of a distracted Oriental empire.

The history of Venice and Genoa had already shown what might be achieved by the power of armed commerce in the hands of small communities greatly superior in wealth and civilization to their neighbours. These towns had grown into independent States by successful monopoly of the Asiatic trade in the European waters; they were originally no stronger than a chartered English Company of the seventeenth century. The decadence of the Byzantine empire enabled the

Italian cities to supplant the Greeks in the Levant, to acquire and fortify the islands and other points of vantage along the coasts, and thus to seize trade and territory in the Mediterranean very much as the Dutch and English established themselves in the Indian seas. Chios belonged entirely to a Genoese Company, whose rule for two hundred and twenty years over several islands of the Greek archipelago bears a curious likeness, in miniature, to the territorial domination of the English East India Company. The ruins of strongholds and other signs of extinct Italian dominion are to be seen all along the shores of Greece and Asia Minor, like the relics of the Dutch and Portuguese settlements on the Indian Ocean or the Persian Gulf.

But neither Greeks nor Italians could resist the torrent of Asiatic conquest that came pouring across Asia from the East. The Italian republics had not the population, capital, or territorial resources sufficient for holding their scattered possessions against the fleets and armies of the Ottoman empire; their territory on the Italian mainland was constantly threatened by powerful neighbours; and the diversion of the Asiatic trade was drying up the springs of their prosperity. Nevertheless, when we consider how much was accomplished by these small trading states so long as the field lay open to them, and even while they were confronted by the Turkish power in its full strength on the mainland, we may moderate our astonishment at the fact that the foundations of a great empire in India could be laid by an English trading Company, at a time when the Moghul Empire was rapidly waning and England was waxing to the plenitude of her maritime supremacy. It is true that the Levant and Greece lay adjacent to Venice and Genoa, while between India and England were six months of sea voyage. But this distance favoured the establishment of British dominion by keeping Indian affairs in the beginning outside the sphere of European politics; and latterly it became a distinct advantage to the nation that could give its commercial colonies a secure base at home, and could hold the sea against all rivals.

In this situation it might have been foreseen without much difficulty that as decay subsided into dilapidation all over the Moghul empire, the vigorous European settlements on the coasts of India would enlarge their borders and affirm their independence. When in 1672 Leibnitz advised Louis XIV not to attack Holland, but to seize Egypt as the stepping-stone to a great Asiatic dominion, he wrote, truly, that "the extreme feebleness of the Orientals is no longer a secret"; and India was now certainly the weakest, perhaps also still the wealthiest, part of South Asia. The quarrels and embarrassments of the local governors already prevented them from paying much attention to trading factories, except when money was to be extorted or assistance needed. It was clearly as probable that the native usurpers and adventurers who were rising into power would seek aid from the Companies as that they would afford them protection or subject them to control; they were more likely, in this manner, to throw

THE NIZAM'S CAPITAL, HAIDARABAD.

open India to the foreigner than to bar the doors against him.

From such circumstances as these two consequences might fairly be inferred: first, that the power of the foreign Companies would steadily expand so long as they could rely on their communications with Europe; secondly, that commercial jealousies in Asia and national antipathies in Europe would before long bring the expanding Companies into collision with each other. Lastly, it might be predicted that whenever this collision should occur, the Company that succeeded in overthrowing its European antagonist would have little to fear from native adversaries, and would have attained an incontestable ascendency in the adjoining provinces of India.

At the opening of the eighteenth century, therefore, the situation may thus be briefly indicated. The Dutch Company, still rich and prospering commercially, held Ceylon and some Indian stations, but the centre of their operations was slowly shifting further eastward, and as the century advanced their naval power declined rapidly, falling from one hundred and fifty-one vessels of war in 1671 to forty-two in 1740. The French Company had suffered heavily from the recent war in Europe, during which they had lost Pondicherry and had recovered it only in 1697; they were deep in debt, and were altogether in no condition for pushing forward enterprises in Asia. The English Company was flourishing and had obtained a firm foothold on the Indian mainland; but the Moghul Empire still held together under Aurangzib, who would have tolerated no serious territorial encroachment.

Up to this time, therefore, the policy of the French and English had remained strictly commercial in so far that all their plans and proceedings for settling upon the Indian coasts were designed in the interests of trade. We are now approaching the period when the growing strength of their position, the weakness of the Indian governments, the increasing keenness and impulse of competition, and, above all, the violent quarrels between France and England in Europe, combined to transform the commercial rivalry into an armed contest for political ascendency. For some twenty years South India became a battle-field of two distant European nations; the war of succession in Austria was made a pretext for taking sides in a dispute over the heritage of the Nizam of Haidarabad; and Indian affairs were entangled in the prolonged struggle between France and England for colonial and naval superiority. When England was eventually left mistress of the situation at the close of that struggle, she found thrown wide open before her the gates leading to immense territorial possessions, and to the consolidation of an Asiatic dominion which is perhaps the most eminent and valuable legacy bequeathed to us by our forefathers in the eighteenth century.

CHAPTER IV

THE FRENCH AND ENGLISH EAST INDIA COMPANIES

THE death of the Spanish king in 1702 had been the signal for a war that ended with a partition of the Spanish monarchy and a general political resettlement of Europe. So with the death of Aurangzib in 1707 began the disruption of the Moghul Empire, followed by a material disturbance of the political system of Asia. The commotion and territorial derangements that were now spreading through the central regions of Asia were evident premonitory tokens of the instability and approaching downfall of the two great dynasties that had ruled Persia and India from the middle of the sixteenth century; the long stationary period was drawing to its end; an era of great conquests was reappearing; and with the troubles fermenting in Central Asia we may undoubtedly connect the events about to follow on the coast of the Indian Peninsula.

There was nothing unusual in the civil war that broke out on the Moghul emperor's death: for the title to a vacant Indian throne was ordinarily determined by the sword; every ruler of the imperial house had fought in turn for his heritage; and in fact the dynasty had owed its strength to the severe competitive trials in which each successor had proved his capacity for kingship. But as Aurangzib died at an advanced age, the contest had long been foreseen and deliberately prepared for. He left his dominions in confusion, with a formidable revolt spreading among the Marathas; his empire was unwieldy and overgrown; and this time the struggle among his heirs brought out no successor capable of holding together the ill-joined provinces and discordant races. The freebooting companies of the Maratha chiefs soon developed into roving armies that overran the central and western regions. The great viceroyalty of the southern provinces was converted into an independent principality under the Nizam. Bengal, the richest province of India, fell away under an Afghan adventurer; the Sikhs were rising in the Panjab; a powerful official was founding his dynasty in Oudh; and various usurpers were setting themselves up in the remoter districts.

A CORNER OF THE DIVAN-I-KHAS AT AMBER.

The dominion which had been planted in the sixteenth century by the vigour and audacity of Babar and his free-lances from the Oxus was now subsiding into emasculate debility. During the flourishing period of the Moghul Empire its outposts were at Kabul and Kandahar; but toward the end of Aurangzib's reign his garrisons had been driven out of Afghanistan. As the maintenance of a strong northwest frontier has always been essential to the security of India, the divorce of Afghanistan from the rulership of the Indian plains was in those days sure to be followed by the recurrence of chronic invasions from Central Asia. Thirty years after Aurangzib's decease, Nadir Shah, a Persian soldier of fortune who had overturned the ruling dynasty in Persia, came down through the Afghan passes with a great army. The Moghul emperor made but a show of resistance. Nadir Shah sacked Delhi in March, 1739, added one more massacre to the blood-stained annals of that ill-fated city, wrenched away from the imperial crown all its possessions west of the Indus, and departed home, leaving the Moghul government, which had received its death-blow, in a state of mortal collapse.

The barriers having been thus broken down, Ahmad Shah, of the Abdalli tribe of Afghans, followed two years later. When Nadir Shah had been assassinated by the Persians in his camp in Khorasan, Ahmad Shah, who commanded a large body of cavalry in Nadir Shah's army, rode off eastward to conquer Afghanistan; and from that base he seized the whole Panjab between 1748 and 1751. Meanwhile the Marathas were spreading over Central India from the southwest like a devastating flood; and wherever the land had been levelled flat by the heavy roller of absolutism, wherever the minor rulerships and petty states had been crushed out by the empire, the whole country was now easily overrun and broken up into anarchy.

The different provinces and viceroyalties went their own natural way; they were parcelled out in a scuffle among revolted governors, rebellious chiefs, leaders of insurgent tribes or sects, religious revivalists, and captains of mercenary bands. The Indian people were becoming a masterless multitude swaying to and fro in the political storm, and clinging to any power, natural or supernatural, that seemed likely to protect them. They were prepared to acquiesce in the assumption of authority by any one who could show himself able to discharge the most elementary functions of government in the preservation of life and property. In short, the people were scattered without a leader or protector; while the political system under which they had long lived was vanishing in complete disorganization.

It was during this period of tumultuary confusion that the French and English first appeared as rivals upon the political arena in India. For the purpose of throwing some additional light on the origin, character, and eventual results of the great transmarine contest between these two nations which stands in the forefront of their history during the eighteenth century, it may not be inappropriate, at this point, to sketch very briefly the earlier development of a commercial and colonial policy in France. This may at any rate lend readers some slight degree of aid toward substituting clear and well-founded conclusions for the complacent commonplaces that are so often repeated about the lack of national aptitudes for that kind of enterprise. It may also serve to bring out and accentuate the wide contrasts of principle and practice exhibited by the annals of French and English adventure beyond sea.

The history of French colonization is ordinarily divided, we are told, into three periods: the period of the great discoveries, which is carried up to the death of Henry IV in 1609; the era of grand colonial expansion in the seventeenth century; and the period of decline during the hundred years that intervene between the Peace of Utrecht in 1713 and the end of the great French wars in 1815. We have seen that the rivalry among the maritime nations began in earnest at the end of the sixteenth century, when the splendid achievements and conquests of Spain and Portugal had fired the imagination of the whole Western world. The spreading curiosity in France about outlandish peoples, distant voyages, and the fabulous wealth of Asia is illustrated by the writings of that age, and by constant allusions to the subject in such authors as Rebelais and Montaigne.

Nevertheless, although at the opening of the seventeenth century commercial and colonizing projects had already been entertained by that active and far-sighted ruler Henry IV, who projected a French East India Company, it was in England and Holland, not in France, that the first important step was taken by founding the two East India Companies that were destined to a long and memorable career. In 1624, however, began the long ministry of Richelieu, in whose powerful mind the conception of endowing France with a great dominion beyond sea reached its maturity, and had issue in successive decrees for the foundation and multiplication of colonizing companies in various parts of the world, from Canada in the West to Madagascar and the East Indies.

It is worth observation that in the charters of these companies may be found the earliest promulgations of principles that were consistently maintained throughout the entire course of French colonization under the old monarchy, but which would be looked for in vain in the commercial records of England or Holland. The Roman Catholic faith was established, to the rigid exclusion of all other religions; but on the other hand converted pagans were to be admitted to the full civil rights of Frenchmen. The propagation of Christianity was placed upon a level with the plantation of colonies, as a direct object of these expeditions. Nevertheless, their real motive was, after all, not so much economic or propagandist, as political; the companies were organized by the great cardinal to counteract the accumulation of vast transmarine possessions by Spain, then France's most dangerous rival, and in order that Spain might not claim for herself the whole non-Christian world.

In this policy, indeed, Richelieu was only imitating the tactics of England and Holland. Both these nations

ARMS OF THE NEW EAST INDIA COMPANY.

From the original grant of arms, dated Oct. 13, 1698.

were already striking at the extremities of the unwieldy Spanish empire, cutting off its gold convoys, harrying its coasts and islands, sweeping the narrow seas by privateers, and generally pursuing that irregular buccaneering warfare of which the memory long lived among mariners in the romantic traditions of the Spanish Main. In these wild adventures the French took little share; but they had borrowed from their neighbours the system of chartered associations; and under Mazarin as under Richelieu, the peopling of new lands beyond the ocean by French Catholics, in the interests of God and as a balance against Spain, was the essential principle of colonial action in France during the first half of the seventeenth century.

At this moment the religious idea was dominant in France. The court and all the fashionable society interested themselves warmly in collecting subscriptions for propagating the true faith among the heathen; missions were sent out, bishops were appointed, and the Jesuits began gradually to acquire great power in all the new colonies of North America. Nor was officialism less active than ecclesiasticism in the direction and superintendence of these projects for the extension of the faith and dominion of France. The system of companies under Church and State patronage was not popular among the men of business, who demanded of their government no more than freedom of trade for themselves and protection from foreign enemies. But official predilections were then, as they have always been in France, adverse to the English practice of chartering a body of pioneers or merchant adventurers and leaving them to plant settlements or factories by their own resources. The expeditions were not only authorized, but energetically promoted by the government, with the result that the governing classes insisted on sharing the investment or taking their part in the speculations, with an eye to the benefits promised in this world and the next. All the administrative and military commands were distributed among the noblesse; and among the hundred associates of the Company of New France we find thirty *seigneurs de la cour*, besides a certain number of ecclesiastic and even princely dignitaries, who were represented on the board by their secretaries.

No chartered association for the single purpose of trade, like the English or Dutch East India Companies, was founded by Richelieu, nor could any such company have been launched upon the system that has just been described. The French mercantile community demurred to conditions which placed all these corporations so completely under the paternal supervision of priests, nobles, and high officials; they also betrayed a perverse mistrust of the religious and propagandist element. They cautiously suggested that in commercial transactions spiritual directorship and ministerial supervision were not altogether desirable. The Chambers of Rouen and Marseilles recommended that at no price, and on no pretext, should the captains of their vessels be nominated by the king; they complained of French consuls abroad and revenue officers at home as equally dictatorial. They asked that religious interests should not rule trading operations, but that their traffic should be protected at sea by the royal navy and that trading factories should be allowed to manage their own affairs. It does not appear, in short, that Richelieu's colonial policy produced any notable results, beyond some remarkable voyages of discovery which gave a considerable impulse to all future colonization, and a great diffusion of missionary literature reporting the successful propagation of the faith in those countries that had been made over to the new companies.

We may thus register, even at this early stage, observations of a distinct and remarkable contrast in origin, character, and practical methods between the colonial systems of France and England. The first French colonies derived their initiative from the Crown; they were formed under strict official regulations; and the note of high orthodoxy was predominant in their constitution. The first English colonies owed their foundation either to men who had left their fatherland to escape the rule of kings and bishops, or to "gentleman adventurers" with a taste for the roving life and freedom of a new country, which they were quite willing to hold as national property so long as they were permitted to use their own ways and means of acquiring it. And at a time when the great commercial companies of England and Holland were already wresting from Spain and Portugal the invaluable prize of the seaborne trade with Asia, the French merchants were deterred from entering into competition with them mainly by the misguided solicitude of their own government.

For the commerce of France, however, better times were coming. The period of greatest colonial expansion, as it is styled by French writers, was inaugurated when Colbert, the famous minister of Louis XIV, launched his two Companies of the East and West Indies in 1664. It has already been explained that in those days the term "Indies" bore an exceedingly wide geographical significance in both hemispheres. Under the general denomination of the East Indies were included all the coasts of Southern Asia, from the Persian Gulf to China, Malacca, Borneo, Java, and all the rich Spice Islands of the China Sea. By the West Indies were meant not only the islands now known under that name, but the whole eastern littoral, and even the interior of Northern and Central America as far as it had been explored. No ship could double the Cape of Good Hope without coming within the trading sphere of the East India Companies; while to cross the Atlantic was to trespass on some West Indian monopoly. In 1600, the charter of the Dutch Company conferred upon them the exclusive privilege of navigation in all Eastern waters, with power to seize and confiscate any vessel that intruded on their domain. The charter of Colbert's East India Company granted a similar monopoly of trade for fifty years in all lands and seas beyond the Cape of Good Hope.

It is not too much to say that the great Companies of the seventeenth century were the champions and delegated agents of their respective nations in the competition for commerce and territory throughout the whole non-Christian world, and from this point of view

A WATER SCENE NEAR GARRETT, JAVA.

the importance of a good colonial policy can hardly be overestimated. The French West Indian Company was an association of the type invented by Richelieu, with authority to conquer and convert the heathen; but the foundation of the East India Company by Colbert on different lines marks a distinct step in advance. This Company, fitted out on the Dutch and English models as a chartered body with exclusive privileges and a large capital, was destined to acquire for France a substantial share of that rich commerce in Asiatic commodities that has made the fortune of so many maritime States.

In those days of corruption and intolerance, official tutelage was everywhere a sore burden; but the French Companies had something even heavier to bear. The king, the royal princes, and the principal courtiers took an active part in floating the concern, and they were good enough to subscribe largely to the investment. High ecclesiastic dignitaries condescended to patronize the East India Company; the prospectus was advertised in the churches and recommended from the pulpits; while royal proclamations exhorted all true Frenchmen to seize this opportunity of making their own fortunes and contributing to their country's prosperity.

Strange to say, however, not even these appeals to patriotism and piety roused any widespread enthusiasm among mercantile men. The capital expected from public subscription came in very slowly, in spite of heavy official pressure upon the great towns; for the traders, who had no guarantee for the good faith or consistency of a despotic government, vainly implored the bureaucracy to reduce the crushing tariffs on foreign imports and to leave the management of the business in private hands. As for the West India Company, it seems to have broken down by 1674, when its charter was revoked. Colbert determined to abandon henceforward, for the purpose of colonization, the agency of Companies, and to substitute direct administration by a minister of the Crown.

For the East Indies, however, Colbert maintained the organization of a chartered Company, although under the close superintendence of the Crown. Yet the legitimate commercial undertakings of this Company had been hampered at the outset by combining them with an expedition for the colonization of Madagascar, which failed disastrously. The first attempts of the French to gain a footing on the Indian coast were also defeated by the Dutch, so that in six years after its foundation this Company was entangled in very serious embarrassment. Nevertheless, if the most liberal support and encouragement from Louis XIV and his great minister could have secured success to the Company—and if a sharp turn of general policy, adverse to Colbert and his commercial views, had not speedily supervened—it is possible that the French might have made good their position in India before the close of the seventeenth century. Their initial difficulty was that the ground had been preoccupied by Holland, against whom Louis XIV declared war in 1674, partly, it is said, on account of the violent opposition of the Dutch to French interference with their Indian trade. But a few years later, when Louvois had plunged his master into interminable continental wars, the light and guidance of Colbert's pacific influence suffered total eclipse, and projects of colonial or commercial expansion were set aside for plans of campaign.

At the opening of the eighteenth century, therefore, the Portuguese, who had started first by priority of discovery, were at a standstill far in the rear. The Dutch, who followed, had wrested from the Portuguese most of their trade and territory, but the strength of Holland had already been broken by the incessant attacks of France, who had been good enough thus to relieve England of her most capable maritime rival. From the beginning of the eighteenth century the grasp of the Dutch upon points along the Indian coast became gradually relaxed; they relinquished the contest for predominance in that region; and their principal trading stations were shifted southeastward to Ceylon, Java, Borneo, and the Spice Islands. The Danish East India Company was extinguished in 1728. In 1722 the Emperor of Austria had granted to the merchants of the Austrian Netherlands a charter authorizing the Ostend East India Company to trade, fit out armed vessels, build forts, and make treaties with Indian princes; but this interference with their trade alarmed the maritime powers. England, France, and Holland united in diplomatic protests and threats of armed resistance to its establishment in the East Indies, until the emperor finally agreed by treaty to suppress the Ostend Company totally. The French, on the other hand, were gradually gaining ground and strengthening their position in India; for although they had been much enfeebled by the disastrous European wars that ended in 1713, their resources and their enterprising spirit revived during the tranquil interval of the next thirty years.

Under the pacific ministries of Fleury and Walpole trade and navigation now began to gather strength on both sides of the Channel; although the speculative mania that supervened in France at the beginning of this long peace had involved her East India Company in some dangerous vicissitudes. They had first been absorbed in 1719 into a gigantic Company of the Indies with exclusive right of trade on the African coast as well as on the shores of the Indian and the Pacific Oceans. The next step was to place this Company, already laden with privileges and monopolies, in charge of the famous Land Bank, with Law as Inspector-General over all their business, commercial and financial. The inevitable result was an enormous inflation of the shares and operations, followed by a sharp and ruinous collapse; nor did the Company right themselves until a royal decree had autocratically cut away all their liabilities, after which they again confined themselves to the East India trade.

Their situation in the Indian waters now began rapidly to improve. In 1715, they had occupied the important island of Mauritius (abandoned by the Dutch), and were steadily taking up their ground side by side with the English on the southeastern or Coromandel coast of India, where Pondicherri, the seat of the governor-general of all the French settlements, was developing into a fine town of seventy thousand inhabitants. This settlement had been established in 1674 by François Martin, who built the town, acquired the lands adjoining, and brought Pondicherri to such a high de-

A PAGODA AT PONDICHERRI.

gree of solid prosperity during twenty-five years of wise and courageous administration from 1681 to 1706—though from 1693 to 1697 the place was in the possession of the Dutch—that he is regarded by some French writers as the true founder of French India.

From 1735 to 1740, the capital and dividends of the

Company showed a substantial increase; they held five chief stations in India and they were trading with China, although it does not appear that they ever established themselves in the Spice Islands or the Malay Archipelago. The earlier governors, Lenoir and Dumas, managed their affairs with prudence and sagacity. Dupleix, who followed them, was a man of larger calibre, full of energy and ambition, who had distinguished himself as chief of the French factory at Chandarnagar on the Hugli River. When he was appointed to succeed Dumas in the governorship of Pondicherri in 1741, with supreme civil and military authority in the settlement, he lost no time in developing his bold and high-reaching projects for the promotion of his Company's interests.

In this manner it came to pass that, not long after the great settlement of Europe which was accomplished at the Peace of Utrecht, France and England alone faced each other as serious competitors for the prize of Indian commerce, having distanced or disabled all other candidates. Not only in the West, but in the East, the commercial and colonial rivalry between the foremost maritime states of Europe had reached its climax toward the middle of the eighteenth century. A high spring tide of maritime enterprise, setting strongly and decisively from Europe toward the unguarded coasts of India, was bearing on its rising wave the ships of these two jealous and powerful nations. So early as 1740 when war between England and France was imminently threatening, though not declared, the

French government had been entertaining the plans of Labourdonnais for destroying the English factories in the East Indies. A few years later, Dupleix was actively encouraged in his grand project of expelling the British from the Coromandel coast. At the same time, the French were making substantial progress in North America, having already formed the design of pushing down the Ohio, in order to appropriate what would now be called the Hinterland in the rear of the English colonies on the seacoast.

Toward the middle of the century, therefore, the territorial position and prospects of France in America and Asia had decidedly improved; and the growing dissensions caused by discordant political interests in Europe were exasperated by quarrels over trade and colonies beyond the sea. The colonial quarrel was fought out, as we know, in North America; the field on which the two nations met to contend for what was at that time the most valuable sea-borne trade in the world was India. And from this time forward the really potent element in Asiatic politics, which has since transformed and may again dominate the whole situation, is the political rivalry and rapidly increasing ascendency of the European Powers.

The contest had begun in a spirit of keen but pacific commercial rivalry. Each nation was represented in India by a substantial and well-equipped Company, which kept to its business, established factories and agencies, and concerned itself very slightly about the internal affairs of the state or province within whose jurisdiction it was settled. But at home the circumstances and constitution of the two bodies reflected the differences of national character and political conditions then prevailing between the two mother countries. It is exceedingly instructive to examine the financial transactions of the French and English Companies, respectively, with their governments at this period, and to observe the remarkable contrast of situation, system, and administrative principles which the comparison brings out.

In France, the East India Company was closely connected with the government; it farmed monopolies, received treasury grants and subsidies, dealt largely in loans and lotteries, and being usually deep in the state's debt, was at the mercy of the Crown. From the year 1723 its directors had been appointed by the king, whose officers exercised such constant control over the management that, as the Company afterward declared, the interference of the government was the cause of all its misfortunes. After 1747 it was constantly borrowing large sums on the security of its privileges or revenue farms; it was from such revenues as these that their dividends were paid and their stock artificially maintained. Under an able minister paying serious attention to Indian affairs, it is quite possible that the administration of the French Company might have been directed on larger political principles and pursued with more force and consistency of aim than could be expected from a private mercantile association. But as the government of Louis XV soon began to sink under the embarrassments, vices, and misfortunes of incapable rulership, official patronage gradually proved fatal to the Company that depended on it.

The English Company, on the other hand, was so far from being in debt to the government that it had aided the public treasury with large loans and contributions that amounted to £4,200,000 in 1750. It was an independent and powerful corporation, trusting not to official favour but to parliamentary influence in transacting business with the Crown; and as it was left to manage its own affairs, the greater responsibility thrown upon its chiefs produced in the long run a body of sound and experienced administrators, guided by long tradition, well versed in foreign trade, and backed by the overflowing capital of a great mercantile community.

In India, the means and resources of the two Companies were fairly equal at the outset. The settlements on the Coromandel coast were not only important as points of attraction for the inland commerce; they were also valuable as entrepôts for the general traffic on both sides of the Bay of Bengal and as naval stations for the protection of the thriving trade with the Malacca Straits and Eastern Asia, Ceylon being then held by the Dutch. Moreover, since the decay at the heart of the Moghul empire was soonest felt at its extremities, the distant provinces had already begun to fall away into confusion. The settlements in the far south of India were thus becoming more independent of the

MANDHATA ISLAND IN THE NARBADA RIVER.

imperial authorities than the factories in Bengal, which were up the estuary of a river with forts below them toward the sea, and in a land where the province was still under effective government. On the west side of India, the Marathas, who held most of the districts along the seashore, were by this time strong enough to keep foreign traders within bounds.

But on the southeast or Coromandel coast, Madras and Pondicherri, the headquarters of the French and English Companies, were fortified and fairly armed places upon open roadsteads, lying within the governorship of the Karnatic, which was the name for a large province attached to the viceroyalty of the Deccan, that is, of South India. This viceroyalty had been conferred by the emperor upon Asaf Jah, with the title of Nizam-al-mulk, who soon made himself so powerful as to excite alarm and jealousy at the Imperial Court. When, however, an attempt was made to remove him, the Nizam, who had been summoned to Delhi, marched back into the Deccan with an army, defeated the officer sent to replace him, established his authority in the south, and became the most powerful feudatory of the empire. A few years later, he took advantage of the disorganization caused by Nadir Shah's irruption into North India to consolidate his great possessions south of the Narbada, including the Karnatic, into a hereditary rulership, owning a nominal allegiance to Delhi, but in fact entirely independent.

In the Karnatic, which had been a governorship under the Deccan viceroyalty, a kind of subordinate principality had been established by one Saadat-Allah; but on his death the succession was disputed, and though the disorders that ensued were temporarily suppressed by the Nizam, they necessarily weakened local authority in the country round the English and French settlements. It was here that the French and English came to blows in 1745, as soon as the news of a declaration of war between France and England reached India. And from this outbreak of hostilities is to be dated the first crossing of swords on Indian soil in a national duel which lasted, with short intervals, for eighteen years, until one of the combatants was disarmed and virtually driven off the field.

When, in 1741, Dupleix was appointed Director-General of the affairs of the French East India Company, he succeeded to an office that had been held by two predecessors of character and capacity, who had shown great tact and judgment in their dealings with the native powers. Mahé and Karikal had been quietly acquired for France; and during the confusion into which the whole Karnatic was thrown by the Maratha invasion in 1740, the Mohammedan princes had found shelter for their families and treasure behind the walls of Pondicherri. But the plans and aims of the French had not travelled beyond the security and extension of their commerce until the stirring and ambitious spirit of Dupleix, who made no secret of his opinion that the French temperament was better suited for conquest than for commerce, led the Company into a more adventurous field of action. He foresaw that in the event of war with England the rising jealousy between the two Companies would kindle hostilities in India; and he accordingly began to negotiate with the neighbouring chiefs, to assume titles granted under the imperial patent, and to imitate the solemn ostentation of Indian grandees, with the object of preparing the way toward a place for his Company in the political system of the country. He spared no pains to reform his military establishments and to fortify Pondicherri against the contingency of an attack from the sea; nor did he desist when the Directors at Paris ordered him to suspend all expenditure on defensive works, to pay the Company's debts, and attend to their trade.

The declaration of war in Europe in 1744 gave the signal for beginning the first act of a dramatic contest that was to determine the issue whether France or England should win a great dominion in South Asia. We have to bear in mind that this issue did not depend, as some writers have imagined, upon the petty fighting that ensued along the Coromandel coast, or on the success or failure of their rival alliances and intrigues with Oriental princes. The issue was determined, in reality, by the result of the struggle between these two nations for superiority on all the seas. Maritime supremacy had laid the corner-stone of the whole fabric of Asiatic commerce upon the Indian mainland, where alone it could find a solid foundation; and while the security of this commerce depended on naval power, that power was also sure to expand with the development of trade. Although, therefore, the story of the Indian contest is but an episode of that great international drama which was played out in the next fifty years with many changes of scene and character, it is interesting, instructive, and of the highest importance for a proper understanding of the events and causes which threw open before the English the way to ascendency in India, and which lie at the base of their success.

CHAPTER V

THE FRENCH IN INDIA UNDER DUPLEIX

THE war between England and Spain, which had begun in 1739 over commercial and maritime quarrels, was now gradually drawing France into open hostilities with England. But as the English had a larger and more powerful navy, the rupture between the two countries placed France in the dangerous position of holding great transmarine possessions and interests by insecure lines of support and communication. In America and the West Indies the colonial dominions of France were more extensive than those of England; in India there was no great difference as to strength or settlements; and the French had the advantage of a most valuable, though rather distant, base of operations at the islands of Bourbon and Mauritius, with a station on the Madagascar coast.

At Mauritius, Labourdonnais, as governor, had been accumulating naval stores since 1740 and preparing, with the aid and approval of the French government, to fall upon the English merchant vessels or to attack the English settlements in India. In 1743, however, the Directors of the French East India Company, anxious to preserve neutrality in the East Indies, had procured the despatch of orders which held back Labourdonnais; and although, when war had actually been declared in 1744, he received authority to take the offensive, he was not ready until 1746, when he mustered his fleet at Madagascar and sailed in June for the Coromandel coast. Meanwhile, a squadron sent out from England had appeared in 1745 off Pondicherri, which had a weak garrison and unfinished fortifications. Dupleix, in order to gain time, induced the Nawab of Karnatic to interpose with an order forbidding hostilities within his jurisdiction; and in deference to this prohibition the English commodore was persuaded by the authorities at Madras to suspend his attack. The stormy season compelled him to leave the coast; but when the British fleet returned next year, it was met by the French squadron from the Mauritius.

The English Company now appealed to the Nawab in their turn, but they found him lukewarm; he had not been properly bribed; his own position was insecure; nor was it possible for him in any case to prevent the two hostile fleets from fighting or bombarding each other's factories on the seashore. After an indecisive naval action, the English ships withdrew to Ceylon. Labourdonnais now landed some two thousand men and Madras was besieged by land and sea, until, in September, 1746, it was surrendered on terms permitting the English to regain their town on payment of a ransom.

But this compromise was violently opposed by Dupleix, who saw plainly enough that if he was to build up solidly a French dominion in India, he must begin by clearing away the English, and who therefore insisted that the fortifications of Madras should be razed to the ground.

The Nawab of the Karnatic also interposed on

THE COLOMBO BREAKWATER, CEYLON.

his side, professing much indignation at this private war within his sovereignty, and demanding that the town should be given up to him, which Dupleix promised to do. After a sharp quarrel over this question Labourdonnais, whose fleet was shattered by a tremendous storm, sailed back with the surviving ships to Mauritius, leaving the French in temporary possession of Madras, under an agreement, made by Labourdonnais, that if the ransom were paid, it should be restored to the English within three months.

The next incident was important. Dupleix, who had now three thousand French soldiers at his disposal, and who had been positively ordered by a secret despatch from his government on no account to give up Madras, had not the least intention of relinquishing it either to the Nawab or the English Company. When the Nawab invested the town, Dupleix drove off the native troops so effectually as to establish, at one blow, an immense military reputation for the French in the Karnatic, since the ease and rapidity with which the Nawab's army was dispersed at this first collision between the regular battalions of Europe and the loose Indian levies proved at once the formidable quality of European arms and discipline.

Dupleix made unsparing and audacious use of his advantage; he declared null and void the agreement with the English, seized all the Company's property, carried the Madras governor and his officers to Pondicherri, where they figured as captives in a triumphal procession, and despatched a large force against the English fortress of St. David, the only fortified post still held by the English, about twelve miles south of Pondicherri. But the French were surprised in their march, and the expedition was so sharply checked that the troops thereafter lay inactively encamped in the neighbourhood of the fort, which they never succeeded in besieging.

In the meantime, as the English squadron was returning with reinforcements from Ceylon, Dupleix sent his four ships out of its way to the west coast, so that the sea was now open. When, therefore, in 1747, the French commander, Paradis, was about to move again on Fort St. David, he was stopped by the appearance of the English squadron, which threw supplies and troops into the place and compelled him to retire to the protection of Pondicherri. From this moment the tide turned. In attempting to take Cuddalore by a dashing blow, the French were outwitted by Lawrence and beaten back with loss; Admiral Boscawen arrived with a formidable fleet and fifteen hundred soldiers; and in 1748 Pondicherri was invested by land and sea. But as the French had failed before Fort St. David, so the English failed before Pondicherri; the place was so clumsily besieged by the English and so gallantly defended by the French that the assailants had at last to draw off with serious loss.

In 1749 the news of the peace of Aix-la-Chapelle stopped the fighting in India and restored Madras to the English in exchange for the restitution of Louisburg in North America to the French. The chief outcome of this sharp wrestle between the two Companies at close quarters on a narrow strip of seacoast was a notable augmentation of the French prestige in India, and great encouragement to Dupleix in his project of employing his troops as irresistible auxiliaries to any native prince whose cause he might choose to adopt. He was already in close correspondence with one of the parties in the civil war that was just beginning to spread over the Karnatic; he took care to keep on foot his disciplined troops, whose decisive value in the field had now been abundantly manifested; he had overawed the neighbouring chiefs, depressed the English credit, and seemed to have struck out with the boldness and perspicacity of political genius the straight way toward establishing a French dominion in the Indian peninsula.

So far as it related to facts and circumstances on the Coromandel coast, his judgment of the situation was correct; the opportunity had come, and Dupleix had discerned the right methods of using it. The Moghul empire had finally disappeared in all the southern provinces; the whole realm was torn by internal dissensions; the Marathas, whose mission it was to prepare the way for a foreign domination by riding down and ruining all the Mohammedan powers, were spoiling the country and bleeding away its strength; the native armies in the south were no better than irregular ill-armed hordes of mercenaries; the coasts lay open and defenceless.

Not only Dupleix, but others (as will be shown later on), were beginning to see the practicability of turning this state of things to the advantage of some European power. But Dupleix had not perceived or taken into account certain larger considerations which inevitably controlled the working out of his ambitious schemes and which soon began to counterbalance his local successes. Any plan of establishing the territorial supremacy of a maritime European power in India must be fundamentally defective and must necessarily suffer from dangerous constitutional weakness so long as it does not rest upon a secure line of communication by sea. Until this prime condition of stability is fulfilled, the aggrandizement of dominion in a distant land only places a heavier and more perilous strain on the weak supports, and the whole fabric is liable to be toppled over by a stroke at its base.

No quarter is given by French writers to Labourdonnais, who is accused of having thwarted the thoroughgoing designs of Dupleix by the half-hearted measure of holding Madras to ransom, by refusing to co-operate energetically in the extirpation of the English settlements, and by sailing away to Mauritius, so that the coast was left clear for the enemy. On his return to France, he was thrown into the Bastille, where he remained three years, though in the end he was honourably acquitted. His quarrel with Dupleix, who was imperious and uncompromising, may have had much to do with his hasty departure from the Indian seaboard. But it is more than doubtful whether, if Labourdonnais had kept his shattered squadron in those waters, he could have held that command of the sea without which all the triumphs of Dupleix over the petty forts on the coast, or over the loose levies of Indian princes, were radically futile.

However this may be, it soon became evident that success on the land would follow superiority at sea. We have seen that when, after the departure of Labourdonnais, a strong English fleet appeared on the scene, the French ships were obliged to leave the coast, while on land the operations of the French were paralyzed at once and they were easily driven back into Pondicherri. Then, also, the restoration of Madras in exchange for Louisburg in North America showed that a mere local advantage counted only as a single move on the vast chessboard, and might promptly be sacrificed to larger combinations. All these signs and tokens

A SCENE IN PONDICHERRI.

were so many warnings to Dupleix of his insecurity and of the fallacy underlying the fair surface of his designs upon India. But either he missed the significance of sea power, or he committed the mistake of imagining that he could shelter himself from naval attacks by carrying his conquests inland, forgetting that the roots of any European dominion in Asia must always be firmly planted in the fatherland. The experience of this first war seems to have brought him nothing but encouragement, for as soon as peace had been proclaimed at home, he lost no time in prosecuting his schemes on a larger scale.

We have to remember, in any case, that Dupleix cannot be supposed to have known the relative strength of the maritime nations, or the conditions to which the naval forces of France had been reduced by the war of the Austrian succession. The English had spent immense sums of money, but their navy had greatly increased in power and capacity; it had attained a clear superiority over the French everywhere, and notwithstanding some reverses, it was far more than a match for the enemy in Indian waters. The resources of Holland were exhausted, and she was threatened by imminent invasion when peace was signed at Aix-la-Chapelle. As for France, her victories in the Low Countries had brought her no substantial profit and much positive loss, for the damage done to Holland by the war told entirely in favour of England's commercial preponderance; while at sea her trade and marine had suffered so heavily, and her naval material at home was so completely spent that, according to Voltaire, she had no warships left.

Such national destitution must have severely affected any great trading enterprise; it was particularly damaging to the interests of the French East India Company which were directly associated with the fortunes of the State. At the end of the war, the Company found themselves deep in debt; their directors, all nominees of the Crown, had been profuse in expenditure, concealed the real state of affairs, and endeavoured to bolster up their credit by magnificent but fictitious dividends, until after 1746 their embarrassments compelled them to make sudden and startling reductions.

The remedy of the French ministers, whenever anything seemed to go wrong with their Company, was to appoint special commissioners to supervise the direction, notwithstanding the Company's protests that all their misfortunes were due to overinterference. In England, the East India Company's administration was managed independently by great merchants, with a long traditional experience of Asiatic affairs, with a strong parliamentary connection, with a very extensive business all over the East, and with a large reserve of capital on hand.

In a comparison of the two systems, we have on the French side of the Channel a Company propped up by lottery privileges and tobacco monopolies, subsisting on grants in aid from the treasury. On the English side, we have a rich corporation making annual loans to the government in aid of war expenses, borrowing millions at a very low interest, and using this great financial leverage to obtain from the ministers exclusive privileges and the extension of their charter. In England, the superior wealth and naval instincts of the nation were directed with all the energy and active play of free institutions; in France, the natural ability and enterprise of a courageous and quick-witted people were fatally hampered by a despotic bureaucracy, by growing financial confusion, and by all the evils of negligent misrule.

To Dupleix in India these things could not be discernible; he saw that his improved position and the increase of his troops gave ample scope to his patriotic ambition; and he now launched out hardily upon the troubled and hitherto unexplored sea of Indian politics. Although the last war had not altered the relative situations of either Company, its effect had been to change their character and to deepen the colour of their rivalry; they had both acquired a taste for Oriental war and intrigue; they had each raised a military force which mutual jealousy prevented them from disbanding, though it was very costly to maintain. The problem of keeping up a standing army without paying for it out of revenue is occasionally solved by an impecunious state at the cost of its neighbours; but there is also the alternative, well known in Indian history, of lending an army for a consideration. The French and English in India could not make direct war on each other while the peace lasted in Europe; they could only prepare for the next rupture by manœuvring against each other politically, by husbanding their forces, extending their spheres of influence, and aiming back strokes indirectly at each other under cover of the *mêlée* that was going on in the country round them.

There was, therefore, everything to invite and nothing to prevent their taking a hand in the incessant fighting for independence and territory among the princes and chiefs who had now discovered the weight of European metal on the war-field, and were quite ready to pay handsomely for a temporary loan of it. The Companies, indeed, found little difficulty in striking a bargain with men whose best title to rulership was their power to take and hold, whose life and the existence of their principality were continually staked upon the issue of a single battle; capable usurpers with no right; rightful heirs with no capacity; military leaders who had seized a few districts; Maratha captains or Afghan adventurers at the head of some thousand horsemen; provincial viceroys who were trying to found dynasties. None of these rivals could afford to look far ahead or to concern themselves, in the face of emergent needs, with the inevitable consequences of calling in the armed European.

The two Companies, on the other hand, were under an irresistible temptation drawing them toward proposals that offered pay and employment for troops that they could not yet use against each other, with the prospect of large profits upon the campaign, extension of trade privileges or even territory, and the chance of doing some material damage to a rival. It must be admitted that the first who yielded to this temptation were the English, when they took up the cause of a raja who had been expelled by his brother from the Maratha kingdom of Tanjore. But the expedition sent to reinstate him managed matters so badly that the Company were well content to withdraw it on payment of their war expenditure in addition to a small cession of land. This was not only a military failure but a political blunder; since the Tanjore intervention furnished Dupleix with an excellent precedent for taking part in the quarrels of the native rulers precisely at a moment when he was meditating similar designs of a much more important and far-reaching character. He

THE MAIN GATEWAY OF THE TEMPLE AT TANJORE.

was now ready to develop his policy of assuring the ascendency of France upon a system of armed intervention among the candidates who were preparing to settle by the sword the open question of the succession to rulership in South India.

His opportunity came in April, 1748, with the death of Asaf Jah, the first Nizam, founder of the dynasty that still reigns over a large territory at Haidarabad. Asaf Jah's succession was disputed between his son

Nasir Jang and his grandson Muzaffar Jang, who both took up arms; whereupon the Karnatic, which had been kept quiet only by Asaf Jah's power of enforcing his authority, at once became the scene of a violent conflict between rival claimants for the subordinate rulership. The entanglement of these two wars of succession threw all South India into confusion, producing that complicated series of intrigues, conspiracies, assassinations, battles, sieges, and desultory skirmishing that is known in Anglo-Indian history as the War in the Karnatic. The whole narrative, in copious and authentic detail, is to be read in Orme's History under the title of "The War of Coromandel," which records the admirable exploits of Clive, Lawrence, and some other stout-hearted but utterly forgotten Englishmen, who at great odds and with small means sustained the fortunes of their country in many a hazardous or desperate situation by their skill, valour, and inflexible fortitude.

Into this medley Dupleix plunged promptly and boldly. His immediate aim was to establish in the Karnatic, the province within whose jurisdiction lay both Madras and Pondicherri, a ruler who should be dependent on the French connection. His ulterior object was the creation of a preponderant French party at the court of the Nizam himself, to whom the Karnatic was still nominally subordinate; and by these two steps he hoped to obtain a firm dominion for his nation in India. In defending himself, afterwards, for having taken a part in these civil broils, he argued, not unfairly, that neutrality was impossible, because if the

French had refused all overtures for European assistance, the contending princes would certainly have got it from the English, who would thus have attained irresistible predominance. However this may be, the result of his policy was that the English Company, who at first expected that the Treaty of 1748 would relieve them from the hostility of France, soon discovered that they were in greater danger than before; for the peace enabled Dupleix to employ his forces in giving such material assistance to Chanda Sahib, one of the competitors for the Karnatic, that the ruling Nawab Anwar-ad-din Khan was speedily attacked, defeated, and slain. The victorious Chanda Sahib joined forces with Muzaffar Jang, who was contending for the Nizamship; and both marched to Pondicherri, where they were magnificently received by the French, to whom they made a substantial grant of territory, with special allotments to Monsieur and Madame Dupleix. The French were now openly supporting Muzaffar Jang for the Nizamship of the Deccan, and Chanda Sahib for the Nawabship of the Karnatic.

The English, who regarded these proceedings with considerable dismay, although their own behaviour at Tanjore made protest embarrassing, became involved in an acrimonious correspondence with the French, obviously leading to a rupture. Their position, which was now seriously threatened, left them no alternative but to take the side opposed to the French candidates in this double war of succession. When Dupleix sent out a strong contingent in support of Muzaffar Jang, Nasir

Jang, his opponent, appealed to the English, who, after some hesitation, supplied a body of six hundred men and also assisted Mohammad Ali, whom Nasir Jang had appointed to contest the Karnatic Nawabship against Chanda Sahib. Thus Nasir Jang and Mohammad Ali were supported by the English for the Nizamship and the Karnatic against Muzaffar Jang and Chanda Sahib, who were backed by the French.

The English Company also sent home urgent requisitions for succour, representing to their directors that the French had "struck at the ruin of your settlements, possessed themselves of several large districts, planted their colours on the very edge of your bounds, and are endeavouring to surround your settlements in such manner as to prevent either provisions or merchandise being brought to us." The murder of Nasir Jang by his own mercenaries seemed indeed to secure the triumph of the French cause; for Muzaffar Jang, whom Dupleix was assisting, was thereby placed for the moment in undisputed possession of the Nizamship; while Chanda Sahib with his French auxiliaries became irresistible in the Karnatic, where only the strong fortress of Trichinopoli held out against him.

It would be very difficult to describe briefly and yet clearly the intricate scrambling campaigns that followed, in which the French and English played the leading parts on either side, for the result of every important action depended on the European contingents engaged. While their troops exchanged volleys in the field, the two Companies exchanged bitter recriminations from Madras and Pondicherri, accusing each other of breaches of international law, denouncing one another's manœuvres, and imploring their respective governments at home to interpose against each other's total disregard of the most ordinary political morality. The French troops had carried the Karnatic for their candidate, had sent Bussy with Muzaffar Jang to establish him as Nizam at Haidarabad, and seemed in a fair way toward general success. The English had thrown a reinforcement into Trichinopoli, where Mohammad Ali defended himself steadily against Chanda Sahib; but the fortress was beleaguered by a greatly superior army with a strong French contingent, and was saved only when Clive made an effective diversion by his daring seizure of Arcot, the capital of the Karnatic.

THE ROCK OF TRICHINOPOLI.

This was the turning-point of the war. A large division of the besieging army, despatched from Trichinopoli to retake Arcot, made some fierce assaults that were repulsed by the desperate valour of Clive's scanty garrison, who made such an obstinate stand behind very feeble defences that the attempt had to be abandoned. The English and their allies, led by Clive and Lawrence, then took the open field against their enemy, cut off the French communications, dispersed Chanda Sahib's army, captured the French officers, and completely relieved Trichinopoli. Chanda Sahib was murdered by the Marathas who had joined Mohammad Ali; and Muzaffar Jang was killed in a skirmish on his march toward Haidarabad.

Meanwhile, Bussy had established himself at Haidarabad, where he had set up a Nizam, had organized a complete *corps d'armée* under his own command, and had made himself so much too powerful for the native government that he necessarily provoked much jealousy, enmity, and plotting against him. Having succeeded, nevertheless, by great dexterity and firmness in maintaining his position, he obtained from the Nizam an assignment of four rich districts lying along the eastern coast above the Karnatic, still called the Northern Sirkars, which yielded ample revenue for the payment of his troops.

Yet Bussy was well aware that his footing at Haidarabad, far inland, was isolated and precarious, dependent entirely on a semi-mutinous army under a few French officers. He had, therefore, consistently advised making peace with the English; and now the campaign in the Karnatic was visibly turning against

Dupleix, who had no military commander to match against Clive and Lawrence.

The French leader in India was beginning to find that practice was making the English no worse players than his own side at the game which he himself had introduced. The whole strength of the French had been exerted and exhausted in vain against Trichinopoli; the protracted siege had brought them nothing but disaster. Not only his native allies, but also the French Government at home, were losing their former confidence in Dupleix; for his policy may be said to have broken down when the French candidates for rulership were worsted, and when, after some years of heavy expenditure on these irregular hostilities, the results fell so far short of the expectations that he had raised. Toward the end of 1753, he made overtures for peace, but as soon as the English discovered that he intended to retain in his own person the Nawabship of the Karnatic, they broke off negotiations. As his policy fell into disrepute, he had naturally been led to disguise the real condition of the Company's finances; so when the directors in Paris were suddenly advised from Pondicherri that they were two millions of francs in debt, they determined at once to recall him.

The English Company at home had long been pressing their government to protest diplomatically against this illegitimate system of private war and against all the Indian proceedings of Dupleix, whose manifest object they declared to be the extirpation of their settlements. They urged that "the trade carried on by the East India Company is the trade of the English nation in the East Indies, and so far a national concern"; that the French power was growing; and that Dupleix had laid claim to the whole southeastern coast from Cape Comorin to the river Kistna.

The French ministry, on the other hand, did not care

A MONOLITHIC TEMPLE AT MAHABALIPUR ON THE SOUTHEAST COAST.

to embroil themselves with England, whose sea power was dangerous to all their colonies, on account of these apparently interminable Indian quarrels. Their finances were low; and they had good reasons for honestly desiring to substitute pacific for warlike relations between the two Companies, to discontinue the practice of lending auxiliary troops to native princes, and to agree upon a mutual return to the old commercial business. So in 1754, having settled an understanding upon this basis with the English government, they deputed to Pondicherri M. Godeheu, who superseded Dupleix, and concluded with the English governor, Saunders, first, a suspension of arms; and secondly, a provisional treaty, afterwards ratified, whereby the Companies bound themselves not to renew attempts at territorial aggrandizement or to interfere in local wars, and covenanted to retain only a few places and districts stipulated in the treaty. Mohammad Ali, whom the English had been supporting throughout the whole contest, was tacitly recognized as Nawab of the Karnatic. This concession virtually dropped the keystone out of the arch upon which the high-reaching policy of Dupleix had been built up, and on his return to France he died, after some vain attempts to obtain justice, in neglect, poverty, and unmerited discredit.

It has been usual to regard this treaty arrangement, which put an end to the unofficial war between the two Indian Companies, as the turning-point of the fortunes of France in the East Indies. The abandonment of the policy of Dupleix has been freely censured as short-sighted and pusillanimous, particularly by recent French writers. The French government is accused of throwing up a game that had been nearly won, and of deserting in the hour of his need the man whose genius had engendered the first conception of founding a great European empire in India, who showed not only the possibility of the achievement but the right method of accomplishing it. We are told, for instance, by Xavier

Raymond that England, in conquering India, has had but to follow the path that the genius of France opened out to her. James Mill, in summarizing the causes why the English succeeded, says that the two important discoveries for conquering India were, first, the weakness of the native armies against European discipline; and secondly, the facility of imparting that discipline to natives in the service of Europeans. He adds: "Both these discoveries were made by the French." And almost all writers on Indian history have repeated this after him, insisting that the failure of Dupleix is to be ascribed to the ineffective co-operation on the part of the French naval officers, to the want of good military commanders, to accidents, to bad luck at critical moments of the campaign, and, above all, to the faint-heartedness of the French ministry.

Now, it is quite true that Dupleix was a man of genius and far political vision, who strove gallantly against all these obstacles. On the other hand, it is also true that the English, with their usual good luck, had in Clive and Lawrence commanders superior to any of the French military officers with Dupleix, except Bussy. Bussy was a very able man, whom French historians delight to honour; but he was evidently intent, under Dupleix as afterwards under Lally, much more upon building up his own fortunes as a military dictator at Haidarabad than on sharing the unprofitable hard-hitting struggle between the two Companies in the Karnatic; and when misfortune overtook Dupleix and Lally he behaved ungenerously to both of them.

We may heartily agree with Elphinstone that Dupleix was " the first who made an extensive use of disciplined sepoys; the first who quitted the ports on the sea and marched an army into the heart of the continent; the first, above all, who discovered the illusion of the Moghul greatness." Nevertheless, although it seems invidious to detract from the posthumous glory of a man so able and yet so unfortunate as Dupleix, he cannot be ranked as an original discoverer in Asiatic warfare and politics, without taking into account surrounding circumstances and conditions that naturally pointed to the use of methods which he developed rather than invented.

The weakness of all Oriental states and armies had long been known; and India has always been, through natural causes, less capable than other great Asiatic countries of resisting foreign invasion. Her indigenous population has rarely furnished armies that could encounter the inrush of the hordes from Central Asia; and the only soldiers upon whom the princes of Southern India could rely were commonly mercenaries from the north. At the end of the seventeenth century, the imperial troops were probably still the best in India; but Bernier writes that a division of Turenne's men would have made short work of the whole Moghul army; nor could any European of military experience have doubted that the loose levies of the Karnatic would be scattered by a few well-armed and disciplined battalions.

Nor was there, in point of fact, any great novelty

in the French introduction of the practice of drilling a few native regiments for their own service. The Moghul army had always contained some European officers, while the Maratha chiefs were forming trained regiments within a very few years after the time of Dupleix; and so soon as the European Companies began to engage in Indian wars, the expedient of giving discipline to the mercenaries who swarmed into their camps was too obviously necessary to rank as a discovery. The real discovery of the value of organized troops had to be made, not by Europeans who knew it already, but by the natives of India, who had never before made trial of such tactics or had met such bodies in the field.

But there is no need to attempt any detraction from the high credit fairly due to Dupleix for having first started on the right road toward European conquest in India. The more interesting question is why, with so much energy, ability, and patriotism, he made so little way. To those who maintain that, but for the blindness of the French government towards the ideas of Dupleix, the blunders of colleagues or subordinates, and the final disavowal of Dupleix, France might have supplanted England in India—the true answer is that these views betray a disregard of historic proportion and an incomplete survey of the whole situation. They proceed on the narrow theory that extensive political changes may hang on the event of a small battle, or on the behaviour of a provincial general or governor at some critical moment. The strength and resources of France and England in their contests for the possession of

A RAJA OF INDIA RECEIVING A REPRESENTATIVE OF FRANCE.

empires are not to be measured after this fashion, or to be weighed in such nice balances.

It may even be questioned whether the result of the confused irregular struggle between the two Companies in the Indian peninsula told decisively one way or the other upon the final event. The Karnatic war, being unofficial, was necessarily inconclusive, for neither French nor English dared openly to strike home at each other's settlements; while even if this had been done indirectly through native auxiliaries, the home governments must have interfered earlier. The system of private or auxiliary war gave Dupleix the temporary advantage against the English that it was necessarily confined to the land, where he was the stronger; for as the two nations were at peace, their fleets could not take part in it. On the outbreak of national hostilities three years later, the naval strength of England came into play with decisive effect.

Dupleix was a man of original and energetic political instincts, and of an imperious and morally intrepid disposition, who embarked upon wide and somewhat audacious schemes of Oriental dominion and lost the stakes for which he played more through want of strength and continuous support than want of skill. He saw that so long as a European Company held its possessions or carried on trade at the pleasure of capricious and ephemeral Indian governments, the position was in the highest degree precarious. The right method, he argued, was to assert independence, to strike in for mastery, and to beat down any European rival who crossed his path; and, if the English had not been too strong for him, he might have succeeded.

He made the commonplace mistake of affecting ostentatious display and resorting to astute intrigues in his dealing with the Indians; whereas a European should meet Orientals not with their weapons, but with his own. His claim to be recognized as Nawab of the Karnatic, under patents of doubtful authenticity, was a grave political blunder, since it was quite impossible for the English to acquiesce in a position that would have placed their settlements in perpetual jeopardy. Major Lawrence, writing from his camp near Trichinopoli of the negotiations that were attempted in January, 1754, said: "It is my opinion there never can be peace in the province while Dupleix stays in India. He neither values men nor money, nor anything but what can gratify his own ambition. The continual ill-success of his troops would have made anybody but him reflect and be glad of the terms offered; but he talks not like the Governor of Pondicherri but as Prince of the Province."

Although some allowance must be made for the prejudice of an adversary, there is much truth in this view of the conduct and attitude of Dupleix. We may regard him, nevertheless, as the most striking figure in the short Indian episode of that long and arduous contest for transmarine dominion which was fought out between France and England in the eighteenth century, although it was far beyond his power to influence the ultimate destiny of either nation in India, and although the result of his plans was, as Clive wrote Lord Bute in 1762, that "we accomplished for ourselves against the French exactly everything that the French intended to accomplish for themselves against us." It is certain, moreover, that the conception of an Indian empire had already been formed by others besides Dupleix, and that more than one clear-headed observer had perceived how easily the whole country might be subdued by a European power.

It is easy to understand that when France and England, in 1753, determined to stop the fighting between their two Companies in India, they were actuated by the obvious expediency of terminating a protracted war between the representatives of two nations who were at peace in Europe, and of compelling their Indian governors to retire from politics and revert to trade. On the scene of action neither side had as yet gained any decisive advantage. In 1754 the French and English had both received reinforcements that brought their respective European forces up to about two thousand men each; but Orme says that the English troops were so superior in quality to the French that, if hostilities had continued, the English must have prevailed. The presence of an English squadron on the coast was also an argument, he observes, that inclined M. Godeheu toward pacific views.

On the other hand, the French held a much larger territory than the English, and apparently a more considerable political connection among the native states. The English governor at Madras, in transmitting to the

London Board the provisional treaty he had made with Godeheu in 1754, warned his Company that the French were in an advantageous position for continuing hostilities; they had, he wrote, a stronger military force

BODY-GUARD OF A NATIVE PRINCE.

—particularly in native cavalry, which could harry the English districts—and "their influence with the country powers far exceeds ours."

Yet the views and motives by which the French ministers were actuated are amply intelligible. The policy of Dupleix had been frustrated in the sense that, after four years of irregular warfare, he had brought the Company no nearer to the triumphant conclusion that was to compensate them for heavy military expenditure; while the English Company, though hard pressed, was by no means beaten; their troops were solid and well led, their finances in very fair condition. Dupleix might have gained ground, at best unstable and slippery, among the native princes; but in Europe the English government was remonstrating strenuously, and would certainly go beyond remonstrance whenever it should become manifest to the English people that their Indian trade and possessions were seriously menaced. The headquarters of each rival Company, at Madras and Pondicherri, lay along an open roadstead, completely exposed to attack by sea. The English fleet under Admiral Watson had just reached the coast, and the French government must have been conscious of the inferiority of their own navy. And since the treaty of 1754, which was published in Madras in January of the following year, maintained the French in possession of much larger territory on the Coromandel coast than was awarded to the English—while Bussy was still at Haidarabad with his division of five thousand well-disciplined troops—we may regard the loss of Dupleix himself, and the recognition of Mohammad Ali in the Karnatic, as the only two points in Godeheu's arrangement that could be said to have placed the French at a distinct disadvantage in India.

The French ministers were actuated, moreover, by the imperious and fundamental necessity of restoring their dilapidated finances; they could not, in justice to their overtaxed people, persist in the unsound and extravagant system of subsidizing a commercial Company that had plunged into the quicksand of Indian wars. In 1754, the French Company were on the verge of insolvency; their affairs were under official inquiry; they were demanding large subsidies from the treasury; and it was clear that the public credit would suffer seriously if they were allowed to go into liquidation. Dupleix had laid down the principle, which he was endeavouring to impress upon his government, that no Company could subsist in India which had not a fixed revenue from territory to provide for the cost of establishments. But at that time it was an axiom in France, and even in England, that conquest was incompatible with commerce; the opinion of all French authorities, mercantile and administrative, was unanimous against allowing a trading Company to acquire large territory; and these views had for years been impressed sedulously, though in vain, upon Dupleix.

Whether his principle was right or wrong need not be discussed, for the real point is that it was just then impracticable. The exhaustion of the Company's resources, the embarrassments of French finance, and the weakness of the French navy must have furnished the government with irresistible arguments against persisting in his policy. The true state and inevitable tendency of the contest between the two nations in India has been recognized by M. Marion, in his study of the history of French finance between 1749 and 1754. In defending Machault d'Arnouville, the controller-general of that period, from the imputation of having sacrificed an empire in Asia by recalling Dupleix, he shows that if the French government had retained his services and supported his policy, the ultimate event could not have been materially changed. The whole fabric of territorial predominance which Dupleix had been building up so industriously was loosely and hastily cemented; it depended upon the superiority of a few mercenary troops, the perilous friendship of Eastern princes, and the personal qualities of those in command on the spot. It was thus exposed to all the winds of fortune and had no sure foundation.

The first thing needful before any solid dominion could be erected by the French in India was to secure their communications with Europe by breaking the power of the English at sea; but this stroke was beyond the strength of the French in 1754. In the last war the French navy had, according to Voltaire, been entirely destroyed; and though since the peace of 1748 it had recovered to some extent, yet we are told that in 1755 France had only sixty-seven ships of the line and thirty-one frigates to set against one hundred and thirty-one English men-of-war and eighty-one frigates. When the Seven Years' War began in 1756, the French did make a vigorous attempt to regain command of the waterways; and it must be clear that to their failure in that direct trial of naval strength, far more than to their abandonment of the policy of Dupleix, must be attributed the eventual disappearance of their prospects of establishing a permanent ascendency in India.

CHAPTER VI

THE SECOND FRENCH WAR

IN 1756, when a rupture with France over the North American colonies was imminent, George II, to save Hanover, made a treaty of alliance with Frederick of Prussia, against whom the Austrian empress, Maria Theresa, had prepared an overpowering hostile coalition. Fortunately for England, the French government, then under the sinister influence of Madame de Pompadour, was persuaded into a rash and unwise conjunction with the Austrians; so that during the war France had to meet the Prussian army on land and the English navy at sea, a very formidable amphibious combination. From the beginning of the year 1756 both the English and the French in India had been expecting war, and each side had been protesting against the other's breaches of Godeheu's treaty; so that when, toward the year's end, news arrived of an open rupture in Europe, the effect was merely to substitute formal hostilities for the indirect skirmishings and threatening manœuvres that the two Companies had been carrying on in the Karnatic. But as most of the English troops had been despatched with Clive to Bengal, and as the

French were expecting strong reinforcements, no immediate collision occurred on the Coromandel coast.

The French government, having resolved to attack the English possessions in the East, laid out their plan of operations, prudently enough, on the principle of a regular military campaign. They committed the charge of a strong expeditionary force to Count Lally, instructing him to abstain from attempting to penetrate inland, to avoid participation in the quarrels of the native princes, and to concentrate his efforts upon seizing the fortified stations of the English on the coast and uprooting their commerce. They warned him, in short, against reverting to the system of Dupleix and Bussy. The directors of the French Company had no wish to set out again on schemes of territorial aggrandizement; they chiefly desired the restoration of their finances and the secure establishment of their commercial monopoly by the total expulsion of the English from the Coromandel coast.

These views are treated somewhat impatiently by M. Tibulle Hamont, the latest French biographer of Lally, who writes that the French directors were better fitted to weigh out pepper than to comprehend the problems of a people's expansion; and who lays very great stress upon Bussy's magniloquent reports of his conquests in the Deccan and of his supreme influence at Haidarabad. It will be recollected that the reigning Nizam (Salabat Jang) had been established on his throne by the French auxiliary troops under Bussy, who from that time forward exercised paramount influence in the state, being commandant of a small disciplined army under French officers, and in full possession of some rich districts assigned for its payment. After the peace of 1753, Bussy, whose position had not been shaken by the fall of Dupleix, went on strengthening himself in the Deccan; but the military dictatorship of a foreign adventurer inevitably aroused great jealousy

THE TEMPLE TANK AT TIRUPATI.

and suspicion; so that not only the ministers and the nobles, but the Nizam himself, were intriguing against him with the Marathas and even with the English. His firmness and ability enabled him to hold his ground, though not without bloodshed, and he had just put down a dangerous attempt to overthrow him in 1758, when he received a letter from Lally ordering him to repair immediately to Pondicherri.

Bussy was now in this serious dilemma, that if he should obey and quit Haidarabad, the field would be left open to his enemies there, whereas if he remained, not only must he take the consequences of insubordination, but Lally's failure on the coast would unquestionably entail ruin, sooner or later, upon the French party at Haidarabad. Very reluctantly, and after much remonstrance, he obeyed the order. It is probable, on the whole, that he was right in believing himself likely to serve Lally better by remaining to assist the French army with supplies drawn from the resources of the Deccan than by joining him on the coast with a small reinforcement; but this is by no means certain. For the fact remains that the one essential point was to drive the English out of the country, that Lally was quite right in declaring no peace or security to be possible for France in India until this had been done, and that when the struggle came Bussy might have not been able to co-operate decisively from so distant a base as Haidarabad. Clearly the first step was to beat the English by adroit and straightforward fighting, whereby the problems of expansion would have been mightily simplified and could have been solved afterwards at leisure.

Unluckily for the French, Lally, a soldier of great bravery and self-devotion, was yet a man totally unfit for the work. The French minister, D'Argenson, when the directors asked the Crown for Lally's services, warned them in words that almost exactly foretold what subsequently ensued that he was a hot-headed, stiff-necked martinet, who would burst out into thunderous fury at the least check or blunder, and would make himself so generally detested that his own officers would thwart him, trip him up, and foil all his operations for the satisfaction of ruining their general.

However, as the directors insisted, Lally was sent out with a force, which, in experienced and capable hands, would have been quite sufficient to have reduced, at least temporarily, all the Coromandel settlements, particularly if it had reached India twelve months before it did arrive. If the expedition, which was determined upon in 1755, had left France in 1756, soon after the declaration of war, it might have descended upon the coast at a very critical moment. For in June, 1756, the English had been driven out of Calcutta by the Nawab Siraj-ad-daulah, losing all their forts and factories in Bengal; and in October Clive had taken all the Company's best troops northward with the fleet from Madras to rescue his countrymen and recover Fort William.

When these troops were despatched, the Madras president and his council fully realized the situation; they knew that war had been declared in Europe, that a strong French force was under preparation for India, that whenever it reached Pondicherri, Bussy at Haidarabad would co-operate with Lally on the coast, and that the southern presidency would be in great danger if this joint attack were made while the troops were absent in Bengal. They decided, nevertheless, with remarkable promptitude and judgment, to run the risk of sending at once a large relieving force under Clive's command, in the hope that it might settle matters in Bengal and return before the French could appear on the Coromandel coast. Their venture met with the success it deserved; for the preparations in France were

BRAHMANS OF BENGAL.

so dilatory and the outward voyage was so slow that Lally did not land at Pondicherri until April, 1758.

By that time the opportunity had been irremediably lost. The English had not only driven Siraj-ad-daulah out of Calcutta and dispersed his army at Plassey, but had dethroned him and set up another Nawab, had become masters of Bengal, the richest province of India, and had expelled the French from all that region. A few months later Clive could report that "perfect tranquillity reigns in Bengal"; so that he was able to co-operate powerfully by supplies of men and money in the gallant defence of Madras. He also made an effective diversion by despatching Colonel Forde to drive the French out of those important districts, the Northern Sirkars, which was done very smartly and successfully. Masulipatam, the headquarters of the French administration, was taken by assault; and the French army was thenceforward deprived of the immense resources which it had been drawing during this war from the advantage of Bussy's influence and possessions. For as these were the districts which had been assigned to him by the Nizam for payment of his troops, their loss was a heavy blow to Bussy's credit at that court; it disclosed the real instability of his imposing position, and gave a strong impulse to the revolution which soon afterwards destroyed all French preponderance at Haidarabad.

Meanwhile Lally had landed his men, had taken Fort St. David, which was not very resolutely defended, and would have marched on Madras if he had not been prevented by want of money and supplies and by the refusal of the French admiral, D'Aché, to co-operate. He was entirely without tact or temper, suspected all the civil authorities of corruption, knew nothing of Oriental feelings or customs, and had precisely that impatient contempt of local experience and provincial soldiering that has so often led second-rate military commanders to disaster in colonial and Asiatic warfare. In order to get money, he made a fruitless raid upon Tanjore, which only plunged him deeper into unpopularity and financial embarrassment.

The English ships of war had now arrived, and several sharp though indecisive encounters with the French squadron had so damaged the French ships and discouraged their admiral, that in September, 1758, D'Aché withdrew, like Labourdonnais before him, to the Isle of France. Neither entreaties nor protests, nor the fury of Lally, could induce him to remain. We have seen that Lally, who saw and said plainly that the French could take no firm hold of the country until the English were beaten out of it, had summoned Bussy to join him from Haidarabad; but with Bussy's departure vanished all the French ascendency at the Nizam's court, where it was immediately supplanted by English influence and was never again restored. Bussy had now arrived, and strove by arguments of every sort, including something like bribery, to persuade Lally to permit him to return, with no better result than a rancorous quarrel, in which Bussy lost patience, became estranged, and made no effort whatever to avert the discomfiture of the unlucky general.

Surrounded by obstacles, almost destitute of means, abhorred by the civil functionaries, and distrusted by the army, Lally marched desperately upon Madras, hoping to reduce it before the English fleet, which had withdrawn during the stormy season, should return to the coast. But the place had been strengthened and well victualled, while Lally was in great straits for men and money, with no hope of reinforcements: his troops were discouraged, and at Pondicherri he was much more hated than helped. A letter from a high Pondicherri official to M. Conflans, dated September 4, 1758, and intercepted by the English, gives some notion of the depression then prevailing at headquarters. Lally furiously accused Bussy of disloyalty in evading his demands for money and active co-operation; nor can it be denied that Bussy, although far superior to Lally in military skill and in the knack of managing Orientals, much preferred remaining at Haidarabad, where he was wealthy and independent, to serving against the English under Lally, who was suspicious, intractable, and manifestly predestined to ruin.

In the course of the next twelve months, Lally's situation grew rapidly worse. A letter written by him from his camp before Madras to the governor of Pondicherri betrays the unhappy general's impotent rage and misery. His cash and gunpowder were both running out, and the country round could furnish no more provisions. He proposed to storm the place by the open breach, but his officers refused to risk the assault, and there was a serious mutiny among his European soldiery; yet he persevered until in February, 1759, the arrival of the English fleet struck such dismay into his army that the siege was hastily raised, to the great damage of the French reputation among the native princes, who were all watching the contest. Admiral D'Aché returned with his ships from Mauritius, threw some insignificant supplies into Pondicherri, and then disappeared finally, leaving French India to its fate. The English forces could now take the field against the French outposts, and they carried by assault the important fort of Vandewash. Clive's letter to Pitt in January, 1759, before the siege of Madras had been raised, shows that he had confidently foreseen that the English power at sea, and their possession of the resources of Bengal, must inevitably bring about Lally's complete discomfiture; and before the year's end this prediction was fulfilled.

The two armies manœuvred against each other in the Karnatic for some months; but Lally, disregarding Bussy's advice, insisted on attempting to recover Vandewash; whereupon he was attacked by Coote, who saw that since the siege chained the French down to one spot, he could choose his own time and tactics for fighting them, whereas, to meet him, Lally would be compelled to divide his force, having to leave a part in the entrenchments. The battle that followed was gallantly contested between the European troops, who were about two thousand strong on each side, by push of bayonet, musketry at close quarters, and artillery. Coote's and Draper's regiments met the battalions of Lorraine and Lally; there was resolute charging and countercharging, until the French fell into some disorder, when the plunging fire of the English cannon, the explosion of a tumbril, the fine handling of their men by Coote and Draper, and the capture of Bussy determined the defeat of the French. The sepoys on both sides were kept back by their commanders and took little share in the action; the Marathas in the French pay hovered uselessly on the outskirts. Lally vainly attempted, with his usual intrepidity, to lead in person a charge of the French cavalry—they could not face the superior artillery of the English; so he rallied his broken lines behind the intrenchments and made good his retreat to Pondicherri in January, 1760.

It was nevertheless a fatal reverse. The French could no longer keep the open field; they lost all their

MILITARY PRACTICE AT OLD FORT JHANSI.

strong places; the districts from which they drew their supplies were gradually occupied by the enemy. The French fleet never returned to the coast, for D'Aché flatly refused to bring back his ships; the English squadron held the sea in great strength, and fresh detachments of English troops were arriving. In this hopeless condition Lally was exposed to the ignoble reproaches and resentment of the civil officials within Pondicherri, which was quite unprovided with magazines or a sufficient garrison, and was now at last blockaded by land and water. The French could make but a feeble resistance, and were completely surrounded and half-starved until they were compelled to surrender at discretion in January, 1761.

From the fall of Pondicherri we may date the complete and final termination of the contest between France and England in India. All that remained to the French in that part of the world, says Voltaire, was their regret at having spent, during more than forty years, immense sums to maintain a Company that had been equally maladroit in commerce and in war, that had never made any profits, and that had paid no genuine dividends either to shareholders or to creditors. The association was dissolved in 1770, after it had been proved from official figures by the Abbé Morellet, who was employed to examine the accounts, that between 1725 and 1769 the Company had lost capital to the amount of 169,000,000 francs. He estimated the sum total of the advances that had been made to the Company by successive French ministries, during those forty-four years, at 376,000,000 francs, but it should be remembered that the abbé seems to have been preparing a case for the Company's dissolution.

The French did indeed recover, at the peace of 1763, the places that had belonged to them before Dupleix entered upon his schemes of territorial extension. Nevertheless, the sinews of their war power were cut by the stipulation against their fortifying these places and against their keeping troops in Bengal, whereby France was permanently shut out of North India and confined to some indefensible points on the seaboard. The two primary conditions of success, whether commercial or military, in India were the establishment of strong *points d'appui* on the coast and the maintenance of a naval force that could keep open communications with Europe; but the English had gained the preponderance at sea, while the French had now lost their footing on land. The real causes of their failure are to be found, not in the ill-luck or incapacity of particular individuals (for that might have been repaired), but rather in the wider combination of circumstances that decided against France her great contest with England at that period.

M. Tibulle Hamont declares that if Lally had thrown into the sea the instructions given him in France, and if he had resumed the policy of Dupleix and followed Bussy's advice, the imperial diadem of India would not have been worn by the English queen. It is more than doubtful whether Lally would have gained anything by imitating Dupleix or by taking counsel with the astute Bussy, since both these able and gallant Frenchmen relied far too much upon spheres of influence and military protectorates over native rulers as the basis of ascendency in India. Such methods provide powerful leverage for the extension of Asiatic dominion, but not for its foundation, which must always rest upon sure and swift support, in times of need, from the mother country. Without this essential resource, it is quite clear that to drive the English out of India during the Seven Years' War was an exploit far beyond Lally's power or capacity.

India was not lost by the French because Dupleix was recalled, or because Labourdonnais and D'Aché

AN INDIAN NATIVE RULER.

both left the coast at critical moments, or because Lally was headstrong and intractable. Still less was the loss due to any national inaptitude for distant and perilous enterprises, in which the French have always displayed high qualities. The record of their exploration and adventure in America and Asia during the seventeenth and eighteenth centuries fully sustains the reputation of this courageous and energetic people. It was through the short-sighted, ill-managed European policy of Louis XV, misguided by his mistresses and by incompetent ministers, that France lost her Indian settlements in the Seven Years' War. When it is remembered that before the end of that war France had surrendered her North American colonies, all her African settlements, and some of her finest West Indian islands, that her campaigns had been unfortunate in Germany, and that she had suffered deplorably at sea, there need be little hesitation in acknowledging that better men than Lally must have failed on the Coromandel coast.

To sum up: the immediate local causes of the English triumphs in India were, first, the conquest of Bengal, which furnished the British with the sinews of war and a firm base of operations on the mainland, whereas the French very soon exhausted their treasure-chest, and their only safe base was at Mauritius. Secondly, the English had the good luck to find a commander of military genius, well versed in Indian affairs, while the French general was inexperienced and without the slightest tincture of the capacity for dealing with Orientals which Frenchmen have often displayed.

The essential underlying causes, the primary reasons, why the French could not hold India are to be discovered in the insolvency of their East India Company, the maladministration of their affairs at home and abroad, the continual sacrifice of colonial and mercantile interests to a disastrous war-policy on the Continent, and above all in the exhaustion of their naval strength, which left all transmarine possessions of France defenceless against the overwhelming superiority of England. The English nation was deeply and ardently interested in the struggle; the lead and direction was in supremely able hands. The whole unfettered energy of a free and fierce people had been wielded by Pitt, the ablest war-minister that England has ever seen, against the careless incapacity of courtiers and the ill-supported efforts of one or two able but irresponsible officials, under such an autocrat as Louis XV. Nor can it be denied that French writers are mainly right in ascribing the success of England at this period, in India and elsewhere, to this signal inequality between the two governments.

It was natural that, after such mishaps and disappointments, the benefit to be derived from distant colonies or Asiatic conquests should be sharply questioned in France. The imposing authority of Montesquieu had been pronounced, a few years earlier, against emigration beyond sea, on the ground that it had a tendency to drain the population at home; although he saw the great advantages of commerce and navigation. The anti-colonial party was now headed by Voltaire, who declared the loss of Canada to be France's gain, mocked at the folly of fighting for a few snow-covered acres more or less, and deplored the shedding of blood to procure coffee, snuff, or spices for the citizens of Paris and London.

In the latter part of this same century, when the

mind of French statesmen and writers had become still more impressed by political idealism, Rousseau followed in a like vein with his discourses on the corrupting effects of luxury and modern civilization. And although these writers varied widely in their points of view, they united in attacking with caustic irony or sombre reprobation the sinister influences of priestly ambition and unscrupulous propagandism. The subordination of civil to ecclesiastical interests had too often hampered the authority of French governors in Canada, where the religious orders were much too strong; nor should we forget that in India the intrigues of the Jesuit Lavaur were held to have fatally accelerated the disgrace and condemnation of the unfortunate Lally.

But while in France the new spirit of humanitarian philosophy was consoling the nation for the loss of foreign trade and distant colonies, in England the tolerant and progressive ideas of the eighteenth century operated favourably rather than otherwise toward the spread of Asiatic dominion. As commerce has invariably bred freethinking in religion and politics all the world over, so rationalism and liberal principles in their turn helped commerce, by saving Englishmen from the mistakes and prejudices that had hampered the commercial enterprise of Spain, Portugal, and, partly, of France. England's conquests in India began at the period, about the middle of the eighteenth century, when, according to Lecky, "a latent skepticism and a wide-spread indifference might be everywhere traced among the cultivated classes."

The habit of treating their own religious differences with equanimity undoubtedly indisposes men to trouble themselves about the conversion of others, and leaves no room for the confusion of temporal with spiritual interests in dealing with heathen folk. No more suitable mental outfit could have been provided for Europeans in the religious climate of India; nor indeed could the charge of subordination to clerical influence, or of impolitic proselytism, ever have been brought home to the East India Company by their bitterest enemy. On the whole, therefore, the calm and open temper of the English mind at this period may be numbered among the moral conditions that were advantageous to the English East India Company in contending for superiority in India.

We have thus seen that, of the three collisions between the French and English upon Indian soil, both parties found themselves after the first, at the Peace of Aix-la-Chapelle in 1748, very much in the same condition as at the beginning of hostilities, with a slight advantage, if any, to the English. On the second occasion, when Dupleix launched his grand political schemes, the French closed the unofficial war in 1754 on terms at least equal; they probably had some local superiority of influence and position. The third war, which was international, finished in 1761 decisively and irremediably against them, as was proved twenty years afterwards. When the French made their last descent upon an India coast in 1781, the long odds were for the moment against England on the sea, for she was fighting single-handed against all the maritime nations; against France, Spain, Holland, and her own American colonies. She was also entangled within India in a very intricate desultory war against Hyder Ali of Mysore and the Marathas; two powers which both held strips of the Indian seaboard and were both corresponding with the enemy.

The French fleet was under Suffren, the best admiral

THE SACRED BULL AT MYSORE.

ever possessed by France, and the military force in the expedition was commanded by Bussy. Suffren was far superior as a naval tactician to the English commander, but the French admiral found on the Indian coast, as Captain Mahan justly observes, "no friendly port or roadstead, no base of supplies or repair." The French settlements had all fallen by 1779; and the invaluable harbour of Trincomali, in Ceylon, had been taken by the English from the Dutch just a month before. It was retaken by Suffren in 1782, but not until after England had made peace with the Marathas. In any event, the English power was by that time too firmly consolidated in India by the acquisition of Bengal, with the rich districts northwestward up to Allahabad, to be shaken by the landing on the southeast coast of a small force, which could hardly have produced more than local damage and temporary political confusion in the peninsula. Suffren's real object must have been no more than to create a diversion by harassing our Eastern possessions while our forces were employed against the colonial revolt in America, and in 1783 his operations were interrupted by news of the Peace of Versailles.

We are therefore entitled to fix on the Peace of Paris in 1763 as the true date after which the maritime powers of Europe finally withdrew from all serious rivalry, either in commerce or conquest, with England in India. The epoch is one of pre-eminent importance in the history of the rise of British dominion in the great Asiatic peninsula, for thenceforward the contest for ascendency was between the English and the native powers only—a contest of which the issue was in reality so far from being doubtful, invisible, or amazing, that it could be and was already foreseen and deliberately foretold.

CHAPTER VII

THE CONQUEST OF BENGAL

IN the foregoing chapter the summary of affairs on the east coast has been carried up to the date of Suffren's expedition in order to present an unbroken view of our relations with the French in India. It is now necessary to go back some years in order to take up the narrative of events in Bengal.

The rise and territorial expansion of the English power may be conveniently divided into two periods, which slightly overlap each other, but on the whole mark two distinct and consecutive stages in the construction of our dominion. The first is the period when the contest lay among the European nations, who began by competing for commercial advantages and ended by fighting for political superiority on the Indian littoral. The commercial competition was going on throughout the whole of the seventeenth century; but the struggle with the French, which laid the foundation of English dominion in India, lasted less than twenty years, for it began in 1745 and was virtually decided in 1763.

The second period, upon which we are now about

SHAH SUTLAJ MOSQUE AT MULTAN IN SIND.

to enter, is that during which England was contending with the native Indian powers, not for commercial preponderance or for strips of territory and spheres of influence along the seaboard, but for supremacy over all India. Reckoning the beginning of this contest from 1756, when Clive and Admiral Watson sailed from Madras to recover Calcutta from the Nawab of Bengal, it may be taken to have been substantially determined in fifty years; although for another fifty years the expansion of British territory went on by great strides, with long halts intervening, until the natural limits of India were attained by the conquest of Sind and the Panjab.

The first thing that must strike the ordinary observer, on looking back over the hundred years from 1757 to 1857, during which the acquisition of our Indian dominion was accomplished, is the magnitude of the exploit; the next is the remarkable ease with which it was achieved. At the present moment, when, from their small island in the West, the English survey the immense Eastern empire that has grown up out of their petty trading settlements on the Indian seaboard, they are apt to be struck with wonder and a kind of dismay at the prospering of their own handiwork.

The thing is, as has been said, so unprecedented in history, and particularly it is so entirely unfamiliar to modern political ideas—we have become so unaccustomed in the Western world to build up empires in the high Roman fashion—that even those who have studied the beginnings of our Indian dominion are inclined to treat the outcome and climax as something passing man's understanding. The magnificent possessions of Great Britain are commonly regarded as a man might look at a great prize he had drawn by luck in a lottery; they are supposed to have been won by incalculable chance. It is surmised that we stumbled forward blindfold on our way to dominion without any expectation that it would lead us to that end; we are assumed to have discovered an empire accidentally and to have obeyed the determination of events with no more foreknowledge than a rolling stone.

But it may fairly be argued that this view, which embodies the general impression on this subject, can be controverted by known facts. The idea that India might easily be conquered and governed, with a very small force, by a race superior in warlike capacity or in civilization, was no novelty at all. In the first place the thing had actually once been done. The Emperor Babar, who invaded India from Central Asia in the sixteenth century, has left us his authentic memoirs; it is a book of great historical interest, and nothing more amusing has ever been written by an Asiatic. He says: "When I invaded the country for the fifth time, overthrew Sultan Ibrahim, and subdued the empire of Hindustan, my servants, the merchants and their servants, and the followers of all friends that were in camp along with me were numbered, and they amounted to twelve thousand men. I placed my foot," he writes, "in the stirrup of resolution and my hands on the reins of confidence in God, and I marched against the possessions of the throne of Delhi and the dominions of Hindustan, whose army was said to amount to one hundred thousand foot, with more than one thousand elephants. The Most High God," he adds, " did not suffer the hardships that I had undergone to be thrown away, but defeated my formidable enemy and made me conqueror of this noble country."

A SIKH WARRIOR.

This was done in 1526; Babar's victory at Panipat gave him the mastery of all Northern India and founded the Moghul Empire. He had really accomplished the enterprise with smaller means and resources than those possessed by the English when they had fixed themselves securely in Bengal with a base on the sea; and the great host which he routed at Panipat at the beginning of his campaign was a far more formidable army than the English ever encountered in India until they met the Sikhs, at the end of a century's fighting. Now, what had been done before could be done again, and was indeed likely to be done again, for the whole country was quite incapable of resisting foreign invasion. So, when at the opening of the eighteenth century the Moghul Empire was evidently declining toward a fall, and people were speculating upon what might come after it, we find floating in the minds of cool observers the idea that the next conquest of India might possibly be made by Europeans.

The key-note had indeed been struck earlier by Bernier, a French physician at the court of Aurangzib toward the close of the seventeenth century, who writes in his book that M. de Condé or M. de Turenne with twenty thousand men could conquer all India; and who in his letter to Colbert lays particular stress first on the riches, secondly on the weakness, of Bengal. But in 1746, one Colonel James Mill, who had been in India twenty years, submitted to the Austrian emperor a scheme for conquering Bengal as a very feasible and profitable undertaking. "The whole country of Hindustan," he says, "or empire of the Great Moghul, is, and ever has been, in a state so feeble and defenceless that it is almost a miracle that no prince of Europe, with a maritime power at command, has not as yet thought of making such acquisitions there as at one stroke would put him and his subjects in possession of infinite wealth. . . . The policy of the Moghul is bad, his military worse, and as to a maritime power to command and protect his coasts, he has none at all. . . . The province of Bengal is at present under the dominion of a rebel subject of the Moghul, whose annual revenue amounts to about two millions. But Bengal, though not to be reduced by the power of the Moghul, is equally indefensible with the rest of Hindustan on the side of the ocean, and consequently may be forced out of the rebel's hand with all its wealth, which is incredibly vast."

If we bear in mind how little could have been accurately known of India as a whole by an Englishman in 1746, we must give Colonel Mill credit for much sagacity and insight into the essential facts of the situation. He discerns the central points; he places his finger upon the elementary causes of India's permanent weakness, her political instability within, and her seacoast exposed and undefended externally. Within ten or twelve years the English had carried out Colonel Mill's scheme; and it will be shown hereafter that when Bengal had been taken, the further expansion of British dominion was quite clearly foreseen. By those on the spot it was treated not as accidental, but as inevitable.

In the year 1716, the English, whose trading factories had long been settled in Bengal, obtained from the Moghul emperor an important *farmān*, or imperial order, permitting them to import and export goods upon payment of a fixed tribute, and protecting them from the heavy and arbitrary taxes laid on them at the caprice of the Nawabs. Bengal was a province under a governor whose ordinary title was the Nawab Nazim, who held office during the pleasure of the emperor, and who was frequently changed, so long as the empire was in its vigour, lest he should become too strong for the central authority. But as the power of the emperor declined, the independence of the Nawabs increased in this distant province, until in the eighteenth century, when Maratha insurrections and the irruptions from Central Asia multiplied the distractions of the state, the Bengal governors paid little obedience and less revenue to Delhi.

Under Murshid Kuli Khan, a man of considerable ability, the governorship became hereditary in the usual fashion; but in 1742 his grandson was overthrown and slain by Ali Vardi Khan, an Afghan adventurer who raised himself from a very humble post to be deputy-governor of Behar, and who won for himself by the sword the rulership of Bengal. During the fourteen years of his strong administration, the foreign merchants had no great reason to complain; for although he levied large subsidies from the English, French, and Dutch factories, he gave them protection and enforced good order, suppressing all quarrels and tolerating no encroachments. On his death, in 1756, he was succeeded by his adopted son, known in English histories as Siraj-ad-daulah, — although the accurate spelling is said to be Chiragh-ad-daulah,—a young man whose savage and suspicious temper was controlled by no experience or natural capacity for rulership, and who had long been jealous of the English, whom he suspected of having corresponded with a possible rival against him for the succession.

The new Nawab had just been proclaimed, when letters reached Calcutta from England informing the president that, as war with France was expected, he should put his settlement into a state of defence; whereupon he began to strengthen the fortifications. But the right to fortify their places had not been conceded to the English in Bengal; and the Nawab, to whom some offence had previously been given by the abrupt dismissal of a messenger, sternly ordered them to desist at once. The English president, Drake, not understanding his danger, answered by explaining that the fortifications were against the French, who had disregarded the neutrality of the Moghul's dominions in the last war by taking Madras, and who might attack Calcutta this time.

This reply Siraj-ad-daulah took to mean that his

THE GOVERNMENT HOUSE AND TREASURY, CALCUTTA, FROM THE OLD COURSE.

protection and sovereign authority were very lightly regarded by the foreigners. In great indignation he seized the factory of Kasimbazar, near his capital, and marched upon Calcutta with a large army. The English defended themselves for a time; but the town was open; the governor and many of the English fled in ships down the river; and the rest surrendered on promise of honourable treatment. Nevertheless, those whom the Nawab captured with the fort were thrown into a kind of prison-room called the Black Hole, from which, after one night's dreadful suffering, on the eve of June 21, 1756, only twenty-three out of one hundred and forty-six emerged alive.

As soon as the news of this dismal catastrophe reached Madras, the president lost no time in despatching the fleet, commanded by Admiral Watson, to Bengal, with troops under Colonel Clive. The force was calculated to be sufficient not only for retaking Calcutta, but also for reducing Hugli, expelling the French from Chandarnagar, and even for attacking the Nawab's capital at Murshidabad; and Clive set out, as he wrote, "with the full intention of settling the Company's estate in those parts in a better and more lasting condition than ever." He had less reason, he added, to apprehend a check from the Nawab's army than from the country and the climate. Nor indeed does it appear that any serious misgivings as to the result of the expedition troubled the government at Madras, where they were only anxious to get the business done in Bengal before the French armament under Lally should arrive on the Coromandel coast.

Clive lost no time in driving the enemy's garrison out of Calcutta and Hugli. The Nawab marched down to encounter him with a very large force, which, after some parleying, was attacked by the English close to Calcutta. The engagement was indecisive, but the Nawab was so far daunted as to sign a treaty restoring to the Company their possessions in Bengal, and promising compensation for losses. This truce, however, was broken very soon. There were strong reasons why the English should return speedily to Madras, but as France

The Black Hole of Calcutta

The Black Hole of Calcutta is the name given to a room in the garrison in which 136 captive British soldiers were incarcerated by Nawab Siraj ad-Daulah when he took the fortress, June 20, 1756. The cell was only twenty feet square and had but two small windows, so that it became almost impossible to live in the stifling air. The next morning all but 23 of the men were found dead after a night of agonizing suffering.

and England were now at open war, it was dangerous to depart while the French held their fortified station of Chandarnagar, within a few miles of Calcutta. So Watson and Clive carried the place by assault; but the Nawab, who had at first acquiesced, at the last moment withdrew his consent to the attack, and was secretly inviting Bussy to march from Haidarabad to his relief. There could be no reasonable doubt that Siraj-ad-daulah would renew hostilities on the first opportunity, while, on the other hand, Lally's expedition must soon reach the eastern coast, and the Madras government was urgently pressing for the return of the troops.

The English in Bengal thus found themselves in a perilous dilemma, since the troops could not return to Madras until Calcutta had been in some way placed beyond danger from the Nawab. When, therefore, overtures were received from certain disaffected chiefs of the Nawab's court, Clive entered into a compact to dethrone Siraj-ad-daulah, and to set up in his stead Mir Jafir, one of the principal conspirators. He then marched up the country against the Nawab, whom he found entrenched at Plassey with about fifteen thousand cavalry, thirty thousand foot, and forty pieces of cannon.

The engagement began with some cannonading, in which a battery managed by Frenchmen gave much annoyance to the English. Early in the afternoon the Nawab fled from the field, and as his army began to fall back, an advance was made against the battery, which alone remained in position. So soon as the

French had been dislodged and some rising ground occupied that commanded the interior of the enemy's fortified camp, Clive delivered his assault at one angle; whereupon the Nawab's whole army dispersed in a general rout, leaving on the field its camp equipage, its artillery, and about five hundred men. Clive's despatch reports the loss on his side to have been twenty-two killed and fifty wounded. Next morning, Mir Jafir, who had merely hovered about the flanks of the engagement with a large body of cavalry, paid a visit to Clive, was saluted as Nawab, and hastened to occupy the capital, Murshidabad, where soon after he put Siraj-ad-daulah to death.

The whole province quietly submitted to the new ruler; the emperor's government at Delhi, which was occupied just then by Ahmad Shah with an Afghan army, was totally incapable of interference; so that by this sudden and violent revolution English ascendency at once became established in Bengal.

The rout of Plassey—for it can hardly be called a battle—is in itself chiefly remarkable as the first important occasion upon which the East India Company's troops were openly arrayed, not as auxiliaries, but as principals, against a considerable native army commanded in person by the ruler of a great province. It stands, in fact, first on the long list of regular actions that have been fought between the English in India and the chiefs or military leaders of the country. The event supplies, therefore, a very striking illustration of the radical weakness of those native governments and armies to whom the English found themselves opposed in the middle of the eighteenth century. This inherent feebleness of the Hindus, and their inability to govern or defend their possessions, obviously explains why the English, who could do both, so rapidly made room for themselves in a country which, though rich and populous, was, in a practical sense, masterless.

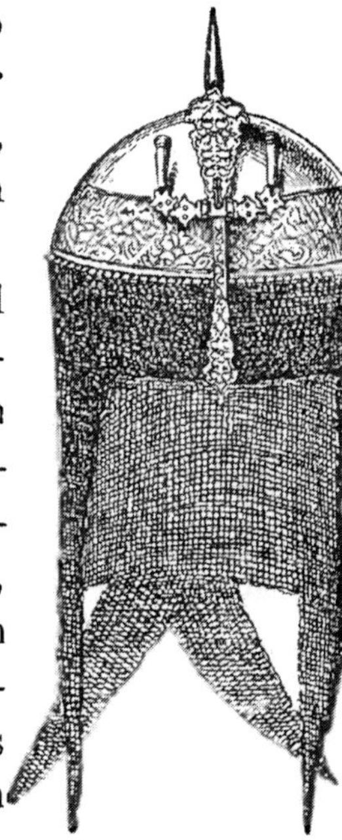

AN INDIAN MOHAMMEDAN HELMET.

It must also be remembered that Bengal and the other provinces bordering on the sea in which the English won these facile triumphs were far more defenceless than the inland country, partly through the dilapidation of the central power, partly because the people of those tracts are naturally less warlike than elsewhere, and partly by the accident that they just then were very ill governed. The army of the later Moghul emperors had always been bad; yet until Aurangzib died it was quite strong enough to repulse any small expeditionary force descending upon the coast. Nor could such a stroke as Clive's at Plassey have been attempted with impunity if Bengal had happened to possess a vigorous and capable viceroy; for a few years later our first campaigns against Hyder Ali in the south and the Marathas in the west showed us that under competent leadership the superior numbers of an Indian army might make it a very dangerous antagonist.

We have to understand, then, that our earliest victories were over troops that were little better than a rabble of hired soldiers, without coherence or loyalty. An Indian army of that period was usually an agglomeration of mercenaries collected by the captains of companies who supplied men to any one able to pay for them, having enlisted them at random out of the swarm of roving freelances and swordsmen, chiefly Asiatic foreigners, by whom all India was infested. These bands had no better stomach for serious fighting than the *condottieri* of Italy in the sixteenth century; the close fire of European musketry was more than they had bargained for; and artillery, properly served, they could not face at all. Their leaders, moreover, changed sides without scruple, if it seemed to their advantage, and were constantly plotting either to betray or supplant their employers.

It is not surprising, therefore, if troops of this kind were such exceedingly perilous weapons in timid or maladroit hands that the prince, governor, or usurper who had retained their services often went into action with a very uncomfortable distrust of his best regiments. In the eighteenth century, most of the revolted provinces of the empire had been appropriated by successful captains of these mercenaries, among whom the best fighting men were the Afghans. Their most celebrated leader was Ahmad Shah Abdali, a mighty warrior of the Afghan nation, and the only great Asiatic soldier who appeared in India during the eighteenth century.

But no sooner had the European appeared upon the Indian arena, than the men of this new immigration were discovered to be distinctly superior to all Asiatic foreigners in the art of war, and far beyond them in those qualities of united, persistent, and scientific action by which a compact and civilized force must always prevail in the long run over incoherent and uninstructed opponents. Against the French or the English the dissolute and rickety Nawabs of Bengal and the Karnatic could take into the field only a crowd of mutinous soldiery, who often dispersed at the first shock and followed their leader in tumultuous flight. The natural and speedy result was that the military classes of the Indian population very soon began to transfer their services to the standard of leaders who always paid and usually won; who were invariably to be seen in the front line of battle, and who did the hardest fighting with a *corps d'élite* of their own countrymen.[1]

The British sepoy army was recruited and gradually developed out of the immense floating mass of profes-

[1] The rank and file of this *corps d'élite*, whose fighting qualities decided for us all our earlier battles, were drawn in those days from strange sources. General Smith, in his evidence before a Committee on the East India Recruiting Bill, told the House of Commons "that in 1769, when he left India, the European army in Bengal was in very good discipline, considering the sort of men who being chiefly raised about London were the riffraff of the people, chiefly boys under seventeen or old men above forty to sixty years old, and fitter on their arrival to fill the hospital than the ranks." He added that the Sepoys were "almost too good." — *Parliamentary Debates, 1771, April.*

sional mercenaries (reckoned by good contemporary authority at two millions) who roved about India in those days. It is on record that any number of foot-soldiers might be enlisted, although they "deserted in shoals" when a very distant march was in prospect; and that the best cavalry of Hindustan (Afghans, Tartars, Persians, or Marathas) might be had in abundance at six weeks' notice, "many of them," as the East India Records state, "out of the very camp of the enemy." The English commanders, however, seem to have relied for their infantry chiefly upon natives of India, who were probably more faithful to their salt, and more amenable to discipline, than the wilder folk of Central Asia. And for a hundred years the Indian sepoy well repaid the confidence placed in his courage and loyalty. With artillery served by men who stood fast to their guns, with a few red-coated English battalions, with a strong contingent of well-drilled native infantry and some excellent native light cavalry, the Company's army presented a combination of war material that only wanted good handling to dispose of any opponent in Southern India.

The foregoing observations on the native armies of this period may help to explain the rapidity with which the English won their earliest battles against Indian adversaries and made their first conquests in the seaboard provinces, especially in Bengal. They had only to upset a few unstable rulers of foreign descent, whose title rested on dexterous usurpation; and to disperse by their trained battalions, European and native, great

SHIVARY HILLS NEAR SALEM IN SOUTHERN INDIA.

bodies of hired troops who usually had no interest in the war beyond their pay. Between the Marathas, who were spreading over the country from the west, and the Afghans, who had broken in from the north, the inland country was being ruined by rapine and exactions; trade and cultivation had fallen low; and the position of the minor native powers was so unsteady through military weakness and financial embarrassments that any of them might be destroyed by the loss of one campaign or even a single battle.

But this course of easy victories on the outskirts of India did not last long; for we shall see that as the English penetrated further into the interior, their progress became very much slower, and was, indeed, arrested for a time. On the west coast, they were already confronted by rivals very different from an incapable Bengali Nawab—by the Marathas, whose power had considerable national character, some political stability, and formidable military organization. Under their great Peshwa, Balaji Bala Rao, they were now attaining the zenith of their predominance; they had conquered great territories; they were pushing forward into North India; they were supreme in the central regions; and while one army was dismembering the Nizam's State, another was extorting heavy subsidies in the Karnatic and Mysore. Their operations had hitherto been very serviceable to the English, with whom they were at this time often in alliance, by weakening all the Mohammedan rulerships, and particularly by checking Bussy's military domination at Haidarabad.

On the whole there is good ground for the opinion that if, at the time of the dissolution of the Moghul Empire, India had been left to herself, if the Europeans had not just then appeared in the field, the whole of Southern and Central India would have fallen under the Maratha dominion. The correctness of this view is attested by a statement in a letter from the President and Council of Madras, who wrote under date of October, 1756: "We look on the Morattoes [Marathas] to be more than a match for the whole (Moghul) Empire, were no European force to interfere." It was very fortunate for the English that they did not come into collision with such antagonists until their own strength had matured; since there can be no doubt that throughout the later stages of the tournament for the prize of ascendency between England and the native powers, the most dangerous challengers of the British were the Marathas.

CHAPTER VIII

THE SITUATION IN BENGAL

CLIVE'S victory in 1757 was followed by the military occupation of Bengal, which had an immense and far-reaching effect upon the position of the English in India. Their resources were so considerably increased that the defeat of the French in the Peninsula became thenceforward certain; for while Lally was cut off by sea and vainly attempting to support himself along a strip of seacoast, the English had their feet firmly planted in the Gangetic delta and the rich alluvial districts of the lower Ganges. The word Bengal must be understood, here and hereafter, to signify the great territory which includes the three provinces of Bengal, Bihar, and Orissa, which were all under the rulership of the Nawab Siraj-ad-daulah. The subordination of the Bengal Nawabs to the English at once extended British predominance northwestward as far as the banks of the Ganges opposite Benares, and the capital of English political dominion was thenceforward established at Calcutta.

This transfer of the headquarters of the Company's government to Calcutta marks a notable step forward, since it was from Bengal, not from Madras or Bombay, that the English power first struck inland into the heart of the country and discovered the right road to supremacy in India. To advance into Bengal was to penetrate India by its soft and unprotected side. From Cape Comorin northward along the east coast there is not a single harbour for large ships; nor are the river estuaries accessible to them.

But at the head of the Bay of Bengal we come upon

A NATIVE BOAT OF BENGAL.

a low-lying deltaic region, pierced by navigable channels which discharge through several mouths the waters of great rivers issuing from the interior. Some of these are merely huge drains of the water-logged soil; others are fed by the Himalayan snows. On this section, and upon no other of the Indian seaboard, the rivers are wide waterways offering fair harbourage and the means of penetrating many miles inland; while around and beyond stretches the rich alluvial plain of Bengal, inhabited by a very industrious and unwarlike people, who produce much and can live on very little.

All authorities agree that in the eighteenth century

the richest province of all India, in agriculture and manufactures, was Bengal. Colonel James Mill, in his memoir already quoted above, points out that it has vast wealth and is indefensible toward the sea. "The immense commerce of Bengal," says Verelst in 1767, "might be considered as the central point to which all the riches of India were attracted. Its manufactures find their way to the remotest parts of Hindustan." It lay out of the regular track of invasion from Central Asia, and remote from the arena of civil wars which surged round the capital cities of the empire, Agra, Delhi, or Lahore. For ages it had been ruled by foreigners from the north; yet it was the province most exposed to maritime attack, and the most valuable in every respect to a seafaring and commercial race like the English. Its rivers lead like main arteries up to the heart of India. From Bengal northwestward, the land lies open, and, with few interruptions, is almost flat, expanding into the great central plain country that we now call the Northwest Provinces and Oudh, and further northward into the Panjab up to the foot of the Himalayan wall. Whoever holds that immense interior champaign country, which spreads from the Himalayas southeastward to the Bay of Bengal, occupies the central position that dominates all the rest of India; and it may accordingly be observed that all the great capital cities founded by successive conquering dynasties have been within this region.

Looking now at a map of India, we perceive that upper or continental (as distinguished from peninsular)

India has been divided off from the rest of Asia by walls of singular strength and height. The whole of the Indian land frontier is fenced and fortified by mountain ranges; and where, in the southwest toward the sea, the mountains subside and have an easier slope, the Indian desert is interposed between the outer frontier and the fertile midland region. It is as if Nature, knowing the richness of the land and the comparative weakness of its people, had taken the greatest possible pains to protect it; for along the whole of that vast line of mountain wall which overhangs the northwest and the northern boundaries of India there are only a very few practicable passes.

These are the outlets through Afghanistan, by which Alexander the Great and all subsequent invaders have descended upon the low country; and any one who, after traversing the interminable hills and stony valleys of Afghanistan, has seen, on mounting the last ridge, the vast plain of India spreading out before him in dusky haze like a sea, may imagine the feelings with which such a prospect was surveyed by those adventurous leaders when they first looked down on it from the edge of the Asiatic highlands. Along the whole northern line of frontier, the Himalayas are practically impassable; for the chain of towering mountains is backed by a lofty tableland, rising at its highest elevation to nearly seventeen thousand feet, which projects northward into Central Asia like the immense glacis of a fortress.

Such are the natural fortifications of India landward. But an invader landing on the seaboard takes all these defences in reverse. He enters, as has been said, by open ill-guarded water-gates; he can penetrate into the centre of the fortress, can march up inside to the foot of the walls, can occupy the posts, and turn the fortifications against others. This is just what the English accomplished between 1757 and 1849, during the century occupied by their wars with the native powers in India. At the beginning of that period, the conquest of Bengal transferred the true centre of government from Southern India to that province; and thus we emerge rapidly into a far wider arena of war and politics.

For the English, after their victory at Plassey, the most urgent and important matter was the restoration of some regular administration. They had invested Mir Jafir with the Nawabship under a treaty which bound him to make heavy money payments to them in compensation for their losses by the seizure of Calcutta and other factories, and for their war expenditure; agreeing in return to supply troops at the Nawab's cost whenever he should require them. The result was to drain the native ruler's treasury and at the same time to reduce him, for the means of enforcing his authority and maintaining his throne, to a condition of dependence upon the irresponsible foreigners who commanded an army stationed within his province. Such a situation was by no means novel in India, where the leaders of well-disciplined troops are often as dangerous to their own government as to its enemies. At this very time, indeed, Bussy, with his French contingent at Haidarabad, was in much the same position as Clive with his English levies in Bengal. But when Lally had recalled Bussy from Haidarabad, the power of the French disappeared from the Deccan, and was soon after extinguished in their general discomfiture;

THE GREAT MOSQUE AT KALBARGAH IN HAIDARABAD.

while the English were now consolidating their supremacy over a kingdom that they had practically conquered.

The difficulty of this consolidation was greatly enhanced by the perplexity and indecision of the English as to their actual situation in the country. Although they were conquerors *de facto*, they neither could nor would assume the attitude of rulers *de jure*; they were merely the representatives of a commercial company with no warrant from their nation to annex territory, and were obliged to pretend deference toward a native ruler who was really subservient to themselves. Nothing more surely leads to misrule than the degradation of a civil government to subserve the will of some arbitrary force or faction within the state; and in Bengal the evils of precarious and divided authority were greatly heightened by special aggravations.

In the first place, the Company and the Nawab were equally hard pressed for money. The Company was making large and emergent remittances to Madras for sustaining the war against the French, and it was obliged, at the same time, to maintain an army of more than six thousand men in Bengal. The Nawab, who did not choose to place himself entirely at the mercy of his foreign allies by disbanding his own forces, was beset by mutinous bands claiming arrears that he could not pay. Meanwhile, he wanted troops to put down disorder within his territories and to repulse attacks from without; for some of the principal landholders were in revolt against him; the Marathas were threatening Bengal on the west; and the heir apparent of the Delhi emperor had appeared with a force in the northwestern districts, on the pretext of reclaiming a province of his father's empire.

Secondly, the Company was not merely the Nawab's too powerful auxiliaries, demanding a large share of his revenue as the price of their annual support; nor were they, like the Marathas or the Afghans, an army of occupation that might be bought out by disbursement of one huge indemnity. They represented an association which insisted upon regular remittances to Europe; their primary interests and objects were still commercial; and as soon as they found themselves irresistible, they began to monopolize the whole trade in some of the most valuable products of the country. By investing themselves with political attributes without discarding their commercial character, they produced an almost unprecedented conjunction which engendered intolerable abuses and confusion in Bengal.

This is the only period of Anglo-Indian history which throws grave and unpardonable discredit on the English name. During the six years from 1760 to 1765, Clive's absence from the country left the Company's affairs in the hands of incapable and inexperienced chiefs, just at the moment when vigorous and statesmanlike management was urgently needed. That Clive himself clearly foresaw that the system would not answer and would not last, is shown by his letter written to Pitt in 1759, in which he suggested to the Prime Minister the acquisition of Bengal in full sovereignty by the English nation, promising him a net revenue of two millions sterling. In the meantime, he had done what he could to revive internal order and had forced the Delhi prince to evacuate the province.

The Dutch in Bengal, who naturally watched English proceedings with the utmost jealousy and alarm, were secretly corresponding with the Nawab and had brought over from Batavia a large body of troops. When their armed ships were prohibited by the English from ascending the river, they began hostilities, and were totally defeated by Colonel Forde in an action described by Clive's report as "short, bloody, and decisive." But after Clive's departure for England in 1760, the invasions from the outside were renewed; and within Bengal the whole administration was paralyzed by acrimonious disputes between the Company's agents and the Nawab, who fought against his effacement and was secretly corresponding with the Dutch. Being intent, as was natural, on asserting his own independent authority, he manœuvred to thwart and embarrass the Company, intrigued with their rivals, and did his best to disconcert their joint operations against the Marathas who were laying his country waste, since a defeat might at least help to shake off the English.

It followed that as neither party could govern tolerably, both soon became equally unpopular, and that during these years the country was in fact without an authoritative ruler. For while the English traders garrisoned the country with a large body of well-paid and well-disciplined troops, the whole duty of filling the military chest and carrying on an executive government fell upon the Nawab, who was distracted between dread of assassination by his own officers and fear of dethronement by the Company.

As the English traders had come to Bengal avowedly with the sole purpose of making money, many of them set sail again for Europe as soon as they had made enough. In the meantime, finding themselves entirely without restraint or responsibility, uncontrolled either by public opinion or legal liabilities (for there was no law in the land), they naturally behaved as, in such circumstances and with such temptations, men would behave in any age or country. Some of them lost all sense of honour, justice, and integrity; they plundered as Moghuls or Marathas had done before them, though in a more systematic and businesslike fashion; the eager pursuit of wealth and its easy acquisition had

LORD CLIVE.

blunted their consciences and produced general insubordination. As Clive wrote later to the Company, describing the state of affairs that he found on his return in 1765, "In a country where money is plenty, where fear is the principle of government, and where your arms are ever victorious, it was no wonder that the lust of riches should readily embrace the proffered means of gratification," or that corruption and extortion should prevail among men who were the uncontrolled depositaries of irresistible force. This universal demoralization necessarily affected the revenues and exasperated the disputes between the Company and Mir Jafir by increasing the financial embarrassments of both parties; especially as the Nawab showed very little zeal in providing money for the troops upon whom rested the Company's whole power of overruling him, and arrears were accumulating dangerously.

At last the president and council determined to put an end to these dissensions by removing the Nawab. An understanding was arranged with Mir Kasim, the Diwan, or chief finance minister, whereby he undertook to provide the necessary funds as a condition of his elevation to the rulership in the place of Mir Jafir, who was dispossessed by a bloodless revolution. But as the new Nawab had gained his elevation by outbidding his predecessor, this rack-renting revolution only made matters infinitely worse. Mir Kasim's performances fell far short of his promises; the quarrels grew fiercer, and nothing was done to remedy the disorganization that was wrecking the administration and emptying the treasuries. The land revenue continued to decrease; commercial intercourse with upper India was checked by the insecurity of traffic; while the English Company was using their political ascendency not only to insist upon its privileged monopoly of the export trade to Europe, but also to enforce an utterly unjust and extravagant claim for special exemption from all duties upon the internal commerce of Bengal. In the assertion of this pretension, the Company's servants, native as well as English, set at nought the Nawab's authority, and their factories were in arms against his revenue officers.

All this violent friction soon culminated in an explosion, brought about by an awkward attempt on the part of Mr. Ellis, chief of the Patna factory, to seize Patna city, with the object of forestalling an attack by the Nawab on his factory. Although Ellis took the place, he could not hold it, and his whole party was captured in their retreat; but the Company's troops marched against and defeated the Nawab, who, in his furious desperation, caused his English prisoners to be massacred and then fled across the frontier to the camp of the Vizir of Oudh. The Company, somewhat sobered by these tragic consequences of misrule, relinquished the more scandalous monopolies and restored Mir Jafir in 1763. When he died in 1765, the ruinous system of puppet Nawabs came practically to an end; for in that year Lord Clive, who had returned to India, assumed, under a grant from the Delhi emperor, direct administration of the revenue of the three provinces of Bengal, Bihar, and Orissa, an office that was entitled the Diwani. The Diwan had been originally the controller-general on behalf of the imperial treasury in each province, with supreme authority over all public expenditure; so that the investiture of the Company with this office added the power of the purse to the power of the sword, and rendered them directly and regularly responsible for the most important departments of government.

We must now turn from internal affairs to the foreign relations of the East India Company and the general aspect of Indian politics. The Vizir of Oudh, when Mir Kasim took refuge with him, had in his camp the titular emperor of Delhi; and he thought the opportunity favourable for an expedition into the Bengal provinces with the professed object of restoring the imperial authority, but really with the intention of annexing such territory as he could seize. At Baxar, on the Ganges, he was met and signally defeated in September, 1764, by the Company's troops under Major Hector Munro, in an engagement of which the eventual and secondary consequences were very important. The success of the English brought the emperor into their camp, intimidated the Vizir, carried the armed forces of the Company across the Ganges to Benares and Allahabad, and acquired for them a new, advanced, and commanding position in relation to the principalities northwest of Bengal, with whom they now found themselves for the first time in contact. By this war the English were drawn into connection with upper India, and were brought out upon a scene of fresh operations that grew rapidly wider.

At this point, therefore, it will be useful to sketch in loose outline the condition, in the middle of the last century, of that vast tract of open plain country, watered by the Jumna, the Ganges, and their affluents, which stretches from Bengal northwestward to the Himalayas, and which is now divided into the three British provinces of Oudh, the Northwest Provinces, and the Panjab. Throughout this vast region, the flood of anarchy that had been rising since Aurangzib's death was now at its height; and as the struggle over the ruins of the fallen empire was sharpest at the capital and the centres of power, the districts round Delhi

THE JAMI' MASJID AT LUCKNOW.

and Agra, Lucknow and Benares, were perhaps more persistently fought over than any other parts of India.

Two centuries of systematic despotism had long since levelled and pulverized the independent chiefships or tribal federations in these flat and fertile plains, traversed by highways open to every successive invader. So when the empire toppled over under the storms of the eighteenth century, there were no local breakwaters to check the inrush of confusion. The Marathas swarmed up, like locusts, from the south, and the Afghans came pouring down from the north through the mountain passes. Within fifty years after the death of Aurangzib, who was at least feared throughout the length and breadth of India, the Moghul emperor had become the shadow of a great name, a mere instrument and figurehead in the hand of treacherous ministers or ambitious usurpers. All the imperial deputies and vicegerents were carving out independencies for themselves, and striving to enlarge their borders at each other's expense.

We have seen that the Nizam, originally Viceroy of the Southern Provinces, had long since made himself *de facto* sovereign of a great domain. In the north-west, the vizir of the empire was strengthening himself east of the Ganges, and had already founded the kingdom of Oudh, which underwent many changes of frontier, but lasted a century. Rohilkhand had been appropriated by some daring adventurers known as Rohillas (or mountain men) from the Afghan hills; a sagacious and fortunate leader of the Hindu Jats was creating the State of Bhartpur across the Jumna River; Agra was held by one high officer of the ruined empire; Delhi, with the emperor's person, had been seized by another; the governors sent from the capital to the Panjab had to fight for possession with the deputies of the Afghan ruler from Kabul, and against the fanatic insurrection of the Sikhs.

These were, roughly speaking, the prominent and stronger competitors in the great scramble for power and lands; but scarcely one of them (except the Sikhs) represented any solid organization, political principle, or title. Most of the rulerships depended on the personality of some chief or leader, who was raised more by the magnitude of his stakes than by the style of his play above the common crowd of plunderers and captains of soldiery. Any one who had money or credit might buy at the imperial treasury a *farmān* authorizing him to collect the revenue of some refractory district. If he overcame the resistance of the landholders, the district usually became his domain, and as his strength increased, he might expand into a territorial magnate; if the peasants rallied under some able headman and drove him off, their own leader often became a mighty man of his tribe and founded a petty chiefship or a ruling family. The traces of this chance medley and fluctuating struggle for the possession of the soil or of the rents were visible long afterwards in the complicated varieties of tenure, title, and proprietary usage that made the recording of landed rights and interests so perplexing a business for English officials in this part of India.

The English reader may now form some notion of the distracted condition of upper India when the Marathas invaded it in 1758 with a numerous army intended to carry out definite plans of conquest. The Moghul Empire was like a wreck among the breakers; the emperor Alamgir, who had long been a state prisoner, had been murdered; and the strife over the spoils had assumed the character of a wide-spreading free fight, open to all comers. But as any such contest, if it lasts, will usually merge into a battle between distinct factions under recognized leaders, so the rapidly increasing power of the Marathas, who came swarming up from the southwest, and the repeated invasions from the northwest of Ahmad Shah Abdali with his Afghan bands, drew together to one or the other of these two camps all the self-made princes and marauding adventurers who were parcelling out the country among themselves. When Ahmad Shah brought an Afghan army to Delhi in 1757, he caused the office of prime minister to be conferred by the emperor on Najib-ad-daulah, one of the few able and politic nobles still attached to the Moghul government, who took a very leading part in subsequent events. At Lahore he appointed a viceroy to govern in his name the very important districts of the Panjab and to keep open his communications.

Having made these arrangements for maintaining his grasp on north India, the Afghan king had returned through the mountain passes to his own country. The Marathas took advantage of his absence with characteristic audacity. They were now overflowing all India with a flood-tide of conquest and pillage; and the supreme control of their confederacy was in the hands of Balaji Baji Rao, the ablest of those hereditary Peshwas, or prime ministers, who long kept their royal family in a state prison. While this powerful and politic ruler was extending Maratha dominion in the centre of India, his brother Raghunath Rao led northward a large army, supported by the federal contingents of Holkar and Sind. Raghunath Rao seized Delhi, expelled Najib-ad-daulah; then marched swiftly with his light troops onward to Lahore, drove out the governor left there by Ahmad Shah, and substituted a Maratha administration in the Panjab.

A MOHAMMEDAN TOMB AT LAHORE.

This achievement marks, as Grant Duff observes in his "History of the Marathas," the apogee of Maratha pre-eminence; "the Deccan horses had quenched their thirst in the waters of the Indus"; but it also marks the turning-point and ebb of their fortunes. By such a bold stroke for the possession of Northern India, they overreached themselves, for the effort drew them very far from their base; the Mohammedans were numerous and hardy in the north, and the Marathas had now provoked a much more formidable antagonist in Ahmad Shah than any of those whom they had encountered heretofore. Their occupation of Delhi threatened all the Mohammedan princes of upper India, who saw that their only chance of preservation lay in a defensive alliance under some strong and warlike leader.

No exertions were spared by Najib-ad-daulah to organize such a league under Ahmad Shah; nor did the Afghan chief hesitate to answer the summons of the Indian Mussulmans, or to resent the provocation he had received. In the winter of 1759 - 1760, he came sweeping down through the northwest passes into the Panjab, followed by all the fighting men of Afghanistan; he retook Lahore at a blow; drove all the Maratha officers out of the northern country; attacked Holkar and Sind, who were plundering the districts farther south; defeated one after the other with heavy loss; occupied Delhi; and continued his march southeastward until he encamped on the Ganges. The Peshwa despatched a very large force from Poona, under his eldest son Visvas Deo, to repair these losses and recover lost ground; it was joined by all the other Maratha commanders, while on the other side the Mohammedan leaguers united with Ahmad Shah.

When the next campaigning season began, the two armies, after some negotiations and much manœuvring, finally met in January, 1761, at Panipat, not far from Delhi. This was the greatest pitched battle that had been fought for several centuries between Hindus and

Mohammedans. Twenty-eight thousand Afghan horsemen rode with Ahmad Shah, whose army was brought up to a total of eighty thousand horse and foot by large bodies of infantry from his own dominions, and by the contingents of the Indian Mohammedans. The regular troops of the Marathas were reckoned at seventy-five thousand horse and fifteen thousand infantry; fifteen thousand Pindaris, or foraging freebooters, followed their standard; a countless swarm of armed banditti thronged their camp; and they had not less than two hundred guns. The artillery on both sides included strong rocket batteries.

The Marathas, who issued out of their entrenched camp at dawn, at first carried all before their furious onset; they broke through the lines of Persian musketeers, camel gunners, and light cavalry. The right wing of the Afghan army was thrown into confusion; its centre gave way under the crushing artillery fire. Ahmad Shah's vizir, who commanded the centre, threw himself from his horse and strove to rally his men on foot, crying to them that their country was far distant and that flight was useless; but to his rage and despair he found himself being overwhelmed by the torrent.

In this peril, the Afghan king, very unlike the half-hearted Nawabs whom the English were routing farther south, proved his courage and high military capacity. With his right wing broken and his centre pierced, he checked or cut down the fugitives, brought up his reserves to the last man, and sent a strong reinforcement to his vizir, with orders to make a desperate charge "sword in hand, in close order, at full gallop." So the vizir remounted, and went storming down upon the Maratha centre under a shower of rockets. The Marathas fought bravely for a short time; but their leader was killed, their line was broken, and they were utterly routed with enormous slaughter; for the pursuit was by swarms of cavalry over a level plain, and the exasperated peasants massacred the Marathas everywhere.

The Peshwa, alarmed by the news of his army's situation in the north, was moving up from the Deccan, and had reached the Narbada River. There his scouts brought him a runner who was carrying a letter from some bankers at Panipat to their correspondents in the south. He opened it and read: "Two pearls [his son and cousin] have been dissolved; twenty-seven gold mohurs lost; of the silver and copper the total cannot be reckoned," an enigmatic message that told him of an immense political, military, and family catastrophe. He never recovered from the shock, which destroyed the baseless fabric of Maratha domination in Northern India. They might plunder towns, levy contributions, and even occupy some of the provinces for a time; but the fate of empires is decided by pitched battles, and in close lists the south-country freebooters would always go down before the hardier races of the northwest.

Such a decisive victory has usually been followed in Asia by the rise of a new dynasty and the establishment of an extensive dominion. Yet although the

Marathas were swept clean out of Northern India for the time, and although Ahmad Shah represented precisely the type of those Asiatic conquerors who had hitherto founded imperial houses at Delhi or Agra, it is a remarkable fact that the results of Panipat were quite disproportionate to the magnitude of the exploit. If Ahmad Shah had consolidated in the Panjab a powerful kingdom resting on Afghanistan beyond the Indus, and stretching southward down to Delhi and the Ganges, the history of India, and the fortunes of the English in that country, might have been very different. But his troops, laden with booty, insisted on retiring to their highlands; his western provinces on the Persian frontier were exposed to invasion and revolt; and so North India gradually slipped out of his grasp.

The Panjab relapsed into confusion for the next forty years, until it was temporarily consolidated under the kingdom of Ranjit Singh. Some inroads were made into India from Afghanistan, subsequently to Ahmad Shah's retirement; but the Afghan ruler's withdrawal practically closed the long line of conquering invaders from Central Asia, at a time very nearly simultaneous with the establishment in Bengal of the first conquerors that entered India by the sea.

CHAPTER IX

THE MARATHAS AND MYSORE

1765 - 1770

TO return to the affairs of the East India Company. The Marathas, in spite of their overthrow at Panipat, were still the most active and dangerous of the native powers in India; but since they embodied the principles of insatiable aggression and of irreconcilable hostility to Mohammedan predominance, the universal dread of their predatory incursions united all other chiefs and princes, especially the Mussulmans, against them. The result was advantageous to the English, for it drew toward them those who drew away from the Marathas. The Vizir of Oudh, who had now become the leading Mohammedan prince in Upper India, and who had been again repulsed in a second attempt upon Bengal in 1765, now showed himself very willing to conclude an alliance with the Company.

Lord Clive, a statesman no less than a soldier, whose despatches show admirable foresight and solidity of judgment, had returned to India in 1765, vested with plenary authority to reform the internal administration and to make peace abroad. He found the springs of government clogged by indiscipline and corruption; he suppressed resolutely the most glaring abuses; he reconstructed the administration with remarkable ability; and by two cardinal acts of public policy he settled the English dominion on a sure foundation within their territory and regulated their foreign relations.

The first of these acts was his acceptance for the Company of the Diwani, which was readily granted by the emperor on the terms of payment to himself of twenty-six lakhs of rupees, equivalent to some £260,000, annually from the Bengal revenues, and the assignment to him of two districts beyond the Ganges. The Company, having thus acquired possession of the whole revenue of the provinces, were at once transformed from irresponsible chiefs of an armed trading association into responsible administrators, with a direct interest in abolishing the peculations, scandalous frauds, and embezzlements that were rife in the country. The measure also put an end to the incessant disputes between the nominal government of the titular Nawab of Bengal and the actual authority of the Company. "The time now approaches," wrote Clive, "when we may be able to determine whether our remaining as merchants, subjected to the jurisdiction, encroachments, and insults of the country government, or the supporting your privileges and possessions by the sword, are likely to prove more beneficial to the

Company,"—in other words, whether the Company should openly take up an attitude of independent authority. And he decided, rightly, that nothing else would give them a stable or legitimate position. They could not continue to maintain themselves by pulling the strings of native government, or by revolutionary methods whenever the machinery broke down; and as they could not abdicate power, they were bound to take charge of its direction.

The second of Clive's measures was the conclusion of the alliance with Oudh. The war of 1764 - 1765 had been disastrous to the vizir, for his strong fortress of Allahabad had been taken by the English troops, who had also compelled him to withdraw from his capital Lucknow, whereupon he had taken refuge with the Marathas. It now lay with the Company to choose between annexing, by right of conquest, some of his important districts situated on their northwestern frontier, or attaching the vizir to their interests by reinstating him in this tract of country, which he held by a very dubious title, and from which he might easily have been ousted.

Lord Clive adopted the latter alternative without hesitation; he restored the districts to Oudh upon the grounds that every motive of sound policy weighed against extending the territorial possessions of the Company. This decision, he found, "disappointed the expectations of many, who thought of nothing but a march with the emperor to Delhi. My resolution however was, and my hopes will be, to confine our assistance, our conquest, and our possessions to Bengal, Bihar, and Orissa. To go further is in my opinion a scheme so extravagantly ambitious and absurd, that no governor and council in their senses can adopt it, unless

THE RESIDENCY AT LUCKNOW.

the whole system of the Company's interest be first entirely new re-modelled." He therefore decided to maintain and strengthen Oudh as a friendly state interposed between Bengal and Northern India. And the barrier-treaty of August, 1765, framed upon this principle by Lord Clive, constituted the basis of British foreign policy upon that frontier up to the end of the century.

It should be understood that the prime object of those who directed the affairs of the English in India at this critical epoch was to place a limit upon the expansion of the Company's possessions, to put a sharp curb upon schemes of conquest, and to avoid any connection with the native princes that might involve the British in foreign war. But this was not because, as some have thought, the Company did not see whither they were drifting; it was because the outcome and irresistible tendencies of their situation were so clearly foreseen. To those who surveyed the prospect now before the English, and who could perceive that all the scattered fragments of the Moghul Empire would be drawn by political gravitation toward any strong and coherent power, it was plain by this time that, if the Company were ready to drop commerce for conquest and to lay out another great dominion over the wide unoccupied spaces left by the subsidence of the Moghul Empire, the site lay open for the builder, the task of those who could do it.

In 1762, before the victory at Baxar, the Calcutta Council had sent home a project of despatching an army with the emperor to replace him on his throne at Delhi and to extend the political influence of the English throughout upper India. And after 1764, when the British success against the Vizir of Oudh carried the arms of England beyond Bengal, it was clearly seen by Clive that the next step forward would commit his countrymen to an enterprise from which there would be no further possibility of drawing back. "We have at last arrived," he wrote in 1765, "at that critical period which I have long foreseen, that period which renders it necessary to determine whether we can or shall take the whole to ourselves. Jafir Ali Khan (the Nawab of Bengal) is dead, and his natural son is a minor; Sujah Daulah (Vizir of Oudh) is beat from his dominions; we are in possession of it; and it is scarcely hyperbole to say that to-morrow the whole Moghul Empire is in our power. The inhabitants of the country have no attachment to any obligation; their forces are neither disciplined, commanded, nor paid as ours are. Can it then be doubted that a large army of Europeans would effectually preserve us sovereigns, not only holding in awe the attempts of any country prince, but rendering us so truly formidable that no French, Dutch, or other enemy will presume to molest us?"

With this remarkable forecast of the possibilities which Clive earnestly counselled his employers to avoid, may be compared an extract from the concluding pages of Dow's history of Hindustan, written in 1770, to show how accurately the possibilities of expansion had been calculated by cool and intelligent observers:—

"Thus we have in a few words endeavoured to give a general idea of the present state of Hindustan. It is apparent, from what has been said, that these immense regions might all be reduced by a handful of regular troops. Ten thousand European infantry, together with the sepoys in the Company's service, are not only sufficient to conquer all India, but, with proper policy, to maintain it for ages as an appendage to the British Crown. This position may at first sight appear a paradox to people unacquainted with the genius and disposition of the inhabitants of Hindustan; but to those who have considered both with attention, the thing seems not only practicable but easy."

And so, indeed, the thing turned out to be; for Dow's political speculations have been literally verified by the result, although his estimates of the military strength required, being founded only on experience of warfare in South India and Bengal, are undoubtedly low. We see, therefore, that in the deliberate opinion of the best judges of the political situation, the English in India were already so strong that no opposition from the native powers could prevent their acquiring complete ascendency. The enterprise was within their capacity, provided that no foreign rival again interfered; the only serious impediment lay in the possible reappearance on the scene of some other European nation, or in the arrival of some powerful invader from Central Asia, who might establish himself securely in Upper India while the English were still near the coasts.

But all risk of transmarine intrusion had ceased for the time with the dislodgment of the French; and the well-trodden path of invasion through Afghanistan, which had been used for two thousand years by conquerors from Alexander the Great to Ahmad Shah Abdali, was at last rapidly closing. Ahmad Shah had now founded the dynasty of the Amirs, who, for nearly one hundred and fifty years, have been the chiefs of a group of tribes firmly planted in the mountains and valleys of Afghanistan. This rugged highland country

MOUNTAIN TRIBES OF THE AFGHAN BORDER.

blocks all the roads from the Oxus and Northeastern Persia into India; it is a country of free and martial races, strong enough to make a great civilized state think twice before attacking them, too weak and poor to give more than occasional annoyance to well-guarded frontiers.

It may be added that the northwestern gates of India were soon to be double-locked against outside invasion. For while this independent Afghan kingdom formed an excellent barrier against all attempts to break into India from Central Asia by the only land routes through which an army can enter, the Afghans themselves were barred off from the Panjab about this time by the Sikhs. The rapid expansion of the power of the Sikhs, who are Hindu sectaries, illustrates the almost invariable process by which every great proselytizing movement in Asia tends to acquire a political and militant character. The two tendencies, of course, interact on each other, for while a religious revival is sure to rally under its flag a good deal of political discontent, civil commotions, on the other hand, usually set up the standard and appeal to the sanction of religious enthusiasm.

Toward the end of the last century, the votaries of the Sikh faith, fanatically hostile to Islam and in open revolt against their Mohammedan rulers, were gathering into a close association, whose stubborn fighting qualities and rapid political development under military chiefs were extending their power across upper India from the Sutlaj to the Indus. They were thus erecting a second and inner barricade against inroads from Central Asia, which cut off the communications between Islam in India and the rest of the Mohammedan world.

Then below the Sutlaj River, further to the south-east, there was a belt of Mohammedan principalities extending from Delhi to beyond Lucknow, holding all the rich central districts along the Jumna and Ganges, but threatened on the north and west by the Sikhs and Marathas. By far the most considerable of these principalities was Oudh, whose territory covered the whole northwestern flank of the Company's possessions in Bengal. We have seen that a treaty of alliance was concluded with Oudh by Lord Clive in 1765; and as at the same time he contented the impoverished Moghul emperor by an ample allotment of revenue, the English had nothing to fear from that quarter for the time being. Thus the jealousies and religious animosities of all these states, Hindu and Mohammedan, in Northwestern India constituted a kind of balance of power, which, in addition to the politic alliances made by Lord Clive, explains the almost entire immunity from disturbance on their Bengal frontier enjoyed by the English for the next forty years.

The year 1765, therefore, when the English thus became firmly settled in Bengal, marks a halting-place in the onward movement of British territorial expansion. Lord Clive so far succeeded in his intention, expressed in a letter to the Directors of the Company, written in this same year, "absolutely to bind our possessions and conquests to Bengal," that the English frontiers, as then fixed by him, did not materially advance until the end of the century, when the irruptions of the Marathas into the plains of Northern India upset the equipoise that had preserved the British from molestation. But the intervening period was by no means one of peace and tranquillity for the English in India. On the contrary, it was a time of constant war that severely strained our resources and occasionally placed our dominion in some jeopardy. After 1765, the scene shifts again; the stress of the English contest with the native powers falls backward toward Madras and Bombay; the centres of urgent political pressure move for a time southward to the peninsula and toward the western seaboard; the conflicts that check and retard British expansion are against the Marathas in the centre of India and the Mohammedan rulers of Mysore.

The character and constitution of these two powers rendered them much more substantial antagonists than those whom the English had hitherto encountered in the Indian field. The incessant warfare prevailing throughout India during the past thirty years, and the great prizes that might be won by the sword, had brought a stronger class of combatants into the arena than most of the men who had found themselves by birth or accident in the front rank at the beginning of the empire's dissolution. Of this stronger class was Hyder Ali of Mysore, a man of great natural genius, who had raised himself entirely by superior daring, military instincts, and a faculty of managing the mercenary bands that were always attracted to the standard of a famous and fortunate leader. Of the same class were the chiefs or leaders of tribes, communities, or military associations—like the Marathas, the Jats of Bhartpur, the Sikhs of the Panjab, or the Rohillas—united by the tie, real or assumed, of common race, religion, or country, and drawn together for defence or attack into compact organizations upon a kind of national or territorial basis.

Such groups were liable to be weakened by internal

THE OLD PALACE AT BHARTPUR.

feuds and dissensions. But as they had some genuine root in the soil and a true bond of popular union, they have always possessed a higher vitality and much stronger resisting capacity than the forces of even such an able military despot as Hyder Ali of Mysore, with whom we began our new series of wars in the south. A skilful commander of mercenary troops may often be hard to beat in a single battle; but it will be found, generally speaking, that all the really hard fighting done by the Anglo-Indian army has been against tribal or quasi-national associations, — against Marathas, Sikhs, Jats, or Afghans.

It was with the greatest reluctance that the English East India Company, after its acquisition of Bengal, again set out upon the road of political adventure and military expeditions. In a letter of 1767 to their President at Calcutta the London Directors say: "The Diwani of Bengal, Bihar, and Orissa, are the utmost limits of our view on that side of India. On the coast the protection of the Karnatic and the possession of the Circars . . . and on the Bombay side the dependencies thereon, with Salsette, Bassein, and the Castle of Surat. If we pass these bounds, we shall be led from one acquisition to another, till we shall find no security but in the subjection of the whole, which, by dividing your force, would lose us the whole, and end in our extirpation from Hindustan."

This letter had been written on receipt of intelligence that had alarmed and displeased the Honourable Court. Although the French had been dislodged, the situation of the English on the southeast coast was still far from secure. In Bengal, the English were recognized masters of a rich inland province, free from any fear of attack by sea, and with their land frontier sheltered on its open side behind the allied kingdom of Oudh. But in Madras their territory ran along the seacoast, and was only covered landward by an indefinite kind of protectorate over the Karnatic principality, then under the rulership of a not very trustworthy Nawab. Two warlike and restless neighbours, Hyder Ali and the Marathas, hovered ominously about our borders; while our only ally, the Nizam of Haidarabad, was embarrassed and wavering politically.

Hyder Ali was the son of a soldier who had risen out of the crowd of common mercenaries to a petty command; and he himself had pushed his own fortunes much further by the ordinary method of employing his troops first in the service of a native state and afterwards in the prosecution of his own independent ambition. He had thus gained notoriety as a military leader, and having secured a great treasure at the sack of Bednor, he had made himself master of Mysore, an ancient Hindu principality lying due west of Madras. From Mysore he had pushed his conquest still further westward to the seacoast of Malabar; and he was now seizing land in South India wherever he could lay hands on it.

The superior craft and courage that he displayed began to alarm his neighbours, most of whom were engaged in similar proceedings. His principal enemies were the Marathas, with whom he had some sharp conflicts, and the Nizam of Haidarabad, from whose state he was tearing off large strips of territory; while from Mysore he was threatening the Karnatic, which the Madras government were seriously concerned to protect.

It was just about this time that Lord Clive, in settling the affairs of Bengal with the emperor Shah Alam, obtained from him a formal grant of the districts to the north of Madras called the Five Circars, which had been assigned by the Nizam to the French, and out of which the English had driven Bussy's garrisons in 1759. The grant cost nothing to an emperor whose sovereignty had become purely nominal; but these districts, though under British occupation since they had been taken from the French, had never been formally ceded to the English by the Nizam, who, not unreasonably, had taken offence at the transaction. However, being in straits for money and in fear of Hyder Ali, the Nizam was soon pacified by a treaty under which the Madras government pledged themselves rather vaguely to support him in case of war. They also entered into a friendly arrangement with a marauding Maratha chief, who had hired out ten thousand horsemen to the Nizam.

Scarcely had the treaty been signed, when Hyder Ali poured a large force into the Haidarabad territory; whereupon the Nizam, acting upon the agreement, at once demanded and obtained from Madras a contingent of troops. Meanwhile, the Maratha chief plundered the Mysore districts on his own account until Hyder Ali bought him off, whereupon he departed home with his booty to evade the Nizam's claim for a share in it. The Nizam next marched, attended by the Madras contingent, toward Mysore; but instead of fighting, he came to a private understanding with Hyder Ali, according to which both turned upon the Company. Some sharp skirmishing followed, in which the Nizam was so roughly handled by the English that he was glad to make terms separately; and the war was pressed against Hyder Ali alone, who soon proved himself an antagonist much more adroit and active than the ordinary Indian princes of whom the Company had military experience.

The campaign was very ill managed from Madras;

A TEMPLE NEAR TINNEVELLI IN THE MADRAS PRESIDENCY.

the commanding officer was hampered by "field deputies" to superintend his movements, and by roguish contractors; while the Marathas took the opportunity of making a plundering tour in the Karnatic. Nor was it until the country had been overrun by the Mysore cavalry close up to the outskirts of Madras, and the finances of the Company considerably deranged, that a protracted and inglorious war was ended in 1769 by a treaty with Hyder Ali, who had taken up his quarters at St. Thomas' Mount, five miles from the

English capital. The revenues of Madras would have been completely exhausted, if they had not been supplemented liberally, during the campaign, from Bengal; and the London Directors were exceedingly displeased at discovering that the money on which they relied for commercial investments in India, and for accommodating his Majesty's ministers with treasury loans at home, had been dissipated in these barren operations, with no other profit than a practical lesson in the ways of Oriental statecraft and the value of Eastern allies.

Moreover, if the beginning of the war was a political blunder, another and worse one was made in ending it. The treaty described all the contracting parties, of whom the principal were the English, Hyder Ali, and the Marathas, as reciprocally friends and allies of each other, provided that they did not become aggressors against one another; so that each party incurred a loose and vaguely worded obligation of assisting the others in the event of future hostilities. And as a similar compact had been made with the Nizam, the position of the Madras government was that they had become liable to be called upon to assist any of three turbulent princes whenever the next quarrel should break out among them. Accordingly, when the Marathas and the Mysore ruler came to blows in the following year, each of these two treaty-parties demanded aid from the English, and each of them proved indisputably that his enemy was the aggressor. The Madras government, having been sharply censured by the Directors for the last war, and being in no way anxious to strengthen either of these two very formidable neighbours at the expense of the other, were compelled to offend both of them by refusing to interfere in any manner whatever. The result was that the Marathas inflicted upon Hyder Ali some humiliating defeats, which he attributed to the faithless desertion of him by the English, and that he became thenceforward a vindictive enemy, watching for an occasion, which he soon found, of gratifying his resentment.

CHAPTER X

ADMINISTRATIVE ORGANIZATION

1770 - 1773

WE have now reached the threshold of that important period in the political history of British India which is covered by the long government of Warren Hastings, from 1772 to 1785. It was in this period that the contest for supremacy between the English and the military powers of India began in earnest, that the attention of Parliament became fixed upon Indian affairs, and that the organization of English government in India was for the first time seriously attempted.

When Lord Clive left in 1767, the Company had become the real rulers of Bengal; but although their position was still dissembled under the cloak of a nominal Nawabship, the disguise was worn almost threadbare. In Calcutta and Madras, the Presidency Councils were exercising some direct authority beyond the town limits, and very large indirect power, as commanders of the troops and collectors of the revenue, throughout Bengal and the Karnatic. Yet in Bengal, although the whole public income was paid to the Company, they were under strict orders from London to

A NATIVE INDIAN PRINCE AND HIS COURT, WITH TWO EUROPEANS.

abstain from all open interference with the rest of the administration. They disbursed to a Deputy Nawab (for the Nawab himself was now a mere pensioner) the costs of establishments; and they left the whole executive and judicial government nominally in his hands. Verelst, who succeeded Clive at Calcutta, writes that the President and Council "are repeatedly and peremptorily forbidden to avow any public authority in our names over the native officers, and enjoined to retain our primitive characters of merchants with the most scrupulous delicacy."

The consequences were but too evidently exemplified in the decline of commerce and cultivation, the diminution of specie, and the general distress; for the native officers were uncontrolled, while the Company received an immense revenue without possessing the means of protecting the people who paid it. Against such a system Verelst protested generously; and a futile attempt to mitigate its evils was made by appointing a few English servants of the Company to supervise the native agency.

It was not, however, until 1773 that the executive and judicial administration of the country was placed on a regular, though imperfect, footing by parliamentary ordinance. Up to this time, Anglo-Indian annals have recorded the vicissitudes of a contest, first, between commercial companies; next, between maritime nations; latterly between one powerful Company, representing the successful nation, and the native Indian princes. This latest stage of the contest was in reality no more than a part of the general disorderly conflict prevailing all over India, in which the weak fragmentary states that had at first been manufactured out of the provinces of the dismembered empire were now being trampled in their turn under the feet of hardier rulerships. The work of the English had hitherto been mainly destructive, because the exigencies of self-defence compelled them to strike down their antagonists. But the era now opening will introduce their first essays at reconstruction, for in Bengal the English had by this time cleared for themselves a good political building site, and the chronicle of interminable straggling wars is henceforward to be varied by attempts at administrative organization.

In England, although state interference with private enterprise had never been a popular duty, a conviction was growing up that it had become necessary to place the doings of the East India Company under national control. The British people had at this time reached a very high degree of settled civilization under institutions that secured to them almost complete civil and religious liberty. They found themselves involuntarily responsible for a country plunged into violent disorder, where no species of government except illimitable personal despotism, usually of foreigners, had been known for many centuries. Into this country they had to import, from a great distance, the principles of civilized polity; so that their first experiment at regulating the affairs of Bengal may be regarded as the beginning of a vast constitutional innovation that has since been extended, with many mistakes and some mishaps, but in the end with remarkable success, throughout the whole of India.

It was the astonishing acquisition of so rich a province as Bengal, and the discreditable sight of a few commercial agents handling the wealth of a kingdom, that roused the attention of the British Parliament and enforced the necessity of looking into the condition of affairs in India. In 1765, Lord Clive had estimated the whole gross revenue of Bengal, from all sources, at four millions sterling, and the net income of the Company, after payment of all expenses, at £1,650,000. Having become the possessors of so magnificent a property, the Court of Directors were raising their dividend; their stock went up to 267; their shareholders divided 12½ per cent. in 1767; and their servants brought home large fortunes to be employed in buying country-seats and parliamentary boroughs. Alderman Beckford expressed in the House of Commons his hope that the rich acquisitions of the Company in the East would be made a means of relieving the people of England from some of their burdens. Nor was the British government backward in acting upon the hint, since the system of granting renewals of the Company's charter for short periods afforded excellent opportunities of making fresh terms in proportion to the market price of the concession.

In 1766, upon an intimation from the Prime Minister that the affairs of the East India Company would probably occupy the attention of Parliament during the approaching session, there ensued a long bargaining discussion between the government and the Company, which produced a law binding the Company for a term of years to pay £400,000 annually to the Crown, "in respect of the territorial acquisition and revenue lately obtained by them in the East Indies." From a subsequent inquiry in 1773, it appeared that the Company's annual expenses had increased since the year 1765 from £700,000 to the enormous sum of £1,700,000. It also appeared that from 1765 the British government had received by the net customs duties, the indemnity upon tea, and the yearly payment of £400,000, little less than two millions annually from the Company; so that the British nation took heavy blackmail upon the Company's gains, however they may have been gotten.

This yearly payment represented, in fact, the tribute or royalty levied by the state upon the great territorial revenues recently acquired by Clive's victories. But with the possession of these revenues had come a change in the Company's commercial system, for in 1767 began the practice of making what were called investments, that is, of employing a large portion of the surplus public revenue collected from the province in buying goods, raw produce and manufactures, for exportation to Europe. It followed, as Burke said, that whereas in other countries revenue arises out of commerce, in Bengal the whole foreign maritime trade, of which the Company had a monopoly, was fed by the revenue. The consequence of this steady drain upon the production of the country soon began to be felt.

Moreover, after Clive's departure from India in 1767, the withdrawal of his resolute, clear-headed dictatorship was immediately felt throughout all departments of the administration; official discipline again became relaxed; the finances suffered a relapse into extravagance and malversation; and the agents of government still meddled in private trade. The Madras

THE FORT OF CHENGALPAT.

Presidency drifted into that ruinous war with Hyder Ali which has already been described, and in 1770 a terrible famine had desolated Bengal.

Under the system of annual elections to the directorship, the Company at home were demoralized by party contests and violent internal dissensions. Yet notwithstanding all these concurrent evils and mishaps, no serious inquiry was taken up in Parliament until the Company declared themselves to be not only unable to continue the annual tribute of £400,000, but also so overloaded with debt as to need a large loan from the

English treasury. Instead of taking tribute or borrowing at easy rates, the British government was actually asked to lend money. Here was a scandalous confession of insolvency which naturally placed the misdoings of the Company before Lord North's ministry in a very different and much stronger light, arrested their earnest attention, and convinced them of the immediate necessity of radical reform.

The general circumstances of the time, also, were bringing about changes and amendments. Lord Clive said truly that the affairs of the East Indies were, in fact, partaking of the general confusion then spreading over the immense transmarine possessions of Great Britain, which had been acquired so recently and rapidly that there had been no time to set them in order. The English people had yet to discover the nature of their responsibility for the tutelage of subject or alien races, and for the proper management of countries differing so widely in origin, character, and situation as North American colonies and Indian provinces. They had as yet no experience in the difficult art of ruling distant and diverse populations on so broad a scale. Nor could the whole range of modern history furnish them with any useful precedent, seeing that all previous experiments in the government of dependencies may be pronounced, by a very moderate standard of ethics and efficiency, to have failed.

The comparatively long interval of peace in Europe, so far as England was concerned, that followed the termination of the Seven Years' War in 1763, gave leisure and opportunity for looking into the state of our outlying property. The nation began to take stock of the vast accession to its estate beyond sea which had been won by its naval and military successes; and the novel sense of duty toward India was undoubtedly stimulated by a general feeling that a trading association had no business with the revenues of a great kingdom.

The urgency of the case and certain symptoms of rising popular indignation combined to press the government into active interference with the Company, whose financial embarrassments left them in no position to resist an inquiry ordered by the House of Commons, or to dispute the right of the nation to deal as it chose with their territorial acquisitions. They tried hard, then and afterwards, to shelter themselves from Parliamentary interposition under the shadow of the nominal sovereignty of the Delhi emperor, from whom they pretended to hold their land. In maintaining this doctrine they acted upon the advice of Lord Clive, who, although he accepted the Diwani in 1765 because the assumption of some kind of legitimate authority over Bengal was unavoidable, nevertheless still affirmed that for the Company to declare themselves politically independent was very far from expedient. Consequently, the law courts and the police were still in charge of native officers, superintended to some little extent by the Company's agents, but under separate judicial and executive departments which the Company did not undertake to administer.

But the essence of executive government is to be one and indivisible, so that the machine will not run unless all the driving power centres ultimately under one prime mover, whether it be an autocratic prince or a democratic assembly. In Bengal, the outcome of this divided responsibility after Clive's departure was masterless confusion. The magistracy, the police, and the revenue officers, being diverse bodies working upon different systems, with conflicting interests, and under no common head, vied with each other in mismanagement; there were no positive laws and there was very little justice in the country.

Moreover, the three Presidencies made wars and alliances independently of each other; the Company's standing army in Bengal amounted to over eleven thousand men; and the increased civil and military establishments involved expenditure that encroached greatly upon the funds for commercial investment. Fortunately, this dilapidation of the Honourable Company's revenue produced a fall of their stock, which brought home to them a conviction that they were on the downward path to some distressing predicament. They applied for financial assistance to the Ministers, who referred the Company to Parliament, and in January, 1772, the king's speech gave notice of an intention to look into their affairs. The result was the appointment of two Select Committees "to inquire into the state, nature, and condition of the Company, and of British affairs in the East Indies."

It is true that Parliament had hitherto been much

more disposed to pass abstract resolutions than to affirm sovereign rights and to act upon them in India. When, in 1762, the French negotiators for peace de-

A MOUNTAIN ROAD AT MAHABLESHWAR, IN THE BOMBAY PRESIDENCY.

manded the restitution of districts that had been taken from them during the war, the English representatives met the claim by demurring to "any right of the Crown of England to interfere in the legal and exclusive property of a body corporate." And subsequently Burke, not being hostile to the Company at the time, described their possessions as "held in virtue of grants from the Delhi emperor, in the nature of offices and jurisdictions dependent on his crown; a very anomalous species of power and property quite unknown to the ancient constitution of England." The East India Company, he observed, had usually dealt in a spirit of equal negotiation with the government for the renewal of their charter; until the Minister (Lord North) set up the Crown's claim to their possessions with the original idea of extracting money to pay off the civil list debts, and Parliament asserted a judicial right to inquire into the question of title in order to alarm the Company.

Burke's view, then, was that the terrors of Parliamentary inquiry were hung over the Company mainly with the object of levying contributions for the Exchequer's benefit. There was much truth in this; and it was partly as a set-off against those contributions that the Company was licensed to export duty-free to North America the tea which the intractable colonists flung into Boston harbour. But Lord North, who now ruled both Houses with an overwhelming majority, was adverse to the Company; the Committees brought up condemnatory reports; and the Commons passed resolutions declaring that all acquisitions made under the influence of a military force, or by treaty with foreign princes, belonged of right to the state. A motion was made arraigning Clive's proceedings in Bengal as dishonourable and detrimental to the nation. Clive defended himself vigorously, laying about him on all sides; and the motion was rejected, without division, in favour of a resolution "that Robert Lord Clive did render great and meritorious services to his country." His death in the following year (November, 1774) closed the career of this high-spirited, courageous, indefatigable man, to whom above all others the English are indebted for the foundation of their empire in India. Never before or since has an Irish peerage been the cheap reward of such invaluable service to the nation. His daring and his sagacity, his singular talent for politics and his genius for war, produced in Lord Clive a rare combination of masculine qualities exactly fitted to the circumstances of his time in India.

Of the two Acts that were eventually passed in 1773, one enabled the Ministers to lend the Company £1,400,000 to discharge their obligations; the other changed the constitution of the Company and gave a Parliamentary title to their administration in India. To these matters, to the re-arrangement of the governing body at home and to the reform of the system abroad, the scope of Lord North's Regulating Act was carefully confined. The territorial acquisitions and revenues were still to be retained by the Company for the term of their charter; and the uncertain ground of sovereign prerogative was evaded by founding the enactment upon "the eminent dominion of Parliament over every British subject in every concern." The Courts of the Directors and Proprietors in London were re-constituted upon a more oligarchic model by raising the money qualifications and reducing the numbers. In India, the Governor-General and Council were estab-

SIMLA, THE SUMMER SEAT OF THE BRITISH GOVERNMENT.

lished for Bengal (the first appointments to be made by Parliament) with a general authority over the three Presidencies, under a rule whereby a majority of votes in the Council determined all disputed questions. And a supreme Court of Justice, having a very ill-defined jurisdiction, was set up side by side with the Governor-Generalship in Calcutta.

It is easy now to perceive that this ill-constructed governing machinery, which stands toward our latest systems in the same relation as does the earliest traction engine to the present locomotive, contravened some primary principles of administrative mechanics. When it becomes necessary to organize a new régime in an Asiatic country acquired from a native ruler by cession or conquest, the first thing needful is to fix the chief local authority, arming him with ample though well-defined powers, to be used in general subordination to the central government.

What these powers should be depends upon the circumstances of the case, upon the character of the people, the state of their society, and often upon the distance of the new province from headquarters. The executive and judicial departments may be quite separate, or they may be more or less under the same superior control; in any case, the jurisdictions and the laws or rules applicable to the community are plainly marked out and promulgated. In all cases, due provision is made for empowering one chief governing person to decide at once, and on his own responsibility, in emergencies.

In 1773, on the other hand, the chief executive authority at Calcutta was vested in a majority of the Council, the Governor-General having only a casting vote, so that in a government where promptitude and unity of action were all-important, every order was arguable, and where opinions differed, no measure passed without violent controversy. Moreover, the boundaries between the executive and judicial powers were also left to be discovered by incessant conflict, producing a kind of border warfare in which each party made encroachments and reprisals. In the midst of all this turmoil, the sovereign power remained ambiguous and formally in abeyance, and Parliament, the only umpire acknowledged by both sides, was at the distance of a six months' voyage.

Thus the main obstacles to the smooth working of the new constitution were, first, the entire dependence of the Governor-General on the votes of his Council; secondly, the conflict of jurisdictions; and lastly, the want of a supreme legislative authority, nearer than England, to arbitrate in these quarrels and to mark off the proper sphere of the executive and judicial departments. The Governor-General could make no laws that the judges condescended to notice. On the other hand, the judges claimed, upon one ground or another, a general power of entertaining complaints against the acts of the executive government and its officers, and of issuing orders tending to reduce the administration to the status of a subaltern agency, whose proceedings might be reviewed by the judges at their discretion.

The capital question of sovereignty stood open to be explained theoretically according to the interests or contentions of either side. It might be colourably

Victoria Station, Bombay.

argued, on the part of the Company, that they held the country by grants from the Delhi emperor and treaties with native princes, whereby the jurisdiction of the judges appointed by the King of England was greatly restricted and, as it were, cut off at the base. Or it might be maintained that all the possessions of the Company fell naturally to the Crown, whence it followed that the writs of the Supreme Court ran wherever the Company exercised public authority, that the judges at Calcutta could control the native courts, and that the procedure of Westminster Hall was applicable to every Bengali landholder. For since jurisdiction was given by the statute over all servants of the Company, it was held by the Court that the whole body of landowners in Bengal, who collected the land revenue and paid over the state's share to the Company, might fall within their purview. At any rate, if any one demurred to the jurisdiction, he was held bound to appear to plead his objection before the judges, although the cost and trouble of answering a summons to Calcutta might be ruinous to a native at a distance in the interior districts and totally ignorant of these technicalities.

With a prolix and costly procedure, with strange unintelligible powers resembling the attributes of some mysterious divinity, the Supreme Court was soon regarded by the natives as an engine of outlandish oppression rather than as a bulwark against executive tyranny. "So far," says Burke's Report, "as your Committee have been able to discover, the Court has been generally terrible to the natives, and has distracted the government of the country without substantially reforming one of its abuses."

In this atmosphere of doubt concerning the country's ownership and its title-deeds, and concerning the limits of the two great administrative provinces, complications, acrimonious controversy, and even collisions necessarily ensued. The Council and the Court were ranged in two hostile camps set over against each other on the borderland of debatable jurisdictions. The Company's officers claimed illimitable authority over the people of Bengal in revenue matters; the judges affirmed the duty of protecting the people from fiscal injustice; and very fair arguments might be found for either contention. The judges were quite as much bent on asserting their own power as on protecting the natives of India, while to the Council any sort of control or check upon their fiscal operations was highly inconvenient. The truth is that, outside Calcutta, there were no laws at all at that period, and that the Company had no regular authority and very little inclination to make any.

Out of these causes and complications arose the celebrated disputes between Warren Hastings and his Council, which kept the Governor-General and his councillors at bitter feud with each other, except when they united in a quarrel with the Supreme Court of Judicature. These matters fall within the scope of this narrative only so far as they illustrate an early stage in the experimental process of adjusting English institutions to the conditions of an Asiatic dependency; for it is otherwise superfluous to tell over again an oft-repeated story.

The system of administration set up by the Act of 1773 embodied the first attempt at giving some definite and recognizable form to the vague and arbitrary ruler-

KATKARI NATIVES ON THE WESTERN GHATS.

ship that had devolved upon the Company. From that date forward, this outline of Anglo-Indian government was gradually filled in. The administrative centre was now at any rate distinctly located at Calcutta with the Governor-General as its acknowledged head, invested with the chief control of the foreign relations of the three Presidencies, and deriving his authority from a statute of the English Parliament. Thus far the foundation had been laid on broad and permanent lines; but the work of interior organization was scarcely begun, and it remained for Warren Hastings to persevere in building up the fabric of administration under the stress of discord in Council, political complications, foreign wars, and every kind of financial embarrassment.

CHAPTER XI

THE GOVERNOR-GENERALSHIP OF WARREN HASTINGS

WARREN HASTINGS did not take his seat as first Governor-General in India until 1774; but from 1772, when he went to Calcutta as Governor of the Bengal Presidency, until his final departure in the spring of 1785, the whole course and character of Anglo-Indian history bear the impress of his personality and are connected with his name.

At the time of his taking office, the power of the Marathas, which had been accumulating for a hundred years, was threatening every prince and state in India from the Sutlaj River southward to Cape Comorin. The shattering overthrow that they had suffered at Panipat in 1761 had expelled them from the Panjab. Yet in Western India they were supreme; in Rajputana and Central India they plundered and ransomed at their leisure; and they were incessantly making predatory excursions northeastward into the fertile plains watered by the Ganges and the Jumna to harry the lands of the Oudh Vizir, of Rohilkhand, and of the Mohammedan chiefships about Delhi, Agra, and Allahabad. Although the Maratha armies subsisted by freebooting, and although their leaders were rough uneducated captains whose business it was to levy contributions and seize territory, their civil administration, especially the whole collection of revenue in conquered lands, was managed by Brahmans, by far the ablest class of officials then existing in India. The Maratha tactics were to overrun a country with swarms of light horsemen, harassing and exhausting their opponents, exacting heavy contributions if they retired, or rack-renting the land scientifically if they settled down on it.

By this combination of skilful irregularity in war and methodical absorption of a country's wealth, the leaders were able to keep on foot great roving armies, which were the terror of every other Indian power. The unwieldy State of Haidarabad, notwithstanding its size, was no match for them; they were too numerous and active even for such an eminent professor of their own predatory science as Hyder Ali of Mysore; and they descended annually, like a chronic plague, upon the Rohillas and the Oudh Vizir, who could barely hold against them the large provinces that they had secured out of the partition of the Empire. Everything pointed to the Marathas as destined to be the foremost rivals of the English in the impending contest for ascendency. And in fact no native power other than the Marathas did oppose any solid resistance to the spread of British dominion in Upper India, until the Sikhs crossed the Sutlaj long afterwards in 1845.

When Warren Hastings assumed the government of Bengal in 1772, the different Maratha chiefs were just beginning to found separate rulerships without abandoning their confederacy under the Peshwa. And from

WARREN HASTINGS, GOVERNOR-GENERAL OF BENGAL.

1774, during the whole of his Governor-Generalship, the state and course of the East India Company's foreign affairs were governed principally by the varying relations of the English with these chiefs. Hastings found that a Maratha army had made its annual irruption into the districts northwest of Bengal, where the emperor Shah Alam, who had been living at Allahabad on the revenues assigned him by Clive in 1765, solicited and obtained their assistance toward recovering his capital. Under their patronage, he had been replaced on his throne in 1771, but the Marathas treated his kingship as a mere pageant, using his name as a pretext for seizing more districts, and leaving him almost destitute in the midst of a plentiful camp. They were now swarming about the north country and rapidly gaining the upper hand of all the Mohammedan princes. What concerned the English more particularly was that they were demanding, in the emperor's name, surrender of the districts of Kora and Allahabad, which had been made over to him by Lord Clive in 1765, when the Diwani of Bengal was granted to the Company. For since these districts bordered on Bengal as well as on Oudh, their occupation by the Marathas would have been equally fatal to the security of both territories.

On the northern frontier of Oudh, in the angle between the line of the Himalayas and the Upper Ganges, lay the country possessed by the Rohilla Afghans. This was a chiefship established about twenty-five years previously by an adventurer of reputed Afghan parentage, who had asserted his independence of the Moghul Empire during the confusion caused by Ahmad Shah's earlier descent upon India. It was now under a confederacy of which Hafiz Rihmat Khan was the leader, and it formed an important section of the general line of defence against the Marathas, who had broken through in 1771 and now reappeared in 1772. As Oudh covered the open side of Bengal, Rohilkhand covered the exposed frontier of Oudh; so when the Rohillas implored the vizir to succour them, the vizir, fearing for his own dominions, asked the English to co-operate against the common enemy. The Calcutta government sent up an English brigade under Sir Robert Barker, instructing him to make a demonstration in support of the vizir and to act generally on his side in any negotiations. A treaty was arranged between the vizir and the Rohillas and attested by the English commander, whereby the vizir agreed to drive off the Marathas on payment of a stipulated subsidy by the Rohillas.

The Marathas soon afterwards retired of their own accord into quarters for the rainy season; but early in 1773 they again menaced Rohilkhand, and this time the combined forces of Oudh, the Rohillas, and the English marched against them. When they had been compelled to withdraw, the vizir demanded payment of his subsidy, but Hafiz Rihmat Khan, the principal Rohilla chief, sent evasive answers; whereupon the vizir addressed himself to the English, whose commander had attested, though he had in no way guaranteed, the engagement.

Out of these transactions arose the Rohilla War, which brought down such violent obloquy and so much loose parliamentary invective upon Hastings, against whom it has always been charged as a dark political crime. The whole situation was overspread by a network of transparent intrigue. The vizir suspected that the Rohilla chiefs, who were a band of Afghan usurpers in an imperial province, might on emergency join the Marathas against him; nor was there, indeed, any particular reason why they should not do so, since the vizir himself had been meditating seriously over a proposal from the Marathas that he should join them in an attack upon the Rohillas and in making a partition of their country. But he was wise enough to see that by joining a band of robbers to plunder his neighbour's house, he would bring them the sooner to his own door; and on the whole he thought the safer step would be an alliance with the English, whose troops would make him sure of success in the field, and whose avowed interest lay in strengthening him as a barrier against the Marathas.

The vizir, therefore, at an interview with the Governor-General at Benares in 1773, desired the assistance of an English force to put him in possession of Rohilkhand, alleging that the Rohillas had broken their treaty by withholding the subsidy from him, and promising liberal payment for the service. To this proposition Hastings, after some deliberation and hesitation on both sides, finally consented. "Our ally," he wrote to his Council, "would obtain by this acquisition a complete compact state shut in effectually from foreign invasions by the Ganges, while he would remain equally accessible to our forces either for hostility or protection. It would give him wealth, of which we shall partake, and give him security without any dangerous increase of power; . . . by bringing his frontier nearer to the Marathas, for whom singly he is no match, it would render him more dependent on us and connect the union more firmly between us."

The united forces accordingly invaded Rohilkhand

in the spring of 1774; the Rohillas, who were well led and fought bravely, would soon have disposed of the vizir's army, but they could not stand against the English troops, and after some gallant charges they were defeated. Hafiz Rihmat Khan was killed fighting courageously at the head of his men, and the short-lived power of the Afghan confederacy was utterly broken. Rohilkhand was annexed to the possessions of the vizir, who thereby acquired the country lying east of the Upper Ganges up to the Himalayas, with a strong frontage on the river against attacks from the west.

The result, from the point of view of English political interests, was to complete our defensive position toward the northwest by substituting a safe and submissive ally for untrustworthy neighbours upon an important section of the barrier, and it is certain that the plan succeeded. For many years afterwards our northwest frontier remained undisturbed, until, in the beginning of the nineteenth century, the English took up ground beyond it. Nevertheless, this advantage was gained by an unprovoked aggression upon the Rohillas, who sought no quarrel with us, and with whom we had been on not unfriendly terms; nor is Warren Hastings's policy in this matter easily justifiable even upon the elastic principle that enjoins the governor of a distant dependency to prefer above all other considerations the security of the territory entrusted to him.

The Rohilla campaign was the only war directly planned and undertaken by Hastings; although he was constantly engaged during seven stormy years, beginning in 1776, with the support and supervision of military operations. From this time forward up to the end of the century, the battle-fields are all in the west and south of India. In Bengal, the subsidiary alliance with Oudh remained the corner-stone of the British defensive system; nor was that province ever invaded, though often threatened, by the Maratha armies. But in Bombay, the President and Council being anxious to distinguish themselves by the acquisition of territory, especially of Salsette, which is close to Bombay, entered into a covenant with a Maratha chief named Raghunath Rao, who had been ejected from power at Poona, to replace him at the head of the Maratha government, stipulating for the cession of certain districts to the Company in return. The object of the Bombay President was to obtain political ascendency at Poona and to make his presidency pay its way by an increase of land revenue; but the plan was very badly laid, and the means adopted proved quite inadequate for the ends in view.

When the Calcutta government received from Bombay a copy of the treaty with Raghunath Rao, they at once totally condemned the measures that had been taken, declaring the war "impolitic, dangerous, unauthorized, and unjust," and protesting that the Bombay Presidency had imposed upon itself "the charge of conquering the whole Maratha empire for a man who appeared incapable of affording effectual assistance in the undertaking." They foretold, rightly, that the enterprise would only embark them upon an indefinite sea of troubles; and they peremptorily ordered the Company's forces to be withdrawn, if it could be done without danger. But before this letter could reach Bombay, the expedition had started; Salsette and Bassein, two very important points, had been forcibly occupied; and the English were committed to the war.

At Arras was fought the first of that long series of battles between the English and the Marathas, almost all of which have been well and honourably contested. The Bombay troops were obliged to fall back in disorder, losing many English officers, who sacrificed themselves with their usual devotion in the attempt to rally their sepoys. It now seemed to Hastings impossible to make peace immediately and honourably, so he insisted that his countrymen must stand their ground and face their reverses; reinforcements were sent across India; and attempts were made at negotiation with the Marathas, who were justly incensed by these proceedings.

RAGHUNATH RAO.

In this manner England became entangled in a long, costly, and unprofitable war, which may be taken to have been the original source of the interminable hostilities which occupied Hastings for the next seven years, straining his finances, damaging his reputation, distracting his administration, and bringing both Bombay and Madras at different moments into serious jeopardy. Any attempt to give a brief and also intelligible narrative of the straggling inconclusive fighting that went on must inevitably fail. The essence of the whole matter is that the Marathas were at this period far too strong and too well united to be shaken or overawed by such forces as the English could despatch against them. They held a position in the centre of India which enabled them to threaten all the three divided English Presidencies, to intrigue successfully against the British at Haidarabad and Mysore, and to communicate with the French by their ports on the western seacoast.

The two minor Presidencies of Bombay and Madras were governed by rash, incompetent persons who were exceedingly jealous of the Governor-General's superior authority, who disregarded his advice or orders, and thwarted his policy; while Hastings himself was hampered by opposition in his own Council and by enemies at headquarters in London. If he had been able to withdraw from the war at once, and to insist on making peace with the Marathas, he might have escaped the graver complications that followed upon the original blunder of attacking them. But the English still held, and were determined to retain, Salsette and Bassein, and although Hastings sent an envoy to Poona, the refusal of the Marathas to cede these two valuable points protracted negotiations up to the end of 1776, when a turn of European politics materially affected, as usual, the situation in India.

By this time the United States had declared their independence, and England had now become so deeply involved in the attempt to put down rebellion in North America that the French determined to use such an apparently excellent opportunity of revenge for the injuries suffered during the Seven Years' War. Providence, said the French minister in a secret state paper, had marked out this moment for the humiliation of England; and accordingly the colonists were actively, though surreptitiously, assisted by France to a degree that made a rupture with that power unavoidable.

A French agent reached India in 1777 to propose alliance with the Marathas on conditions including the cession of a seaport on the west coast. His overtures, which were naturally encouraged by the Peshwa at Poona, filled with alarm and indignation the English, to whom the actual state of affairs in Europe, India, and America rendered the prospect of such a combination exceedingly disagreeable. In the same year, Hastings received secret information from the British embassy at Paris that the French were concerting a scheme for an expedition to India in support of the enemies of the English there. In 1778, came news that Burgoyne had surrendered to the Americans at Saratoga, and that France, probably also Spain, was declaring war; while a French ship from Bourbon Island had actually landed officers and military stores on the south coast for Hyder Ali.

Although at this moment the dissension between Hastings and Philip Francis in the Calcutta Council was fierce and bitter, yet the Governor-General carried with a high hand his energetic measures for meeting these dangers. All the French settlements in India were seized; a force was despatched from Bengal to reinforce Bombay, and under the stress of the emergency the Governor-General determined to throw aside

THE GREAT CAVE AT ELEPHANTA, NEAR BOMBAY.

a treaty just settled with the Marathas and to sanction another march upon Poona in support of Raghunath Rao. In modern times, the device of supporting pretenders to a foreign throne has fallen into disuse among civilized states, even when they are at war; partly because international law disapproves, if it does not condemn, the proceeding, but mainly because a long series of experiments has proved that such enterprises only exasperate the enemy and as political expedients are generally foredoomed to failure. Yet in Europe it was once an ordinary method of vexing or weakening an antagonist, and in Asia it is still a very popular kind of adventure; while Anglo-Indian history contains several examples that are invariably warnings.

Thus the backing of Raghunath Rao for the Maratha premiership turned out a disastrous speculation, for the second expedition ended in ignominious failure. Its leaders, civil and military, blundered signally and retreated disgracefully; the pretender fled back into exile; and nothing was gained except the just and enduring resentment of the Marathas. The Bombay government, says Grant Duff, had desperately sent a handful of men against the Maratha empire and had committed the conduct of such an enterprise to men totally unfit for such a charge; the truth being that the Marathas were at that time, and nearly up to the end of the century, at least a match for the English.

After this second discomfiture in the field, and after the miscarriage of some very diplomatic attempts to detach certain of the leading chiefs from the Maratha confederacy—attempts in which he was outwitted by those adepts in subtle statecraft — Hastings found himself caught in the meshes of protracted war with a loose, active, shifty, and indefatigable enemy, who well knew how to stir up trouble for him in various parts of India. Hyder Ali of Mysore, who for some years had been husbanding his resources and biding his time in the peninsula, now began to disclose ominous symptoms of the vindictive spirit that had been fermenting in his implacable mind ever since the English had abandoned him to the Marathas in 1769.

When the Calcutta government determined to seize the French settlements, orders had been sent to Madras that Mahé, which belonged to France, should be occupied without delay; because this port, in the extreme southwest of the Indian peninsula, might become an important channel of communication between the French and Mysore. It is conceivable that this may have been precisely the reason why Hyder Ali preferred that the place should be left under his protection; at any rate he desired the Madras authorities not to meddle with it, adding that since Mahé was within his jurisdiction and the inhabitants were his subjects, he might find it necessary to defend them if they were attacked. Nevertheless, Mahé was taken by an English detachment in 1779, at a moment when Hyder Ali was engaged in picking off some outlying districts belonging to the Marathas, having naturally availed himself of the quarrel between them and the English to round off his own possessions. Such a disregard of his express interdict gave the Mysore ruler serious umbrage, which was not lessened by the imprudent attempt of an English force to march across a part of his territory without his permission.

Throughout all this period — that is, during the last quarter of the eighteenth century — the balance of power in India rested upon a kind of triangular equipoise between the English, the Marathas, and Mysore. If two of these powers quarrelled, the third became predominant for the time; if two of them united, the third was in jeopardy. This is what had happened in 1778, when the alarm of war with France drove the Anglo-Indian government into precipitate measures that embroiled us first with the Marathas and secondly with Mysore, and consequently brought down upon us the combined hostility of both.

By the summer of 1780, the fortunes of the English in India had fallen to their lowest watermark. At Calcutta the resources of Bengal were drained by the cost of distant and protracted war, and cramped, as Hastings said, by internal imbecility; for the Governor-General was still contending against perverse and obstructive colleagues, one of whom, Francis, he at last quieted by a pistol-shot, wounding him severely, though not fatally, in a duel at Calcutta, August 17, 1780. At Bombay, the funds were so completely exhausted that the Council reported, as their best reason for keeping the troops on active service abroad, their inability to pay them at home. In the south, Hyder Ali had made common cause with the Marathas, had drawn the Nizam of Haidarabad into the triple alliance against the English, had obtained promises of French co-operation on the seacoast, and in July, 1780, had descended from the hills upon the plains of the Karnatic with an army of eighty thousand men.

All premonitory signs of coming danger had been treated at Madras with inattention and contempt. Sir Thomas Rumbold, a corrupt and incapable governor, departing homeward in the spring, had recorded in a farewell minute his satisfaction at leaving the southern Presidency in perfect tranquillity; yet a few months later Hyder Ali, whose preparations had long been notorious, burst upon the low country like a thunder-storm, and his cavalry ravaged the Karnatic up to the suburbs of Madras, in an irruption which Burke describes with splendid rhetoric in his speech on the Nawab of Arkot's debts. The English troops sent to oppose him were surrounded and almost annihilated; the treasury was empty; and there were no supplies in the town, which might easily have been taken if Hyder Ali had resolutely assailed it in force.

Hastings lost no time in despatching money and reinforcements from Calcutta under Sir Eyre Coote, who defeated Hyder Ali in the battle of Porto Novo, in July, 1781, and managed to drive him off from the vicinity of the Presidency town; but the irruption had dislocated all the Governor-General's plans. He now had both Mysore and the Marathas simultaneously on his hands. His finances were exhausted; his military strength overstrained; his attempts to create disunion among the Maratha chiefs had been frustrated; he had to fight one of them, Sind, in the northwest near Gwalior, another, the Peshwa, near Bombay; and his offers of peace, on terms very favourable to the Marathas, were ill received.

The utmost military exertions hardly kept the Marathas in check on the western coast, while at Madras the army which was confronting Hyder Ali was in the greatest straits for provisions, and the Presidency treasure-chest was empty. Sind, who was fast becoming the most powerful chief of the Maratha federation, had by this time extended his conquests from Central

A CASTLE ON THE BARWA SAGAR, GWALIOR.

India northward toward Agra and Delhi; but although this forward movement threatened the flank of Bengal, yet it also brought him within striking distance of the strongest position of the British. After several sharp skirmishes with the English troops, and the loss of the fortress of Gwalior taken by escalade (a brilliant and daring exploit of Captain Popham, one of the forgotten Anglo-Indian heroes), Sind discovered that his interest lay in coming to an understanding. It was arranged that he should be allowed to prosecute his designs upon the few districts round Delhi still retained by the Moghul emperor, on condition of his mediating between the English and the Maratha government.

In this manner, after considerable sacrifices, Hastings at last succeeded in terminating, by a treaty made with the Marathas in May, 1782, a war that was neither honourable to the English name nor advantageous to their interests, and out of which arose those exigencies which drove him into the transactions that formed the main grounds of his subsequent impeachment. In 1780, the vast expense for the subsistence and defence of both Madras and Bombay had, as he wrote, reduced him to the most mortifying financial extremities; the two Presidencies depended almost entirely on Bengal for money; and in 1781 the treasury had been drained, although every kind of expedient for raising funds had been tried.

It was under the pressure of these embarrassments that he demanded a heavy subsidy from the Raja of Benares, which aroused a famous insurrection. When the raja evaded payment of the subsidy, Hastings went in person to Benares, imposed a still heavier fine upon him, and placed him under arrest. The result was an outbreak which for the moment placed the Governor-

General in some jeopardy, but it was vigorously suppressed without any permanent damage to the political situation. Under the same stress of financial hunger caused by an empty military chest, Hastings subjected the Oudh Begums and their eunuchs to coercion for the purpose of compelling the payment of money which the Begums had no right to withhold, although it is more than questionable whether the Governor-General should have used such means to obtain it. The particulars of these two transactions have been so repeatedly and recently given, that an allusion to them seems here sufficient.

The diffusion and versatility of the Maratha armies had made them very troublesome enemies; and from their headquarters at Poona, above the passes leading down to the western coast, they overhung and could always menace Bombay. But their coalition was weakened for consistent action by mutual distrust among the chiefs, who were now supplanting the Peshwa's authority in the Maratha empire, as the Peshwa had previously wrested the sovereignty from the heirs of Sivaji; whereas Hyder Ali's forces obeyed the will of one ruler—strongly entrenched with an effective army in the angle of the Indian peninsula, commanding access to the plains round Madras and to the seacoast on both sides,—whose position, ability, and warlike energy all rendered him a most formidable antagonist in any single campaign. Hyder Ali had long perceived that the weakness of India and the strength of England lay in the defenceless condition of the Indian seaboard.

He had himself made strenuous exertions to organize a naval armament; and in his present war against the English he was relying upon the arrival of a French squadron which was known to be fitting out at Bourbon Island with the design of breaking the communications between England and India.

HILT OF TIPPU'S SWORD.
Now in His Majesty's Collection at Windsor.

When this squadron appeared on the Coromandel coast, in 1781, Hyder Ali was employing himself in reducing the scattered posts of the English in the Karnatic, which were wholly at his mercy; and if the French could have co-operated, he would have taken the important town of Cuddalore, which, indeed, surrendered to his son Tippu in 1782. But the French admiral sailed back to Bourbon; Hyder Ali was pressed by Sir Eyre Coote, and at last brought to bay at Porto Novo, where he was crippled by a heavy defeat which restored the open country to the English. Thus it came to pass that when Suffren, than whom France has never had a better admiral, returned to the coast in 1782 with a much larger fleet, he was met by a strong though unequal force of English ships under Sir Edward Hughes, and he found Hyder comparatively disabled. All the possessions of the French and the Dutch had been occupied by the English; so that Suffren had no base of supplies or repair upon the Indian seaboard.

He succeeded in landing two thousand French troops, which were soon joined by a large contingent from Hyder Ali, when a large force, including four hundred Frenchmen, under Tippu, Hyder Ali's son, surprised Colonel Braithwaite's detachment and almost destroyed it after a stubborn and desperate resistance. Meanwhile, five obstinately contested naval engagements took place in the Bay of Bengal between Suffren and Hughes. Suffren, an admirable naval tactician, might have beaten the English squadron if he had not been ill supported by his captains. On the other side, Hughes and all his men fought their ships with stubborn fierceness, until the superior seamanship and unconquerable endurance of the English sailors so far prevailed that the French fleet was prevented from affording any material assistance to the army on land.

Early in 1783, Bussy arrived from France with a large reinforcement of French infantry. But the death of Hyder Ali in December, 1782, had just relieved the English from their inveterate foe; and although his son and successor Tippu Sahib, acting with the French troops, reduced the English army before Cuddalore to a very awkward predicament, yet no effective blow had been struck when in July, 1783, the news of peace between England and France arrived. Thereupon Suffren sailed for Europe, and Tippu of Mysore, finding himself alone, very reluctantly came to terms somewhat later. Thus ended a war of seven years, during which the

English power in India underwent some perilous vicissitudes; but the ring of enemies by which Hastings had been encompassed was at last broken, and in the spring of 1785, when he resigned the Governor-Generalship, the English were at peace with all the native powers of India.

It will be observed that throughout the eighteenth century the main alternations of peace and war in India

SOME OF TIPPU'S FORCES.
After Gold's Oriental Drawings.

keep time with the successive ruptures and renewals of amity between France and England. So long as the French were rivals of the English in the country, the two Companies necessarily took the word of command, for peace or war, from their home governments. After this rivalry had ceased, the French kept their coast settlements; but their navy could always threaten the British Indian seaboard, and the safety of all English communications with India depended entirely upon the result of the maritime wars between the two nations.

The Anglo-Indian governments were, therefore, so keenly sensitive to any apprehension of war with France that the mere rumour of a French descent on the coast aroused them to warlike activity. A native ruler who might be detected in correspondence with Mauritius was sure to be treated as a dangerous enemy, to be attacked and disabled with all possible speed. The consequence had been that each repeated demonstration of France against the English dominion in India had accelerated instead of retarding its expansion; excepting only the war that ended in 1783 with the Peace of Versailles. During the greater part of that stormy period the English were too heavily overmatched, too closely pressed in all parts of the world, to do more than hold their ground in India.

In 1781, England, without an ally, and with great odds against her, was confronted by all the great naval powers of Europe, France, Spain, and Holland, and by the North American colonies. In Asia, she was locked in a fierce struggle with the two most warlike and skilful Indian powers, both of whom were dealing with the French, who on their side had brought into play against England in India the same strategy that was proving eminently successful against her in America. England lost her American colonies not through the resistance on land, which might and would have been worn down, but through the pressure of her naval enemies upon her communications across the Atlantic. This was the weapon used against her in the east by Suffren, who had learnt from her the lesson that in regions distant from Europe superiority of sea power meant the control of the issues upon the land. The French made great exertions to stop England's sea-roads to India, to drive her fleet off the Indian coasts, and to throw reinforcements into the camps of her Indian opponents; they captured the only good harbour that commands the Indian peninsula, Tricomali in Ceylon, and in conjunction with Hyder Ali they might have taken Madras, if Suffren could have shaken off the English admiral's indomitable grip.

It is no wonder that, during such a struggle, and for some time afterwards, the territorial landmarks of England in India remained stationary, since her resources in men and money barely sufficed to preserve Madras and Bombay from destruction. But the centre and heart of the English power lay in Bengal, which the war never reached at all, and which was governed by a man of rare talent and organizing capacity. No Anglo-Indian government of that time could carry on a campaign by war loans, as in Europe; for its public credit, the sphere within which it could borrow, was confined to the Presidency town. The main cost had to be provided out of revenue, or by requiring subsidies from allied native rulers; and it was Bengal that furnished not only the money and the men, but also the chief political direction and military leadership which surmounted the difficulties and repaired the calamities of the English in the western and southern Presidencies.

When at last the Marathas made peace, when Hyder Ali died, and Suffren, with all his courage and genius, could not master the English fleet in the Bay of Bengal, there could be no doubt that the war had proved the strength of the English position in India and had tested the firmness of its foundation. Although the tidings of peace reached India in 1783, just in time to release the English army in South India from considerable difficulties, and though the French ships still outnumbered the English on the coast, yet Suffren, on receiving the despatches, exclaimed: "God be praised for the peace! for it was clear that in India, though we had the means to impose the law, all would have been lost."

With the termination of this war ended the only period, in the long contest between England and the native powers, during which the British position in India was seriously jeoparded for a time. That the English dominion emerged from this prolonged struggle uninjured, though not unshaken, is a result due to the political intrepidity of Warren Hastings. It seems unnecessary to continue here the discussions, which have now lasted more than a century, over the career of this remarkable Englishman. What chiefly concerns us to understand is that Hastings carried the government of India safely through one of the sharpest crises in England's national history, when her transmarine possessions were in great peril all over the world, because all the naval powers of Europe were banded against her.

When, in the course of the Seven Years' War, the successes of the British against the French in India and North America had freed England from her only powerful rival, it might have been supposed that she should remain in comparatively peaceful occupation. But so soon as foreign competition ceased, internal troubles began in both hemispheres; the colonists struck for independence in the West; the native powers combined to dispute English predominance in the East; and France, evicted and disappointed, naturally encouraged and aided both movements. In America, the insurgents, after an arduous struggle, tore down the British flag; in India, the end of a long and exhausting contest found the English flag not only flying still, but planted more firmly than ever; nor had either the vindictive hostility of Mysore, or the indefatigable activity of the Marathas, succeeded in wresting an acre of British territory from the grasp of Warren Hastings.

Hastings had no aristocratic connections or parliamentary influence at a time when the great families and the House of Commons held immense power; he was surrounded by enemies in his own Council; and his immediate masters, the East India Company, gave him very fluctuating support. Fiercely opposed by his own colleagues, and very ill-obeyed by the subordinate Presidencies, he had to maintain the Company's commercial investments, and at the same time to find money for carrying on distant and impolitic wars in which he had been involved by blunders at Madras or Bombay. These funds he had been expected to provide out of current revenues, after buying and despatching the merchandise on which the Company's home dividends depended; for the resource of raising public loans, so freely used in England, was scarcely available to him; but because his war expenses exceeded the scale of his peace establishment, he was accused of lavish dissipation of the public income.

Hastings was thus inevitably driven to the financial transactions at Benares and Lucknow that were now

UMBRELLA TREE AND GRANITE BOULDER AT BELLARY IN THE MADRAS PRESIDENCY.

so bitterly stigmatized as crimes by men who made no allowance for a perilous situation in a distant land, or for the weight of enormous national interests committed to the charge of the one man capable of sustaining them. When the storm had blown over in India, and he had piloted his vessel into calm water, he was sacrificed with little or no hesitation to party exigencies in England; the Ministry would have recalled him; they consented to his impeachment; they left him to be baited by the Opposition and to be ruined by the law's delay, by the incredible procrastination, and the obsolete formalities of a seven years' trial before the House of Lords. Upon such a career, upon the value of the services rendered by Hastings to his country and the injustice with which he was requited, the English people must by this time have formed a judgment too broadly based to be much affected by any fresh scrutiny of the reckless calumnies flung at him while he stood at bay against false and vindictive accusers. like Nuncomar and Francis, or fought at great odds against Hyder Ali and the Maratha league.

It may be added, as a curious proof of the reputation acquired by Hastings in Europe, that in 1785, when he was just leaving Bengal, the French ambassador in London seriously proposed to his government a plan of secretly encouraging Hastings to make himself an independent ruler in India by means of his native army and of French support. The ambassador, having evidently in his mind the success with which France had abetted the revolt of the American colonists, argued confidently that a man who held "almost a royal position" in India, who had been recalled with indignity and threatened with impeachment, would be found easily accessible to such overtures; and the peremptory refusal of the French minister to entertain his ingenious plot was a bitter disappointment to him.

CHAPTER XII

THE INTERVAL BETWEEN HASTINGS AND CORNWALLIS

1785-1786

IT is an observation of Sir James Mackintosh that in the course of one generation the English lost one empire in the West and gained another in the East; and it may be added that England owes not only the loss but its compensation to the policy of the French Government. In the long war that had now ended, their navy broke the hold of England on the North American colonies, as repeated blows on a man's arms make him let go his antagonist in a furious struggle. But they had so enfeebled themselves by their exertions to fight England on behalf of American independence that they were left powerless to interfere with her thenceforward in Asia, or to maintain their rivalry at sea.

From 1783 begins a kind of pause in Anglo-Indian affairs, varied in India only by a preliminary trial of strength with Mysore, and in England by violent party-warfare over Indian questions. The French Government still continued, according to the reports of British diplomatists, to watch for an opportunity of interfering again in India, but their foreign policy was now suffering incipient paralysis from their growing internal complications. With France, therefore, England had a truce that lasted for ten years, to our great advantage in India, until in the final decade of the eighteenth century a fresh and furious storm broke over Europe with such violence that it rebounded upon India, and levelled most of the remaining obstacles to the expansion of the English dominion in that country.

If we are to measure the growth of the British power in India by the expansion of its territorial dominion, the interval of twenty years between Clive's acceptance of the Diwani in 1765 and the departure of Warren Hastings from India in 1785 may be reckoned as a stationary period. It is true that from Oudh we acquired Benares and Ghazipur on the northwest of Bengal in 1775—although the transfer merely registered our possession of two districts which had long been under our political control—and that we also obtained Bassein and Salsette, small though important points close to Bombay. But during the Governor-Generalship of Hastings, we had been so far from extending our Indian domain that our hold upon our actual possessions had been severely strained, our territory had been invaded, our arms had suffered some reverses, and the safety of one Presidency capital, Madras, had been gravely endangered. In point of fact, the English ascendency in India at this time had by no means been conclusively established; for although we were proving ourselves the strongest of the powers that were now definitely rising into prominence out of the confusion of the previous half-century, yet we were still confronted by jealous rivals, and our dominions were not large in proportion to those of other states.

Two things, nevertheless, had been demonstrated by the struggle that had been sustained by the English nation. It had been proved in the first place that the united naval forces of Europe could not drive England from the sea, or wrest from her the command of the great routes across the ocean between Europe and Asia. Secondly, it had become clear by this time that, so long as their transmarine communications with the mother country could be preserved, and so long as their invaluable possession of Bengal remained undisturbed, the English ran no risk of permanent or vital injury either from the Marathas or from Mysore. The position of these two formidable fighting powers in the centre and south of India undoubtedly still operated as a check upon the English, and they could have diverted our forces to an extent which might have placed us in some jeopardy, if any hostile state of heavy warlike calibre had become established about this time in Upper India. This might easily have happened, for the wide and wealthy plains of the northwest had hitherto been always the seat, and the source, of the largest and strongest military rulerships. But it so chanced, by the good luck which has always attended the English in India, that toward the end of the eighteenth century, when the Marathas and the Mysore dynasty were strong and threatening, England had little or nothing to fear beyond her northwestern frontier. The ghost of the Moghul Empire, sitting crowned among the ruins of its ancient splendour, still reigned over Delhi. And although the imperial authority had lost all substance, the shadow of that great name still so far overspread

CENOTAPH OF A NATIVE RULER AT JAIPUR.

the surrounding districts as to prevent their absorption under a new dominion.

Yet the political vacuum created by the final disintegration of the Moghul Empire, and the withdrawal of the Afghans, was already filling up in the Panjab, by the rapid rise and compact organization of the Sikhs. Under this new Hindu federation, much more closely knit together by ties of race and common faith than the Marathas, the people became animated by a martial spirit and a fiery enthusiasm such as the Hindus had not hitherto displayed. The history of the Sikhs illustrates a phenomenon well known in Asia, where an insurrectionary movement is always particularly dangerous if it takes a religious complexion, and where fanaticism may endure and accumulate under a spiritual leader until it explodes in the world of politics with the force of dynamite.

The martyrdom of their first prophet, and their persecution by the later Moghul emperors, had engendered in the hardy Sikh peasants a fierce hatred of Islam. They had been repressed and broken by the Afghan armies of Ahmad Shah, who routed them with great slaughter in 1761. But in 1762 they defeated and slew his governor at Sirhind; and in 1764 Ahmad Shah was recalled to his western provinces by a revolt in Kandahar. He died in 1773, after which date the grasp of his successors on the Panjab relaxed, and the Sikh confederation became closer and more vigorous. They were subdivided into *misls*, or military confederacies, under different chiefs, who fought among themselves and against the Mohammedans, until, by 1785, the Sikhs had mastered the whole country between the Jihlam and the Sutlaj Rivers in the centre of the Panjab, were threatening the Mohammedan princes about Delhi, and had made pillaging excursions eastward across the Ganges into Rohilkhand.

To the English in Bengal this revival of Hindu nationality in upper India was exceedingly serviceable and opportune. For, in the first place, their real danger, the only substantial obstacle to their rising ascendency, lay always, then as now, in the possibility of some foreign invasion by the army of some rival power led by a chief at the head of the fighting tribes of Central Asia. But the Sikhs were making it impossible for any such Asiatic army to penetrate into the heart of the Panjab without encountering the obstinate resistance of men united to defend their faith and their fatherland, in a spirit very unfamiliar to the quiescence of ordinary Hinduism.

The kingdom founded by Ahmad Shah had extended, from its citadel in the Afghan mountains, on the west over Khorasan, and on the east over the Upper Panjab. It had thus been built up by wresting one frontier province from Persia and the other from India, and as the Afghan ruler was cordially detested in both these countries, whenever he was engaged by invasion or revolt on one flank, the opportunity was sure to be taken by his enemies on the other. Even Ahmad Shah failed to hold such a position without great exertions, and after his death it became quite untenable. Twenty years later Zaman Shah, a very able Afghan king, was obliged to retire from Lahore. This last abortive expedition closed the long series of irruptions by the Mohammedan conquerors, who for seven hundred years had swept down from the north upon the plains of India, and had founded dynasties which were only sustained by constant recruitment from their native countries beyond the mountains. Thenceforward the Sikhs were not only able to hold the line of the Indus River against fresh invaders; they also cut off the channels of supply between Central Asia and the Mohammedan powers to the south of the Sutlaj, who were, moreover, kept in constant alarm by this actively aggressive Hindu community on their northern frontier.

The effect was to maintain among the fighting powers in Northern India an equilibrium that was of signal advantage to the English by preserving their northwest frontier unmolested during the last quarter of the eighteenth century, a critical period when they were fully occupied with Mysore and the western Marathas. The barrier of Oudh set up by Hastings, although it had been sufficiently effective against the predatory Maratha hordes, would have been of little use for withstanding the much heavier metal of attacks from Central Asia. But the fierce enmity of the Sikhs kept out the foreign Mohammedan, and prevented the resuscitation of any fresh Islamite dynasty upon the ruins of the old empire at Delhi or Lahore. By the time that the Sikh power had become consolidated under Ranjit Singh, in the first years of the nineteenth century, the English had met and overcome their southern rivals, and could then turn their forces northward without fear of any serious diversion on their flanks or rear.

The position of the Sikhs on both sides of the Sutlaj was also useful at this period in setting bounds to the encroachments of the Marathas, who were now again pushing northward under Sindhia. This ambitious and able chief was endeavouring to carve out for himself an independent principality in the upper provinces. He had attached himself to one of the parties that were contending for the possession of imperial authority at Delhi, and had rewarded himself by marching up with a large army in 1785 to obtain his own nomination as vicegerent of the empire. The emperor's eldest son had applied to the English for assistance; and Hastings had been much tempted, just before he quitted India, by the project of sending an expedition to Delhi for the purpose of setting the Great Moghul again on his feet, and of making English influence paramount at his capital.

But the Company, though alarmed at this notable aggrandizement of the Marathas in a new quarter, could not yet venture to oppose Sindhia's enterprise, and the project of reviving the moribund empire under European influence—which had passed across the vision of Dupleix, of Bussy, and of Clive—was once more reluctantly abandoned by Hastings as impracticable. Yet it was in fact only premature, for twenty years later the march to Delhi and the expulsion of the Marathas were actually accomplished under Lord Wellesley's orders. In the meantime, Sindhia, who occupied both Agra and Delhi after Hastings's departure, became so confident as to send to the English Government, in his Majesty's name, a requisition for tribute on account of their administration of the imperial province of Bengal.

The year 1786, therefore, when Lord Cornwallis reached India, found the English still confronting the Marathas in the west and northwest, and Tippu Sultan, the Mysore ruler, in the south, but with no other rivals of importance in the political or military field against them.

We have seen how, from the time when the European nations first acquired valuable interests in India, the course of events in India has gradually been drawn

LORD CORNWALLIS.

more and more within European influences. The weaker Asiatic states have felt the attraction of the larger and more active political bodies; wars in the west have kindled wars in the east; and the clash of arms has reverberated from one to the other continent. The outcome of the contest was, as has been said, that England now held undisputed supremacy, as against other European nations, in India. Then, as the connection between the British nation and its great dependency grew to be closer, as the points of contact multiplied, and as the value of her magnificent acquisition became known to England, her clearer recognition of national rights and duties brought Indian affairs within the current of domestic politics.

Not only foreign wars, but the struggle of Parliamentary parties at home had lately affected India. In 1780 Lord North moved in the House of Commons for an order that the three years' statutory notice of intention to dissolve their charter should be given to the Company. The motion was carried against the strenuous opposition of Fox, who asked the minister whether he was not content with having lost America, and of Burke, who warned the House not to throw away the East after the West in another chase after revenue. Nevertheless, by 1783, when the period of notice was expiring, the point of view taken up by these great orators, who were then in office, had materially changed. The conclusion of peace in Europe and America in 1783 had now given the English, after an interval of ten years, a second opportunity of looking into the condition and management of their distant possessions; the loss of the western colonies had sharpened their solicitude for the new dominion that had been gained in the East.

There could now be no doubt that England had acquired a great Indian sovereignty; for although the wars and perpetual contests of the last seven years had for the time imperilled her position in the country, the general result was to prove its stability under severe pressure, and thus to confirm rather than impair British ascendency. Warren Hastings, in reviewing the state of Bengal at the end of his Governor-Generalship, wrote that the late war had proved to all the leading states of India "that their combined strength and politics, assisted by our great enemy the French, have not been able to destroy the solid fabric of the English power in the East, nor even to deprive it of any portion of its territories."

It was this conviction that the Company were now masters in India, that they had grown too powerful for a trading association—so powerful, indeed, as to have become an anomaly under the British constitution and even a danger to it—that gave weight and momentum to Burke's assault upon the whole system. In his speech delivered in December, 1783, upon Fox's East India Bill, which was to transfer the Company's authority to Parliamentary Commissioners, he enlarges upon the extent of the Company's territory and the immense range of their arbitrary despotism. "With very few, and those inconsiderable, intervals, the British dominion, either in the Company's name or in the names of princes absolutely dependent on the Company, extends from the mountains that separate India from Tartary (the Himalayas) to Cape Comorin, that is, one and twenty degrees of latitude. . . . If I were to take the whole aggregate of our possessions there, I should compare it, as the nearest parallel I could find, to the empire of Germany. Our immediate possessions I shall compare with the Austrian dominions, and they would not suffer in the comparison. . . . Through all that vast extent of country there is not a man who eats a mouthful of rice but by permission of the East India Company."

There is great exaggeration in this description, and the German parallel is substantially erroneous; nevertheless, it is worth observing that more than a century ago, within twenty-five years after the battle of Plassey, the predominance of the Company throughout India was treated as a fact only too completely accomplished. Nor can it be doubted that Burke's survey of the situation was, in the main, correct; the weakness of all the native states had been ascertained; the groundwork of empire had already been firmly constructed. And subsequent events rapidly verified the judgment of Hastings that "nothing but attention, protection, and forbearance," an equal, vigorous, and fixed administration, and free play for its vast natural resources and advantages was needed to secure the rise of India, under British ascendency, to a high and permanent level of national prosperity.

For some years the constitution and conduct of the East India Company had been undergoing thorough investigation before committees of the House of Commons, with the result that the need of many reforms, and the expediency of imposing more control on the management of Anglo-Indian possessions, had been agreed upon unanimously. The reports of the committees were submitted, and resolutions proposed, in 1782, at a moment when the old political parties were breaking up and reconstituting themselves into new groups under fresh leaders, when the famous Coalition Ministry was in process of formation, and when the bitter contentions between hostile factions were at their height. In these resolutions the whole recent administration of the Company was severely condemned, the

A VILLAGE GOD IN THE BOMBAY PRESIDENCY.

directors were required to recall Warren Hastings, and it was further resolved that the powers given to the Governor-General and Council must be more distinctly ascertained.

When the Coalition Ministry took office, Fox introduced a bill altering the whole of the Company's constitution, which was supported by Burke in a speech loaded with furious invective against Hastings and the

Company, both of whom he charged with the most abominable tyranny and corruption. Against some of the Company's servants the true record of misdeeds and errors was sufficiently long; but Hastings was a man of the highest character and capacity, an incorruptible administrator who had done his country great and meritorious services. Yet his integrity was virulently aspersed, and all his public acts wantonly distorted, in speeches that invoked against him the moral indignation of partisans engaged in the ignoble wrangle over places, pensions, and sinecures, among whom none had been exposed to similar trials of a man's courage or constancy, and only a very few would have resisted similar temptations.

In this manner the report and resolutions were used as fuel for the engines of party-warfare to drive the bill through Parliament against some very solid opposition. Nevertheless, the essential question before the Commons and the country was not so much whether the Company and their officers were guilty of crimes that were for the most part incredible, as whether the patronage of India should be the prize of politicians, who, after furiously denouncing each other's measures and principles, had made a very dishonourable coalition to obtain office. On this point the king, with a majority of his people, was against the ministry that had been formed under the Duke of Portland by Lord North's association with Fox and Burke.

It thus came to pass that the pitched battles of the memorable Parliamentary campaigns of 1783-1784

The Ghat Temple, Cawnpur.

were fought upon Indian ground; Fox and Burke were defeated and driven out of office; the East Indian Bill was rejected; the Coalition was upset by George III and by Pitt, who rose at once to the summit of ministerial power. In 1784 Pitt carried through Parliament his act which vested full superintendence over all civil, military, and revenue affairs of the Company in six commissioners appointed by the Crown. The chief government in India was placed in the hands of the Governor-General with three councillors, whose authority over the minor Presidencies was complete on all matters of diplomacy, of peace and war, and of the application of the revenues; and by a subsequent act of 1786 the Governor-General was empowered to act on his own responsibility in extraordinary cases, without the concurrence of his Council.

This system of double government, by the Company under the control of a minister directly responsible to Parliament, lasted until 1858, when the Crown assumed the sole and direct administration of India, a project that had been under the consideration of the elder Pitt a hundred years earlier. The immediate effect of Pitt's act was a great and manifest improvement in the mechanics of Indian government, removing most of the ill-contrived checks and hindrances which had brought Hastings into collision with his Council and the subordinate governments, abolishing the defects that he had pointed out, and applying the remedies that he had proposed. All preceding governors had been servants of the East India Company; and Hastings, the first and last of the Company's Governors-General, had been the scapegoat of an awkward and unmanageable governing apparatus, hampered by divided authority, and distracted by party feuds in Calcutta and in London. The position and powers of the chief executive authority in India were henceforward very differently constituted, and the increased force of the new machinery very soon became visible in the results.

CHAPTER XIII

THE ADMINISTRATION OF LORD CORNWALLIS

1786 - 1839

BUT the essence of the new governing constitution conferred upon British India did not only lie in the vigour which it infused into the executive by placing power and responsibility upon a plain incontestable basis; it also strengthened the Governor-General immensely by bringing him into close political relations with the ministry at home. Lord Cornwallis, the first of the new dynasty of Parliamentary Governors-General, went to India with a high reputation as a soldier and a diplomatist, sure of the support of the strongest ministry that had ever governed England, and invested with well-defined supreme authority, military as well as civil, under a full statutory title. He was Governor-General over all three Presidencies, and he was also appointed Commander-in-Chief.

Such a concentration of power in one man, his rank, his reputation, his intimacy with Pitt and Dundas, all combined to sweep away the obstacles that had blocked the path of Hastings, and for the first time to clothe the representative of England in India with the attributes of genuine rulership. In the exercise of these ample powers he was materially aided by the political situation in Europe and Asia. The unfortunate and misconducted wars of Lord North's government had ceased; they had been succeeded, in the East and in the West, by a period of peace for England; it was the interval of cloudy stillness before the explosion of the great revolutionary cyclone in Europe, which was not felt in India until 1793.

Such a breathing-time and interval of calm was well suited for carrying out wide internal reforms in India, for consolidating England's position by a stroke at her foremost and most intractable Indian antagonist in Mysore, and for inaugurating a scheme of peaceful alliances with the other native princes, which lasted with the fair weather, but collapsed as soon as the storm-wave of European commotions reached the shores of India.

In the year 1786, therefore, we find the English sovereignty openly established in India under a Governor-General entrusted with plenary authority by the representatives of the English nation. The transformation of the chief governorship of a chartered commercial company into a senatorial proconsulship was now virtually accomplished; and with the accession of Cornwallis there sets in a new era of accelerated advance. It was Hastings who first set in order the chaos of Bengal misrule, and who drew the ground-plan of regular systematic procedure in almost all departments of executive government. But the administration of

Hastings had been constantly interrupted by quarrels at home and wars abroad.

Henceforward internal organization goes on continuously; laws are passed, abuses are firmly repressed, and the settlement of the land revenue of Bengal is the administrative achievement by which the name of Lord Cornwallis is now chiefly remembered in India. In fixing for ever the land-tax of the districts then included within the regular jurisdiction of the Presidency, he followed the natural bent of a statesman familiar only with the property tenures of England, where a Parliament of landlords was just about to make their own land-tax a perpetual charge at a fixed rate of valuation. And although the measure has cut off the Indian treasury from all share in the increase of rents and the immense spread of cultivation, although it has prevented the equitable raising of the land revenue in proportion with the fall in value of the currency in which it is paid, yet it has undoubtedly maintained Bengal as the wealthiest province of the empire.

From this time forward, also, political insecurity within British territory gradually gives way to a sense of stable and enduring dominion, and to that feeling of confidence in a government which is the mainspring of industry. While the people begin to adjust themselves at home to these novel conditions of Western sovereignty, abroad the British frontier is rarely threatened and hardly ever crossed by a serious enemy. The British government has now taken undisguised rank among the first-class powers of India. There is as yet, however, no formal assertion of superiority; the native states still make war and peace with England on equal terms; they receive special missions, negotiate alliances, and with their internal affairs we pretend to no concern.

When Lord Cornwallis assumed office, there was

TIPPU'S TOMB AT SERINGAPATAM.

peace between the English and the native powers; although the Marathas had joined the Nizam of Haidarabad in an attack on Tippu of Mysore, whose fanaticism and arrogance had alarmed and alienated all his neighbours. In this attack Cornwallis refused to join, but he set about bringing his army up to a war-footing; and Tippu, who was clear-sighted enough to foresee danger from the English, spared no pains on his side to strengthen himself against them. The Mysore ruler, who had witnessed the last appearance of the French, as his allies, on the coast, who still had access to the seaboard and was in touch with the French settlements, had by no means abandoned his father's policy of endeavouring to check the growth of English predominance by calling in the assistance of other European nations.

Tippu's ignorance of the real condition of European affairs, however, led him to make plans that were entirely futile, and that only accelerated his own destruction. In 1787 he sent to Constantinople an embassy which, though it effected nothing at all, obtained from the Sultan so ostentatious a reception that it probably encouraged the unfortunate ruler of Mysore in miscalculating his own power and the intrinsic value of such politic courtesies. In the same year his ambassadors were civilly welcomed at Paris by Louis XVI, at a moment when the relations between France and England were decidedly strained. These most unsubstantial diplomatic amenities seem to have deluded him into a very false reckoning of his situation; while they confirmed the English in their attitude of vigilant suspicion and in their determination to cut off such dangerous communications at the first opportunity.

In such an environment of reciprocal distrust the futility of attempting to arrest the natural current of affairs in India by Acts of Parliament, or to resist the converging pressure of circumstances, was soon demonstrated. It had been declared by Pitt's act that as the pursuit of schemes of conquest was repugnant to the wish, to the honour, and to the policy of the British nation, the Governor-General must not declare hostilities or enter into any treaty for making war against a native state, or for guaranteeing it against an enemy, except for the defence of British territory or of allies from imminent attack. But Cornwallis had scarcely landed when his protection against Tippu was claimed by the Nizam.

There being no immediate menace of war, the Governor-General held himself precluded by the act from according the Nizam a defensive alliance which might have checked Tippu's machinations. What he did, however, was to give the Nizam's envoy a written promise that he would furnish the Nizam, under an old treaty, with an auxiliary force whenever he should need it, making the reservation that it must not be employed against powers in alliance with the Company. These powers were specifically named; and as Mysore was not among them, the engagement tended rather to promote than prevent hostilities, since Tippu not unreasonably treated it as a preliminary to some direct movement against himself.

All these jealousies and mutual preparations were evidently making for war between the British and the Mysore Sultan, who soon relieved Lord Cornwallis from all further doubt in regard to the act's interpretation. In defiance of formal warnings he proceeded to make an utterly unjustifiable and unsuccessful attack upon the Raja of Travancore, a state under English protection. Lord Cornwallis thereupon formed a league against him with the Marathas and the Nizam of Haidarabad, and the allied armies marched into the Mysore country. Very little was effected by the first season's operations, and in 1791, when Lord Cornwallis took command in person, the advance upon Seringapatam failed. But in the following year's campaign Tippu was over-

AN ACTION AT SERINGAPATAM.

powered, besieged in his capital, and compelled to sign a treaty in 1792 which crippled his resources and stripped him of half his territory, including Coorg and the Malabar district along the western seacoast.

From that time forward he was constantly seeking ways and means of revenge; and he clung desperately to the vain hope of foreign alliances that might strengthen his hands against the English. He negotiated with the Marathas, with Zaman Shah, the Afghan king, and with the French, who entertained his overtures and made a show of helping him up to a point just sufficient to annoy and irritate the English. The only serious consequence of Tippu's dealings with France was that when, in 1793, the French Revolution produced a violent rupture between the two nations in Europe, Mysore was soon left exposed to the full force of England's hostility.

In the meantime the Maratha chief Mahadaji Sindhia, on whom the Moghul emperor had been induced to confer the title of vicegerent of the empire, who had made large conquests in the north, and had defeated his rival, Holkar, in a desperate fight, was becoming all-powerful in Upper India. His political aim was to maintain his own independence of the Maratha confederation without dissolving it. And as he was sagacious enough to perceive that the English were fast rising to superiority in India, he had been exceedingly distrustful of any alliance with them for the purpose of aiding them to crush a rival, even though that rival should be the Mohammedan ruler of Mysore.

Now that Tippu (with whom Sindhia was corresponding) had been humbled, it was becoming manifest that the Marathas were the only military power, from the Sutlaj River to the sea, from which the English had any opposition to apprehend. They were masters of immense territory, and their leaders were at the head of numerous well-equipped armies, which easily overcame the weak incoherent resistance of the Rajput clans, and would have certainly routed with small difficulty the mercenary troops of the two principal Mohammedan states, Oudh and Haidarabad. But the natural tendency of the commanders of separate armies to carve independent domains for themselves out of the provinces they had occupied, and to turn their camps into separate capitals, inevitably created great mutual jealousy and constantly embarrassed the common action of the confederation.

Mahadaji Sindhia, whose independence had been recognized in 1786, had since increased rapidly his possessions and his military armaments, and he now occupied the country round Delhi with a large and well-appointed army. The expediency of placing some check on Sindhia's aggrandizement, before it should bring him into collision with the British, had been pressed upon the Governor-General by his political agents. But in this case, as in others, Pitt's act, which strictly bound down the British government to non-interference unless war should be imminent, had the effect of holding the English in a position of enforced immobility that often encouraged a rash and ambitious prince to push forward to the point at which hostilities became inevitable. Sindhia's policy was now manifestly aiming at combinations against the English as against a foreign power which threatened the subjugation of all India. But his predominance alarmed the Maratha chiefs quite as much as the British government, so that the Peshwa was in no haste to follow his lead or to fall in with his projects.

In 1794, however, Mahadaji Sindhia died suddenly;

a man of great ambition, political capacity, and talent for war, who had carried out on a larger scale than any other Indian prince the new system of raising dis-

TOMB OF THE SINDHIAS, AT LASHKAR.

ciplined battalions under European officers, supported by effective artillery. But it had already been seen and said by the more far-sighted leaders among the Marathas themselves that this system, which rendered them irresistible to all other native antagonists, to the loose feudatory militia of Rajputana, and to the raw levies of the Mohammedan princes, was more likely to harm than to help them whenever they should be matched against their only serious opponents. These men saw that it was an attempt to play the game of war by European methods and to beat the English by their own weapons. The regular troops and the cannon hampered those rapid daring marches and manœuvres of light-armed cavalry — their dashing charges and dexterous retreats—which for a hundred years had won for the Marathas their victories over the unwieldy Moghul armies and had on various occasions perplexed and discomfited the English commanders.

In the days of Duplcix and Clive the employment of disciplined troops was equivalent to the introduction of a new military weapon of great efficacy, known to no one except the French and English; and unexpected superiority of this kind always secures a triumph, at first, to the side that possesses it. But the armament and tactics of civilized nations imply high proficiency in the art of war, abundant supplies of costly material, and a strong reserve of well-trained officers; they cannot be hurriedly adopted by an Asiatic chief whose people are totally unaccustomed to such inventions. All military history, up to the latest time, has shown that for a rough uncivilized people, destitute of experience and resources, but strong in numbers, by far the best chance of successfully resisting a small well-trained force lies in irregular evasive warfare. The severest reverses suffered by disciplined English troops in America, Asia, and Africa—from Braddock's defeat on the Ohio to the recent disasters in Afghanistan and the Transvaal—have always been in fighting against active irregulars, who used their own arms and methods.

Moreover, in proportion as the Marathas adopted the armament and tactics of European warfare, they lost the advantage that comes out of unanimity of national, religious, or tribal sentiment, out of the bond of a common country or tradition. The new system required professional soldiers, who must be enlisted wherever they could be found; and especially it needed foreign officers. In this manner the foreign or alien element grew rapidly, until the later Maratha armies became principally a miscellaneous collection of mercenaries, enlisted from all parts of India, with trained infantry and artillery commanded by adventurers of different races and countries.

From this time forward, indeed, it is a marked characteristic of the British battles with the Marathas, as afterwards with the Sikhs, that although they were always sharply contested and often gained at a heavy cost, yet the victories were decisive; the blows were crushing because they were delivered at close quarters upon compact and organized bodies of troops which, when they were once dispersed or destroyed, could not be replaced.

And inasmuch as all the Indian states and dynasties with whom we fought depended for their existence on success in war, an overthrow placed them entirely at our mercy. For in almost every case their territorial title was derived only from recent occupation, and their possession was cemented by little or no national sympathies; so that, unless the conqueror thought fit to set up again the fallen ruler, the people merely underwent a change of masters.

The whole attempt of the native powers to imitate the military methods of Europe proved a delusion and a snare. It led them to suppose that they could put themselves on an equality with the English by a system that really placed them at a disadvantage, and to maintain, upon a false estimate of their strength, large military establishments under foreign officers, which it soon became the chief object of the English government to disband or destroy. Nothing was easier for the English, with their command of money and war material, than to increase their own disciplined army in India up to whatever point might be necessary for maintaining superiority. Nothing, on the other hand, was more difficult than for an Indian prince to repair his losses of cannon and trained soldiers.

Nor is it hard to understand how, in these conditions of military and political inequality, every successive campaign in India for the last hundred years has resulted in an increase of the English territory. In fact the whole country has thus passed gradually under the dominion of the government which excelled all the other leading states in the art of disciplined fighting, and whose stability did not in any event depend upon the life or luck of a single ruler or general or upon the issue of a single battle, because its resources were drawn from an immense reserve of civilized wealth and energy beyond the sea.

After his campaign against Mysore, the chief object of Lord Cornwallis had been to provide for the peace of South India by inducing the Marathas and the Nizam

A STREET-CORNER IN BHOPAL.

of Haidarabad to join him in a treaty guaranteeing against Tippu the territories that each of them possessed at the close of the war. To this proposition the Nizam readily agreed, being much afraid of the Marathas; but the Marathas declined it because they meditated plundering the Nizam. The two great Mohammedan States of Oudh and Haidarabad were remarkably weak in proportion to their territory and revenue; they carried little weight in the political balance; and the chief concern of the British government was to prevent their premature dissolution. By this time Oudh had fallen entirely under the British protectorate; a system which, while it upholds the native dynasty, is necessarily incompatible with the independent sovereignty of the prince; for the military defence of the country is undertaken by the protecting power, and the ruler binds himself by a subsidiary treaty to defray the expenses of an army which he does not command.

Moreover, no Asiatic dynasty can endure which does not produce a succession of able men, tried and selected by proof of individual capacity to rule. But the system of protectorates, which maintains hereditary right and does not permit an incapable heir to be set aside by energetic usurpers, cannot fail to seat on the throne, sooner or later, a prince who has no natural right to be there. The decline of governing ability was already visible in Oudh, which was falling into internal confusion and financial straits. Security from internal revolt and foreign attack bred indolence and irresponsibility; mismanagement of the revenue increased the burden of the subsidy; and the maladministration that was partly the consequence of the protective system became a reason for continuing it. Similar symptoms showed themselves later in Haidarabad, when that state also passed under the British protectorate.

The history of these complicated transactions serves mainly to illustrate the extraordinary and ever-recurring difficulties which have beset the British government in India, where the policy of neutrality and non-interference only ripened the seeds of eventual discord, compelling the English to step in at last for the cure of evils that might have been prevented. No other considerable power in the country was interested in the preservation of order; the stronger preyed, as a matter of course, upon the weaker; and there was always the danger, almost the certainty, that any military chief who should succeed in trampling down his rivals would before long turn his accumulated force against British territory.

We may remember that the British Islands had never been able to abstain from taking part in any great war, during the eighteenth century, among the neighbouring nations of the European continent, where England owned no land except Gibraltar. There is little cause, then, for surprise that the English in India, with possessions scattered, isolated, remote from each other, intermixed with foreign territory, and exposed to easy attack on every side, except from the sea—in a country where, as Arthur Wellesley later said, no such thing as a frontier really existed—were invariably, though often reluctantly, drawn into participation with the quarrels and scrambling for dominion which in those days were continually upsetting the balance of power and the tranquillity of the country.

Thus the acts and results of Lord Cornwallis's administration show how difficult it had become for the English to stand still, or to look on indifferently at the conflicts that broke out all round them in India.

It had been a general charge in England against the Company's governors that they plunged into unjust or unnecessary wars, and were troubled by an insatiable appetite for their neighbours' provinces. But it was understood to be one unquestionable advantage of the regime inaugurated in 1786 that temperance, political self-denial, the renunciation of all ambitious enterprises, and the preservation of peace would have been secured by placing the conduct of affairs under direct ministerial control.

No Governor-General ever set out for India under more earnest injunctions to be moderate, and above all things pacific, than Lord Cornwallis; and these general orders were ratified by a specific Act of Parliament, framed with the express purpose of restraining warlike ardour or projects for the extension of dominion. Pitt's act of 1784 was emphatic in this sense, and in 1793 another act declared that: "Forasmuch as to pursue schemes of conquest and extension of dominion in India are measures repugnant to the wish, the honour, and the policy of this nation, it shall not be lawful for the Governor-General in Council to declare war, or to enter into any treaty for making war, or for guaranteeing the possessions of any country princes or states (except where hostilities against the British nation in India have been actually commenced or prepared), without express command and authority from the home government."

Yet Lord Cornwallis, whose moderation and judgment have never been doubted, found himself obliged to prepare for hostilities almost immediately after his arrival at Calcutta; and he soon discovered that the restraining statutes operated to promote the very evils they were intended to prevent. Under their restrictions the English Governor-General was obliged to look on with tied hands at violent aggressions and dangerous combinations among the native states, and was held back from interposing until matters had reached a pitch at which the security of his own territory was actually and unmistakably threatened. The Mysore war, and a considerable extension of dominion, followed in spite of all injunctions and honest efforts to the contrary. Yet such was the confidence in the good intentions of Cornwallis that, when he left India in 1793, there was a general impression in England that he had merely taken the necessary steps for inaugurating a pacific and stationary policy; whereas in fact the British were on the threshold of an era of wide-ranging hostilities and immense annexations.

Nothing, indeed, is more remarkable, as illustrating the persistence of the natural forces that propelled the onward movement of English dominion, than the fact that the immediate consequence of bringing India under direct Parliamentary control was to stimulate, not to slacken, the expansion of British territories. Mr. Spencer Walpole has declared in his "History of England" that every prominent statesman of the time disliked and forbade further additions to the Company's territories; and we have seen that frequent laws were passed to check the unfortunate propensity for fighting that was supposed to have marred the administration of the Company. Nevertheless, it is historically certain that a period of unprecedented war and conquest began when the Crown superseded the Company in the supreme direction of Indian affairs.

The beginning of our Indian wars on a large scale dates from 1789; and the period between 1786 and 1805, during which British India was ruled (with a brief interval) by the first two Parliamentary Governors-General, Cornwallis and Wellesley—by Governors-General, that is, who were appointed by ministers responsible to Parliament, and for party reasons—comprises some of the longest wars and largest acquisitions by conquest or cession. It stands on record that the greatest development of British dominion in India (up to the time of Lord Dalhousie) coincides precisely with these two Governor-Generalships. The foundations of the Indian empire were marked out in haphazard piecework fashion by merchants, the corner-stone was laid by Clive in Bengal, and the earlier stages were consolidated by Hastings; but the lofty superstructure was raised entirely by a distinguished line of Parliamentary proconsuls and generals. For the last hundred years every important annexation in India has been made under the sanction and the deliberate orders of the national government in England.

The closer connection of India with England, and the importance of the English stake in the country, had now brought our Asiatic dependency so much more within the current of European politics that the rising tide of hostilities between France and England dashed over it, and swept forward the course of events. In 1793 began the long war with revolutionary France, which soon affected the temper of English politics in

THE ATTACK ON THE SIALKOT MUTINEERS BY GEN. NICHOLSON'S IRREGULAR CAVALRY, JULY 12, 1857.

Asia. A few years afterwards Buonaparte was marching toward military despotism in the spirit of an Asiatic conqueror, upsetting thrones and uprooting landmarks, overriding national traditions and hereditary rights, carving out new kingdoms by his sword, and laying out their boundaries as one might divide an estate into convenient farms or properties. His delight in this pastime attracted him instinctively toward Asia, where he saw that a genius for interminable war and autocratic administration would find illimitable scope in knocking down the old-fashioned rickety governments and rebuilding them symmetrically at leisure. His inclinations tallied, moreover, with his interests, since he could combine a taste for Asiatic adventure with an ardent desire to strike a blow at the English somewhere on the land, as he could make nothing of them at sea.

The project of an expedition against British India was constantly in his mind; but his first and last attempt at Asiatic conquest was the abortive occupation of Egypt and the march into Syria in 1798, with the declared object, among others, of "hunting the English out of all their Eastern possessions and cutting the Isthmus of Suez." The menace only served, as usual, to hasten English annexations in India. For on one side it accentuated the alarm and resentment with which the English were watching the intrigues of the French with the Marathas and the Sultan of Mysore, and the recruitment of French officers for the armies of those states. On the other side, the rapidly increasing predominance of the English and the overtures of the French misled the native princes into venturing for their self-protection upon the very steps that helped to precipitate their downfall. Now that England had completely recognized the immense value of her Asiatic possessions, her traditional jealousy of interference by the only European nation that had repeatedly challenged her ascendency in India naturally reached its acutest stage during a desperate war with France.

The last act of Lord Cornwallis before he left India, in 1793, had been to seize all the French settlements; Ceylon was taken from the Dutch in 1796; and the English now treated any symptom of an understanding with France, or even of a leaning in that direction, as a dangerous spark to be extinguished at once. Sir John Shore (Lord Teignmouth), who held the Governor-Generalship *ad interim* until Lord Mornington arrived in 1798, was a very cautious and overprudent politician. Being averse, on principle, to extending British relations or responsibilities, he refused, rather ungenerously, to assist the Nizam when the Marathas attacked him, thereby estranging our principal ally and encouraging our principal rivals. When the Nizam, who was very anxious for a British alliance, proposed a defensive treaty on the basis of mutual territorial guarantee, the English government drew back, not wishing to defend Haidarabad at the risk of offending the Marathas, who might retaliate by a league with Tippu.

The consequences of this half-hearted attitude were serious; for the Marathas invaded the Haidarabad country, dispersed the Nizam's army, and at Kurdla, in 1795, enforced on him an ignominious surrender to very extortionate terms. This triumph brought the Marathas a considerable increase of strength and reputation, while the Nizam was so deeply incensed at our desertion of him that he largely increased his trained battalions and relied more than ever on the French officers who commanded them, and who fomented his alienation from the English. Yet as soon as the Nizam began to augment and reform his regular troops, under Raymond and other French officers, Sir John Shore at once interposed to prevent him.

What the Governor-General feared was a combination against him between Mysore and the Marathas; and what he hoped was that these two jealous and mutually suspicious powers would sooner or later fall to blows against each other. But in fighting times the pacific bystander's attitude rarely suits the interest or dignity of a neighbouring state. In the present instance it only stimulated the combative instincts of both rivals, who soon became more aggressive and more formidable to the British. The impolicy of having abandoned the Nizam to the Marathas now began to appear; for the Marathas had gained great augmentation of wealth and predominance, and their audacity increased as their respect for the English diminished.

Moreover, Tippu of Mysore, who nourished wild hopes of revenge and of recovering his losses in the late war, believed the Nizam's strength to have been so reduced that he might seize all the Haidarabad country if the English could be prevented from opposing him. And for the purpose of counteracting the English power he pursued his futile endeavours to negotiate foreign alliances. He pressed the Afghan Amir, Shah Zaman, to invade India, and he received in reply a sympathetic assurance that the Amir would soon come to exterminate all infidels and polytheists. In 1797 Shah Zaman did march through the Panjab and occupy Lahore, to the great alarm of the Anglo-Indian government; for the whole of North India was stirred by his coming, the Mohammedans were preparing to join his standard, the Oudh ruler was totally incapable of making any effective resistance, and if the Afghan had pushed on to Delhi, there would have been an outbreak of anarchy and perilous commotion. Such a formidable diversion would undoubtedly have drawn northward every available English regiment for the protection of the Bengal frontier; but in 1798 Shah Zaman was obliged to return hurriedly to guard his own western provinces from the Persians.

Meanwhile Tippu had sent a secret mission across the Indian Ocean to the Isle of France, as Mauritius was then called, with letters for the Directory in Paris, proposing an offensive and defensive alliance with the French Republic for the purposes of destroying the English in India and dividing the country between himself and France. The governor of the French islands gave his envoys a public reception, and on January 30, 1798, issued a proclamation calling for volunteers to serve under the Mysore flag against the common enemy, England. In 1799 Buonaparte addressed to him a letter, dated Headquarters, Cairo, saying: "You have been already informed of my arrival on the shores of the Red Sea, with an innumerable and invincible army, full of the desire of releasing you from the iron yoke of the English," and asking Tippu to send him an agent. But the French were themselves soon cut off in Egypt; and as the rumours of foreign intervention by sea or land died away, the Mysore Sultan, abandoned to the hostility of the English whom he had seriously alarmed, soon underwent the certain fate of Oriental rulers who venture among the quarrels of European nations.

THE KIND OF VESSEL CALLED GHRAB.

CHAPTER XIV

THE GOVERNOR-GENERALSHIP OF LORD WELLESLEY

1798 - 1805

LORD MORNINGTON, afterwards Marquis Wellesley, landed at Madras on his way to Calcutta in April, 1798, on the same day when the ambassadors of Tippu disembarked at Mangalore on their return from the Isle of France, bringing a rather shabby collection of volunteers and an assurance from the French governor that his Republic would soon entertain with pleasure Tippu's offer of alliance and amity. The instructions which had followed the Governor-General unquestionably warranted him in treating these dealings with the French as an act of war on the part of Mysore. "As a general principle," wrote Henry Dundas, President of the Board of Commissioners for Indian affairs, in a letter addressed to him, "I have no hesitation in stating that we are entitled under the circumstances of the present time to consider the admission of any French force into Tippu's army, be it greater or smaller, as direct hostility to us"; and within a few months after reaching Calcutta, Lord Mornington declared that the growth of a French party in the councils and armies of the native Indian powers was an alarming evil that demanded extirpation.

When, therefore, it became known that Tippu's embassy to the Isle of France had brought back not only the promise of an offensive and defensive alliance with the French, "for the express purpose of expelling the British nation from India," but also some French officers and recruits for the Mysore army, the Governor-General concluded that he had just ground of hostility. His warlike ardour was easily heated, and he was deterred from attacking Tippu at once only by finding himself unprepared. The finances showed a standing deficit, the Company's credit in the money-market had fallen very low, the Madras army was not fit to take the field; and Lord Mornington was so far from relying on the co-operation of his allies, the Nizam and the Marathas, that he recognized the impossibility of calling them in.

The fruits of the non-interference policy had now shown themselves in the weakness and disaffection of the Nizam, in the ominous preparations of Tippu, and in the spreading power of the Marathas. The six years of English neutrality—from 1792 to 1798—had been employed by the two last-mentioned states in augmenting their war-resources and extending their territory at the expense of weaker neighbours. The defeat and capitulation of the Nizam at Kurdla had reduced him from the condition of a great and leading power in Hindustan to that of a tributary to the Marathas; the corps of fourteen thousand men under

French officers was the only support of his authority. Mornington wrote that these trained battalions at Haidarabad were the main root of the Nizam's disaffection; he believed that if they were brought into the field to take part in a battle against Tippu, they would almost certainly march over at once to Tippu's side.

THE JAMI' MASJID, OR GREAT MOSQUE, AT DELHI.

At Poona, the Maratha capital, the influence of Daulat Rao Sindhia (Mahadaji's successor) was now complete; he also held in sovereignty large tracts in Central India; and had extended his territorial annexations northwestward up to Delhi, outflanking Oudh and the English possessions in Bengal. He was, in short, the most considerable prince in Central and Northern India, where he maintained an ambiguous attitude, overawing both the Peshwa's government and the Nizam, and denouncing the impolicy of Marathas assisting the English to destroy Mysore. About this time, moreover, Lord Mornington received a letter from the Afghan king, Zaman Shah, announcing his intention of invading Hindustan, and demanding aid for the purpose of rescuing the Moghul emperor, Shah Alam, from the hands of the Marathas.

In these circumstances the Governor-General determined to temporize with Mysore by confining his first communication to a demand for satisfaction, while he employed himself in strengthening the Triple Alliance —as he very diplomatically termed the precarious relations of the British with the courts of Haidarabad and Poona—in restoring his finances and reinforcing the Madras army. His first step was to conclude a treaty with the Nizam for the disbandment of the French battalions at Haidarabad, which was then carried out with great skill and resolution; the Nizam receiving instead a force commanded by English officers, to be stationed permanently in his country. At Poona, however, where similar proposals were made, the Maratha government was much more distrustful of the British ascendency and much less in need of British assistance. The Peshwa naturally found very little attraction in the suggestion of an arrangement which, under the name of a subsidiary alliance, manifestly placed the state that furnished the money under military subordination to the state that provided the men.

The Nizam and the Peshwa both consented, nevertheless, to join the league against Mysore; and the Mysore Sultan was required, in reasonable terms, to disarm and abandon his alliance with the French. As he ignored or evaded these demands, a combined army marched against him early in 1799. After some futile attempts to keep the field against his enemy, Tippu was driven into Seringapatam and besieged there until the fortress was taken by assault in May; when the Sultan's death (he was killed in a hand-to-hand medley at one of the gates) brought the short Mohammedan dynasty of Mysore to a violent end. Lord Mornington broke up the kingdom by allotting certain shares of territory to the English and their allies; reconstituting the remainder into a state under the old Hindu reigning family whom Hyder Ali had expelled, and by whom Mysore, after a long interval of sequestration, is well and quietly governed at the present day.

The success of these military and political exploits was largely due to the presence in this campaign of Colonel Arthur Wellesley, who now made his first appearance among scenes where he was destined to attain a most brilliant reputation as a soldier and a statesman. Although he held only subordinate military command, his clear and commanding intellect, and his energy and skill in action, were displayed in the advice which he constantly gave to Lord Mornington, in his able reorganization of all the army departments, and in the rapidly decisive operations with which he terminated the war. The Governor-General was rewarded by the thanks voted to him in the House of Commons in October, 1799, "for counteracting with equal promptitude and ability the dangerous intrigues and projects of the French, particularly by destroying their power and influence in the Deccan," whereby, said the resolution, "he has established on a basis of permanent security the tranquillity and prosperity of the British Empire in India." The imperial note here sounded—probably for the first time in a public document—contrasts remarkably with the hesitating, almost apologetic tone in which our position and the growth of our responsibilities had been discussed in Parliament twenty years earlier.

It may truly be said that the stars in their courses fought against Tippu—a fierce, fanatic, and ignorant Mohammedan, who was, nevertheless, sufficiently endowed with some of the sterner qualities required for Asiatic rulership to have made himself a name among the Indian princes of his time. But he had no political ability of the higher sort; still less had he any touch of that instinct which has occasionally warned the ablest and strongest Asiatic chiefs to avoid collision with Europeans. He was swept away by a flood that was overwhelming far greater states than Mysore, that had taken its rise in a distant part of the world, out of events beyond his comprehension and totally beyond his control, and that was now running full in the channel which carried the English, by a natural determination of converging consequences, to supreme ascendency in India.

He had thrown in his lot with the French just at

the moment when they were at bitter, irreconcilable enmity with the English, and were actually proclaiming their intention of striking, if possible, at the British possessions in the East. He received the plainest warning that the English would wrest the sword out of any hand that showed the slightest intention of drawing it against them in such a quarrel; and he might have reflected that while his friends were far distant, the English, backed by the native powers whom he had alarmed, were close on his frontier. But he knew that submission to the English demands meant subordination to their power, disarmament, the loss of his independence, and reduction to the rank of a prince, whose foreign relations and military establishments would be regulated strictly by English policy; and his fierce intractable temper drove him into a hopeless struggle.

The same situation has frequently recurred since, though not with the same intensity; the same option has been offered to other states and rulers. And the present form and constitution of the British Empire in India, with its vast provinces and numerous feudatories, represents historically the gradual incorporation under one dominion of states that have submitted and states that have been forcibly subdued. As the old Moghul Empire had been built up by a very similar process of gradual conquest, so, when that great edifice fell to pieces, it was certain that the fragments would soon gravitate again toward the attraction of some central rulership, whose protection would be sought by all the weaker chiefships, and whose superiority the stronger rivals must inevitably be compelled, by fair means or forcible, to acknowledge.

When the acquisition of Bengal had given the English power a focus and a firm centralization, this assimilating process began steadily with a slow movement against stiff obstacles, but by the end of the century it had acquired great impetus and velocity. For the English viceroys were now supported by the direct strength and resolution of the nation in securing their Indian possessions; and the temper of those stormy times coloured all their proceedings. What in Hastings would have been reckoned an act of rank iniquity was in Lord Mornington (now Marquis Wellesley) no more than an energetic measure of public necessity. The views and policy of these two statesmen were essentially identical; but Hastings was striving painfully, with slender resources, on the defensive, while Wellesley, backed by a war ministry at home, boldly assumed the offensive on a magnificent scale of operations.

The dissolution of Mysore set the British dominion forward by two important steps. It finally removed an inveterate enemy, whose position had endangered the English possessions in South India for thirty years; it also gave the British complete command over the seacoast of the lower peninsula, and thus greatly diminished any risk of molestation by the French. It led, moreover, directly to the virtual extinction of that power for the control of which the English and French had fought so sharply in the days of Dupleix and Clive, the Nawabship of the Karnatic. From the time when that contest had been decided in favour of the English, the Nawab had gradually descended, through the stages of a protected ally and a subordinate ruler, to the situation of a prince with nominal authority, and with a revenue heavily mortgaged for the payment of the subsidy that was the price of his protection by the Company. In this unhappy condition he naturally kept up a secret correspondence with the Mysore Sultan, his creditor's enemy, and when Mysore was taken, the Nawab's letters were discovered. Thereupon Lord Wellesley found himself amply justified, upon the double ground of political intrigue and internal misgovernment, in bringing the Karnatic wholly under British administration. The system of divided authority was, he observed, a serious calamity to the country, and for the same incontestable reason he annexed Tanjore and Surat.

The declared object of the Governor-General was now to establish the ascendency of the English power over all other states in India by a system of subsidiary treaties, so framed, as he himself stated in one of his despatches, as "to deprive them of the means of prosecuting any measure or of forming any confederacy hazardous to the security of the British Empire, and to enable us to preserve the tranquillity of India by exercising a general control over the restless spirit of ambition and violence which is characteristic of every Asiatic government." This general control he desired to impose "through the medium of alliances contracted with those states on the basis of the security and protection of their respective rights." In plain words, Lord Wellesley, to whom restless ambition was a thing

THE ATAL TOWER AT AMRITSAR.

intolerable in Asiatics, had already resolved to extend the British Protectorate over all the rulerships with which the English government then had any connection, by insisting that each ruler should reduce his army, and should rely for external defence and internal security mainly upon the paramount military strength of the British sovereignty.

The system of subsidiary treaties is worth some brief explanation, for it has played a very important part in the expansion of British dominion. It has been seen that English participation in Indian wars began when we lent the aid of a military contingent to assist some native potentate. The next stage came when we took the field on our own account, usually assisted by the levies of some prince who made common cause with us, and whose soldiery were undisciplined, untrustworthy, and very clumsily handled. The English commander often found it necessary to look behind as well as before him on the field of battle; his allies showed unseasonable impartiality by holding aloof at critical moments and reappearing to plunder in both camps indiscriminately, giving preference to the defeated side. What was needed was a body of men that could be relied upon for some kind of tactical precision and steadiness under fire; but for this purpose it was of little use even to place sepoys under European officers unless they could be regularly paid and taught to obey one master.

The system, therefore, soon reached the stage where the native ally was required to supply not men but money, and the English undertook to raise, train, and pay a fixed number of troops on receiving a subsidy equivalent to their cost. The subsidiary treaties made in India differed, accordingly, from those made by England with European states in this respect, that whereas Austria or Russia raised armies on funds provided by England, Oudh or Haidarabad provided funds on which the British government raised armies. Large sums had hitherto been spent by the native princes in maintaining ill-managed and insubordinate bodies of troops, and in constant wars against each other; they might economize their revenues, be rid of a mutinous soldiery, and sit much more quietly at home by entering into contracts with a skilful and solvent administration that would undertake all serious military business for a fixed subsidy.

But as punctuality in money matters has never been a princely quality, this subsidy was apt to be paid very irregularly; so the next stage was to revive the long-standing practice of Asiatic governments, the assignment of lands for the payment of troops. There were now in India (excluding the Panjab, with which England had had no dealings as yet) only three states whose size or strength could give the English government any concern. One of these, the Maratha federation, was still strong and solvent, but the two Mohammedan states of Oudh and Haidarabad were in no condition to resist the proposals of Lord Wellesley, nor is it likely that either of them could have long maintained itself without British protection. The Nizam of Haidarabad had been very liberally treated in the partition of Mysore, and Tippu's destruction had relieved him of an inveterate foe. In 1800 he transferred considerable districts in perpetuity to the British government, "for the regular payment of the expenses of the augmented subsidiary force."

The position of the Vizir of Oudh was much more important. We have seen that Clive and Hastings maintained this prince for the safety of the northwest frontier of the British, which was still covered by his dominions. But the Afghan king, Zaman Shah, was now making his last inroad into the Panjab, and the Maratha chief Sindhia was in possession of Delhi; while the Oudh vizir was a weak ruler whose country was in confusion, whose troops were mutinous, and whose finances were disordered by the heavy strain of the English subsidy. In these circumstances Lord Wellesley required the vizir to disband his disorderly forces, in order that more British troops might be subsidized for the effective defence of his dominions. The vizir, under pressure of many perplexities, declared that he would abdicate, but afterwards retracted, and the Governor-General, who would willingly have had a free hand in Oudh, received the retractation with "astonishment, regret, and indignation."

It must be admitted that Lord Wellesley subordinated the feelings and interests of his ally to paramount considerations of British policy in a manner that showed very little patience, forbearance, or generosity. Nevertheless, it was really most necessary to set in order the affairs of Oudh, and the result of Lord Wellesley's somewhat dictatorial negotiations was that the vizir ceded all his frontier provinces, including Rohilkhand, to the Company; the revenue of the territory thus transferred being taken as an equivalent to the subsidy payable for troops. This arrangement finally superseded the barrier policy of Hastings, which had effectually served its purpose for thirty years. Instead of placing Oudh in charge of the districts exposed to attack from the Marathas and invaders from the north-west, Lord Wellesley now obtained by cession the whole belt of exterior territory; and Oudh was thenceforward enveloped by the English dominion.

This most important augmentation of territory transferred to the British government some of the richest and most populous districts in the heart of India, lying along the Ganges and its tributaries above Benares up to the foot of the Himalayan range. It consolidated English power on a broader foundation, brought us a very large increase of revenue, and confronted us with the Maratha chief Sindhia along the whole line of his possessions in upper India. These very trenchant strokes of policy were severely criticized by the Directors of the East India Company and cordially approved by his Majesty's ministers.

The evacuation of Egypt by the French and the Peace of Amiens necessarily dislocated the mainspring of Lord Wellesley's martial activity. Hitherto he had been able to describe his policy as purely self-defensive and pacific, to explain that he was compelled to extend the dominion of England by the need of counteracting the design of France, and to declare that he had insisted on reducing the armies of the native princes in order to preserve them against a nation who, as he wrote Tippu

Sultan in 1799, "considered all the thrones of the world as the sport and prey of their boundless ambition and insatiable rapine." But Mysore, Haidarabad, and Oudh had now been placed beyond danger of the French contagion; and Lord Wellesley was able to record that "the only native powers of importance now remaining in India independent of British protection are the confederate Maratha states."

It could only be through a perverse contrariety of spirit that, notwithstanding his solemn warnings against the machinations of France, the European power which the Marathas persisted in regarding with uneasiness was England. Their restless character, the advantages presented by their local position to the future intrigues of France, and the number of French officers in the service of Sindhia, convinced the Governor-General that it was a matter of indispensable precaution to acquire an ascendency in the councils of the Maratha Empire, and to frame a system of political connection that should preserve a powerful barrier against them. This barrier had now been erected by the subsidiary treaties with the Mohammedan states; and as the three leading Maratha chiefs—Sindhia, Holkar, and the Raja of Nagpur—were contending in arms among themselves for supremacy, the time was opportune for interposing with an offer of protection to the nominal chief of their confederacy at Poona, where the government was threatened by three predatory armies, subsisting at large on the country. If the chiefs of these armies combined to upset the Peshwa, they might seize command of the whole Maratha Empire; and, what was still more important, their next step would probably be a combination against the English.

The Peshwa, Baji Rao, had hitherto evaded all overtures from the English for a subsidiary treaty; but there was bitter feud between him and Holkar, whose brother he had cruelly executed, and who was now marching upon his capital. When Sindhia came to the Peshwa's assistance, there was a great battle, in which Holkar was nearly defeated, until he charged the enemy at the head of his cavalry with such desperate energy that the allied army was driven off the field with the loss of all their guns and baggage. The Peshwa fled to a fortress, whence he despatched a messenger to solicit help from the English; and soon afterward he took refuge in Bassein, close to Bombay, where, in December, 1802, he signed a treaty of general defensive alliance with the British government, under which he ceded districts yielding a revenue equivalent to the cost of a strong subsidiary force to be stationed permanently within his territory, while all his foreign relations were to be subordinated to the policy of England.

The treaty of Bassein also accomplished another leading object of Lord Wellesley's policy, for by admitting the British government to mediate in all the exorbitant claims that the Marathas were pressing against the Nizam, it placed the Haidarabad state definitely under the protection of the English, to whom all such demands were to be referred in future. No time was lost in acting upon this important engagement. The

Peshwa was escorted back to Poona by a British force under General Arthur Wellesley; and it was signified to the contending Maratha chiefs that their central government had been taken under British protection. This masterful proceeding alarmed even Lord Castle-

THE RESIDENCY AT LUCKNOW.

reagh, who wrote to the Governor-General some remonstrances against a step which "tended to involve us in the endless and complicated distractions of the turbulent Maratha Empire." He replied that the influence of the French in the Maratha camp was still to be feared, an argument that easily prevailed over an English ministry who were just bracing up the national strength, after a short breathing time, for a second and still closer wrestle with Buonaparte.

Lord Wellesley's political system was now reaching its climax. His subsidiary troops were encamped at the capitals of the four great Indian powers which had been his political rivals, at Mysore, Haidarabad, Lucknow, and Poona; all disputes among these states were to be submitted to his arbitration; and the interference of all other European nations was to be rigidly excluded. Upon these pillars he was firmly building up the inevitable preponderance of a steady, civilized, orderly administration over the jarring, incoherent rulerships by which it was surrounded. But it was not to be expected that the Treaty of Bassein would be otherwise than unpalatable to the Maratha chiefs, who saw that a blow had been struck at the root of their confederacy, and that the establishment of paramount British influence at Poona not only checkmated their movement against the capital, but was a sure step toward the subversion of their own independence. The maintenance of the head of the Maratha Empire in a condition of dependent relation to the British government would naturally, in the course of time, tend to reduce the other Maratha powers into a similar condition of subordination, which was precisely what they feared and were determined to resist. They withheld acknowledgment of the treaty, questioned the Peshwa's right to conclude it without their consent, suspended their internal feuds, and seemed inclined to combine against the common danger.

The Maratha chief of Nagpur (commonly called the Raja of Berar), who had great influence over all the other leaders, succeeded in organizing a league against the British; but Holkar, although he agreed to a truce with Sindhia, refused to join, and the Gaikwar of Baroda kept apart. Sindhia, however, effected his junction with the Nagpur raja, whereupon both chiefs evaded the demand of the British envoy for a direct explanation of their intentions and marched up to the frontier of Haidarabad. It was in the interest of the Marathas to gain time, for they hoped that Holkar might be persuaded to enter the league; for the same reason it was important to the British that the two chiefs should be forced to decide speedily between peace or war. The Governor-General was now in his element again, for in Europe a renewal of the French war was evidently at hand; the English ministers had warned him that a French squadron was preparing at Brest for the East Indies; they had authorized him to retain possession of the French settlements that were to be restored under the Amiens Treaty; and they had desired him to keep his forces on a war-footing. At the same time, some observations, which appeared to the Governor-General particularly inopportune, were conveyed to him upon the increase of his military expenditure and the diversion of funds on which the Company relied for their trade.

Lord Wellesley, who had offered to resign, requested the ministers to "consider the alarm and anger of the Court of Directors on this latter subject with the indulgence which true wisdom extends to the infirmities of prejudice, ignorance, and passion"; while he prepared with alacrity to attack the Maratha confederates simultaneously in various quarters, and to open the impending war on the largest possible scale. The rupture with France intensified, as usual, his sense of the emergent necessity of bringing all the military powers of India under the supreme control of the British. For although there was little real danger, as Arthur Wellesley pointed out, of the French being able to join forces with the Marathas—since their troops, even if they could land, would be destitute of equipments and would be cut off from their base of supply—yet undoubtedly a great European war must always add risks to the English position in India.

Lord Wellesley also saw clearly enough that the security of the dominion that he was establishing on land depended essentially upon the British maintaining a commanding superiority at sea. He urged upon the ministry at home that so long as the Cape of Good Hope and Mauritius were in French hands (for the Dutch were entirely under French influence), the coasts of India could be molested, or the inland enemies of the English might be encouraged by expectations of aid from France. He spared, in short, no pains or preparations that might enable him so to use this opportunity of renewed hostilities in Asia and Europe as to accomplish "the complete consolidation of the British Empire in India and the future tranquillity of Hindustan." Whatever may be thought of the methods occasionally used by Lord Wellesley to compass these ends, it is impossible to withhold our admiration from so large a conception and from so clear and far-ranging a survey of the political horizon.

With these views and intentions the Governor-General issued his orders to General Wellesley, who was facing Sindhia in Western India, and to General Lake, who was moving upon Sindhia's possessions in the northwest. The main objective was to be either the entire reduction of Sindhia's power, or a peace that should transfer to the British government so much of his territory as should be sufficient to isolate him in Central India, to cut him off from the western seacoast, to expel him from Delhi (where he was still Vicegerent of the Empire), and to throw him back into Central India by interposing a barrier between his provinces in that region and in the north country. At Delhi Monsieur Perron, one of Sindhia's ablest French officers, commanded a large body of regular troops, with which he held the fortress, kept the Emperor Shah Alam in custody, and exercised authority in his name. It was one of Lord Wellesley's principal objects to disband this formidable standing army, which was well officered by Frenchmen; and his anxiety to cross swords with Sindhia was intensified by his knowledge of constant intrigues and correspondence between the Marathas and the agents of France.

Under the leadership of the two very able generals who led the English armies, and who were also invested with full diplomatic authority, the war which now began was brilliantly successful, and its objects were completely fulfilled. In July, 1803, General Wellesley signified to Sindhia and the Nagpur raja that they must withdraw their army from its station upon the Nizam's frontier or abide his attack. They replied by desiring him first to retire; but as this would have exposed the territory which their movements were threatening, the English army advanced, and war was formally declared. The scene of the campaign that followed was in that part of Central India where the northern frontiers of the Haidarabad state adjoined the possessions of the two Maratha chiefs. At Assaye, where the collision took place in September, 1803, Sindhia's troops fought well and fiercely; the veteran battalions of De Boigne made a resolute stand; the artillery inflicted heavy loss on the English infantry, and died, stubbornly fighting, at their guns; but Wellesley's victory was decisive. Marching onward into Berar, he inflicted a severe defeat upon the troops of the Nagpur raja at Argaum in November of the same year; he then took by storm the hill fort of Gawilgarh; and before the year's end peace had been concluded with both the Maratha belligerents on terms dictated by the British commander.

General Lake's successes in the northwest were of equal importance. He took Aligarh by assault, dispersed Sindhia's force before Delhi, occupied the town, and assumed charge of the emperor's person. Agra was besieged and captured; and finally, in November, 1803, the British force met at Laswari seventeen battalions of trained infantry with excellent artillery, the last of Sindhia's regular army. These troops behaved so gallantly that the event (Lake wrote) would have been extremely doubtful if they had still been commanded by their French officers; but Perron and the Frenchmen had left the Maratha service. Nevertheless, their vigorous resistance proved the high military spirit which the soldier of Northern India has so often displayed; they held their ground until all their guns were lost, and finally suffered a most honourable defeat.

A MOSQUE AT ALIGARH.

The result of these well-contested and hardly won victories was to shatter the whole military organization upon which Sindhia's predominance had been built up, to break down his connection with the Moghul court in the north, and to destroy his influence at Poona as the most formidable member of the Maratha confederacy. At the beginning of the war Sindhia's regular brigades had amounted to nearly forty thousand disciplined men, with a very large train of artillery, acting entirely under the control of a French commander, and supported by the revenues of the finest provinces in

India. This army had now ceased to exist; and both Sindhia and the Nagpur raja, finding themselves in imminent danger of losing all their possessions, acquiesced reluctantly in the terms that were dictated to them after the destruction of their armies.

The Treaty of Bassein was formally recognized; they entered into defensive treaties and made large cessions of territory; Sindhia gave up to the British all his northern districts lying along both sides of the Jumna River; he ceded his seaports and his conquests on the west coast; he made over to them the city of Delhi and the custody of the Moghul Emperor; he dismissed all his French officers, and accepted the establishment, at his cost, of a large British force to be stationed near his frontier. The Raja of Nagpur restored Berar to the Nizam, and surrendered to the British government the province of Cuttack, on the Bay of Bengal, which lay interposed between the upper districts of Madras and the southwestern districts of Bengal.

But Jaswant Rao Holkar, who had held aloof from the war in the hope of profiting by the discomfiture of Sindhia, his rival and enemy, had been living at free quarters with a large Maratha horde in Rajputana and had put to death the English officers in his service. As he now showed some intention of taking advantage of Sindhia's defenceless condition, he was summoned by Lord Lake to retire within his own country, and on his refusal was attacked by the British troops. Holkar, who had always adhered to the traditional Maratha tactics of rapid cavalry movements, systematic pillaging, and sudden harassing incursions, proved a very active and troublesome enemy. Colonel Monson advanced against him into Central India, and Holkar drew him onward by a simulated retreat, until Monson found himself at a long distance from his base, with only two days' supplies, and in front of an enemy numerically very superior. Then, when he attempted to retire, Holkar turned on him suddenly and destroyed nearly the whole of the British force as it struggled back toward Agra through some difficult country, intersected by rivers. A few months afterward, in November, 1804, Holkar fought a severe action against the British troops at Dig; and his ally, the Bhartpur raja, repulsed three attempts to carry by assault the strong fortress of Bhartpur, so that Lord Lake was obliged to retire with considerable loss. But Lake's flying columns pursued Holkar with indefatigable rapidity until his bands were surprised and at last dispersed, when he himself took refuge in the Panjab. He returned only to sign a treaty on terms similar to those on which peace had been made with the other belligerents.

The result of these operations was to establish beyond the possibility of future opposition the political and military superiority of the English throughout India. The campaigns of Wellesley and Lake dissolved the last of the trained armies which had been set on foot, in imitation of the European system, during the past twenty years by the native princes of India; and the weapon upon which the Marathas had been relying for resistance in the field was thus broken in their hands. In the place of the numerous battalions, many thousands strong, that had been maintained under foreign officers by the foremost Mohammedan and Maratha states, Lord Wellesley's subsidiary treaties now substituted several divisions of Anglo-Indian troops, amounting in all to twenty-two thousand men, cantoned within the jurisdictions or on the borders of these very native states, and paid from their revenues. The employment of foreign officers, unless by permission, was thenceforward prohibited; while the effect of the treaties was to interdict any hostilities between state and state—since all disputes must be referred to British arbitration—to confine their rulers within the territorial limits authorized by the supreme government, to prevent their future combination for any purpose injurious to British interests, and finally to block up all avenues of communication between these states and any foreign power.

Up to this time the acquisitions of the Maratha chiefs in Central India, which had been wrested bit by bit from different owners at various times, had been so intermixed with the lands of the Nizam, of the Peshwa, and of the Rajput princes as to produce an entanglement of territorial and revenue rights that furnished, as it was intended to furnish, ample pretexts for further quarrel and encroachment. Lord Wellesley's policy was, in the first place, to rearrange the political map in this part of India so as to circumscribe each Maratha chiefship within distinct boundaries. His secondary objects were to interrupt the chain of their confederate possessions by interposing the lands of some non-Maratha state, and to raise a barrier between Maratha and British territory in Northern India by maintaining under British guarantee the independence of the petty states along their frontier. Lastly, he desired so to rearrange the map of Southern India as to link the important British possessions in Madras with the central dominion in Bengal.

This work of consolidation and connection was pushed still further by Lord Hastings twelve years later, and was finally consummated by Lord Dalhousie; but Lord Wellesley's settlement laid out the territorial distribution of all India (excepting the Panjab and Sind) on the general plan which was followed for the next forty years, and which survives in its main outlines to this day. By occupying the imperial cities of Agra and Delhi, with the contiguous tracts on both sides of the Jumna, and by annexing the whole country between the Ganges and the Jumna Rivers, he advanced British territory from Bengal northwestward to the mountains, with a frontier resting on the upper course of the Jumna. By his acquisition of the Cuttack province he secured the continuity of British territory southeastward along the seacoast, joined the two Presidencies of Bengal and Madras, and established sure communication between them. The English dominions were thus prolonged in a broad unbroken belt from the Himalayas downward to the Bay of Bengal and the southernmost district of Madras; while the cessions obtained on the west coast went far toward completing British command of the whole Indian littoral.

Above all, when Lord Wellesley expelled the Marathas from Delhi and assumed charge of the person and family of the Moghul Emperor, he inaugurated a significant change of policy. For at least forty years the imperial sign manual had been at the disposal of any adventurer or usurper who could occupy the capital, overawe the powerless court, and dictate his own investiture with some lofty office or with a grant of the provinces that he had appropriated. At an earlier period the European trading companies, English and French, had been careful to obtain title-deeds from the Great Moghul. It was known that when Pondicherri was restored to the French at the Peace of Amiens, Buonaparte used the opportunity to send out to the French settlements in India a considerable military staff, whose mission was to communicate with the Emperor of Delhi through the French officers in Sindhia's service. And it was part of a wild project submitted to Buonaparte in 1803 that an expedition should be sent overland to India with the ostensible mission of rescuing the imperial house from its enemies and oppressors.

Lord Wellesley was at any rate quite satisfied that he was threatened by "the aggrandizement of the French power in India to a degree that compelled him to lose no time in placing the person, family, and nominal authority of his Majesty Shah Alam under the protection of the British Government." He formally renounced any intention of using the royal prerogative as a pretext for asserting English claims to ascendency over feudatories or to the exercise of rulership. With the avowed object of abolishing a titular sovereignty that hardly retained the shadow of its former substance,

GEN. HAVELOCK'S ATTACK ON NANA SAHIB AT FATHPUR.

and whose representative had been rescued by British arms from a state of extreme degradation and distress, he relegated Shah Alam to the position of a state pensioner, with royal rank and an ample income assured him. The arrangement lasted fifty years until it was suddenly extinguished in 1857, when the storm raised by the Sepoy Mutiny swept away the last relics of the Moghul throne and dynasty.

The political outcome of Lord Wellesley's Governor-Generalship is well summarized in the final paragraph of the long despatch of July, 1804, in which he reported to the Court of Directors, in the lofty language of a triumphant proconsul, the general result of the wars and treaties that he had made for the consolidation of our Eastern empire and the pacification of all India—"A general bond of connection is now established between the British government and the principal states of India, on principles which render it the interest of every state to maintain its alliance with the British Government, which preclude the inordinate aggrandizement of any one of those states by usurpation of the rights and possessions of others, and which secure to every state the unmolested exercise of its separate authority within the limits of its established dominion, under the general protection of the British power."

It is indeed from this period, and from the great augmentations of territory obtained by Lord Wellesley's high-handed and clear-headed policy, that we may date the substantial formation of the three Indian Presidencies. Up to 1792 the Madras Presidency administered in full jurisdiction no more than a few districts on the coast. But between 1799 and 1804 the partition of Mysore, the lapse of Tanjore, the cessions from Haidarabad, and the transfer of the whole Karnatic to the Company, brought large and fertile tracts within the administrative circle of Madras and constituted it the headquarters of a large government in South India, which has received no very important subsequent accretions. In Western India the Bombay Presidency, which had hitherto been almost entirely confined to the sea-board, and whose principal importance had been derived from its harbour and trading-mart, now acquired valuable districts in Gujarat; and the influence of its government rose to undisputed predominance throughout the adjoining native states, especially at the Maratha capitals of Poona and Baroda.

In North India the Marathas had lost all power; the important province of Bundelkhand, containing a number of minor chiefships, had been brought entirely under British influence and partly under British rule; the ceded and conquered districts obtained from Oudh and from Sindhia were settling down under regular English administration. The Presidency at Calcutta, which now extended, as has been said, from the Bay of Bengal northwestward to the Himalayas and the Panjab frontier, became henceforward the centre and the chief controlling power of a vast dominion, ruling directly over the richest and most populous region of India, indirectly imposing its presence over every other state or group of chiefships south of the Sutlaj River, drawing them all within its orbit, and enveloping them all within the external bounds of its sovereignty. The only Indian rulerships completely outside the sphere of this paramount influence were those which occupied the Panjab (where the Sikh power was now drawing to a head), the country along the Indus River, and the mountains of Nepal.

The seven years of Lord Wellesley's Governor-

THE ROYAL PALACE AT BARODA.

Generalship, from May, 1798, to July, 1805, constitute the most important and critical stage in the building up of our Indian dominion on the foundations that had been laid by Clive and Hastings. He had reached India at a moment when the British government was halting dubiously between two political ways, before a horizon that was cloudy and unsettled. On the one hand lay the course that had been prescribed by Parliament, of holding aloof from the quarrels of the native powers and of maintaining an attitude of defensive isolation within our own borders. On the other was the course of going forward to meet dangers and disarm rivals, of striking boldly into the medley before disorder or disaffection could gather strength, and of securing the tranquillity of the British possessions by enforcing peace and submission among our neighbours.

Lord Cornwallis and Sir John Shore, his predecessors, had followed, so far as was possible, the former course. But even before arriving in India, Lord Wellesley had discovered (as he wrote long afterward to Lord Ellenborough) "how vain and idle was poor old Cornwallis's reliance on the good faith of Tippu, and on the strength to be derived from treaties with the Marathas or the Nizam." With such proconceived notions he immediately adopted, without hesitation, the latter course, and it must be admitted that his choice was rewarded by triumphant success. He crushed the Sultan of Mysore in a single brief campaign; he disarmed and disbanded the formidable *corps d'armée* of fourteen thousand sepoys under French officers that was maintained by the Nizam; he took possession of the Karnatic, annexed half the dominions of the Oudh Vizir, forced all the great military states into subjection or subsidiary alliance, and by completely breaking down the power of the Maratha confederacy he removed the last important obstacle to the accomplishment of England's undisputed supremacy.

We may regard with just admiration the high qualities shown by the Governor-General in the prosecution of this magnificent career, his rapid apprehension of a complicated political situation, and the vigour and address with which he carried out not only military operations and diplomatic strokes, but also the reforms of internal administration and the organization of government in the ceded or conquered provinces. No man was ever a better subject for panegyric; nor is it worth while to scan too closely, at this distance of time, the defects of a great public servant by whose strenuous qualities the nation has profited very largely.

It is essential, however, to lay stress, for historical purposes, on the peculiar combination of circumstances which gave scope and encouragement to Lord Wellesley's ardent and masterful statesmanship, and which enabled him to treat those who opposed him or criticized him with the supreme contempt that his home correspondence invariably discloses. He had left England and reached India in the darkest hour of the fierce struggle between the French and English nations, when Buonaparte's star was in the ascendent over Europe, when he was invading Egypt and meditating Asiatic conquests, and when a powerful Tory Ministry was governing at home by measures that in these days would be denounced as the most arbitrary coercion.

At such a conjunction there was little time or inclination to look narrowly into Wellesley's declarations that the intrigues of the French in India and the incapacity or disaffection of the native rulers reduced him to the necessity of dethroning or disarming them, and that for British rule to be secure it must be paramount. As a matter of fact, he was applauded and supported in measures ten times more high-handed and dictatorial than those for which Hastings had been impeached a dozen years earlier. During that interval the temper of the English Parliament had so completely changed that he could afford to ride roughshod over all opposition in India, and to regard the pacific directors of the East India Company as a pack of narrow-minded old women.

The avowed object of Lord Wellesley had been to enforce peace throughout India, and to provide for the permanent security of the British possessions by imposing upon every native state the authoritative superiority of the British government, binding them forcibly or through friendly engagements to subordinate relations with a paramount power, and effectively forestalling any future attempts to challenge England's exercise of arbitration or control. In short, whereas up to his time the British government had usually dealt with all states in India upon a footing of at least nominal political equality, Lord Wellesley revived and proclaimed the imperial principle of political supremacy. All his views and measures pointed toward the reconstruction of another empire in India, which he rightly believed to be the natural outcome of the British position in the country and the only guarantee of its lasting consolidation. It must be acknowledged that Wellesley's trenchant operations only accelerated the sure and irresistible consequences of establishing a strong civilized government among the native states that had risen upon the ruins of the Moghul Empire; for by swift means or slow, by fair means or forcible, the British dominion was certain to expand, and the armed opposition of its rivals could not fail to be beaten down at each successive collision with a growing European power.

CHAPTER XV

THE STATIONARY PERIOD

1806-1814

BUT Lord Wellesley's career of military triumphs and magnificent annexations had alarmed the Court of Directors, who protested against the increase of debt and demurred to the increase of dominion. The Governor-General professed utter contempt for their opinion, and wrote to Lord Castlereagh that no additional outrage or insult "from the most loathsome den of the India House" should accelerate his departure so long as the public safety required his aid. Nevertheless, he discovered, after Monson's disaster, that even the Ministers found reason to apprehend that he was going too fast and too far, that Lord Castlereagh was remonstrating, and that the nation at large was startled by his grandiose reports of Indian wars, conquests, and prodigious accessions of territory. Toward the close of his term of office his measures became much more moderate. In 1805 the return of Lord Cornwallis to India brought about a change of policy which checked and altered the whole movement; for although his second Governor-Generalship was very short, he had time to lay down the pacific principles that were acted upon by his successors.

When Lord Cornwallis reached Calcutta, he found

THE KALI GHAT, CALCUTTA.

an empty treasury, an increasing debt, the export trade of the Company arrested by the demand of specie for the military chest, and the British ascendency openly proclaimed and in process of enforcement by ways and means that evidently involved us in a rapidly expanding circle of fresh political liabilities. His own ideas, and the instructions that he had brought out, pointed in a contrary direction. He thought that the subsidiary treaties only entangled us in responsibility for defending and laboriously propping up impotent or unruly princes, impairing their independence and retarding the natural development of stronger organizations. Nor did our interests seem to him to require that we should undertake the preservation of the smaller chiefships adjacent to our frontiers from absorption by the larger predatory states. It seems, on the contrary, to have been his view that the English protectorate should not extend beyond the actual limits of British possessions —a rule of political fortification that has never been practised in India; for England has always found it necessary to throw forward a kind of glacis in advance of her administrative border-line, so as to interpose a belt of protected states or tribes between British territory proper and the country of some turbulent or formidable neighbour.

Lord Cornwallis lost no time in declaring his intention of removing the "unfavourable and dangerous impression" that the British government contemplated establishing its control and authority over every state in India. He died, however, on October 5, 1805, within three months after his arrival, before he could do more than indicate this change of policy. But his views — which represented the reaction in England against Lord Wellesley's costly and masterful operations—so far prevailed that for the next ten years following his decease the experiment of isolation was fairly tried by the British government in India. Sir George Barlow, whom the death of Cornwallis made Governor-General for a time, laid down the principle that a certain extent of dominion, local power, and revenue would be cheaply sacrificed for tranquillity and security within a contracted circle; and he withdrew from every kind of relation with the native states to which the English were not specifically pledged by treaty. It will be found that whenever the Governor-Generalship has been held by an Anglo-Indian official, annexations have been exceedingly rare and the expanding movement has slackened; but Sir George Barlow even took a step backward. The subsidiary alliance with Sindhia, projected by Lord Wellesley, was abandoned; the minor principalities adjacent to or intermixed with the Maratha possessions were left to their fate; the English proclaimed an intention of living apart from broils, of dissociating themselves from the general concerns of India at large, and of improving their own property without taking part in the quarrels or grievances of their neighbours.

If, indeed, Sir George Barlow had adopted to their full extent the views that were pressed upon him by the authorities in England at this period, he would have disconnected the British government from the subsidiary treaties which invested it with paramount influence in the affairs of the two great Maratha and Mohammedan states, ruled by the Peshwa at Poona and by the Nizam at Haidarabad. But the result would have been to undo the work of Lord Wellesley, to abdicate the ascendency that the British had attained, and to throw open again the field of Central India to the Marathas, who would at once have reoccupied all the ground that the English should have abandoned.

THE HUGLI RIVER AT CALCUTTA.

It was, indeed, so manifest to those actually watching the situation in India that the consequence would be a reversion to political confusion and would discredit England's public faith and encourage her enemies, that the Governor-General insisted on maintaining the treaties, and even found himself obliged, against the logical tenor of his principles, to interpose vigorously in support of British diplomatic authority at Haidarabad. In 1807 Sir George Barlow was succeeded in the Governor-Generalship by Lord Minto.

In the meanwhile, although the French had at last been effectively barred out from approaching India by sea, and although every native state accessible to hostile intrigues by the seacoast had been bound over under heavy recognizances to the English alliance, yet signs and warnings of danger now began to reappear in a different quarter of the stormy political horizon.

The Persian king, who had suffered heavily from a war with Russia in 1804 - 1805, appealed for succour to Napoleon in Europe and also sent a similar application to Calcutta. From India, where the policy of retrenchment and retractation prevailed at that moment, no encouragement was forthcoming. The French, however, who were just then in the midst of a desperate war with Russia, readily responded to the advances of Persia by sending an embassy for the conclusion of an offensive alliance against the common foe. Napoleon, who had just fought with heavy loss the drawn battle of Eylau, eagerly welcomed an opportunity of harassing the Russians in Asia and also of resuscitating his favourite schemes of Asiatic conquest. His envoy to Teheran was instructed that his chief aim should be to form a triple alliance between France, Turkey, and Persia for the purpose of opening out a road to India. He was also directed to ascertain what co-operation might be expected within the country, particularly from the Marathas, if India could be reached by a French army.

Then came, in 1807, the battle of Friedland, when Napoleon used his victory to convert the Russian Emperor from an enemy into an ally of France. The offensive league with Persia was quietly transformed into an offer of mediation between that kingdom and Russia; and Napoleon set about organizing with Alexander I a fresh and much more formidable confederation against the English in India. Russia was already an Asiatic power, with a distinct inclination and momentum eastward. It is, therefore, no wonder that this ominous conjunction of France, at that moment supreme in Western Europe, with the only European state that could further her designs upon India should have aroused and substantiated the alarms of an invasion by land; alarms that have never since ceased to recur periodically, gaining strength in proportion as their fulfilment has become by degrees less manifestly impracticable.

The inevitable effect of this chronic disquietude has been, from the beginning, to fix the attention of the Anglo-Indian governments more and more, in the course of the present century, upon the northwest angle of

India. And the concentration of England's whole foreign policy upon that point undoubtedly accelerated the expansion of her dominion in that direction, because in her anxiety about the only vulnerable side of her land frontier, she naturally pushed forward to secure it. No sooner, in fact, had the spectre of French troop-ships hovering about her seacoast been finally laid under the waters of Trafalgar, than the apparition of European armies marching from the Caspian to the Oxus began to trouble the prophetic imagination of English statesmen.

From the day when the Emperors of France and Russia exchanged pledges of immutable personal friendship at Tilsit, Napoleon incessantly pressed upon Alexander his grand scheme of a joint expedition through Turkey and Persia against the English in India, with the object of subverting their dominion and destroying the sources of their commercial prosperity. In 1807 the pre-eminence of France on the European Continent had reached its climax. Napoleon had defeated every army that had successively met him in the field; he had dissolved every league that had been made against him; and he had forced every leading state to join in a coalition for the rigid exclusion of English commerce from all their seaports. When, however, it became clear that these roundabout methods of attacking England were futile, and that nothing short of a direct home-thrust would disable his indefatigable enemy, the French emperor naturally turned his eyes toward the only important English possession whose frontier was not absolutely inaccessible to invasion from Europe by land. His imagination was fired by the recollection that Asia had more than once been traversed by conquering armies.

That Napoleon should seriously have contemplated marching across Europe and half Asia to invade the territory of an island within twenty miles of the French coast, that he should have thought it on the whole less impracticable to send a force from the Danube or Constantinople to Delhi than to transport his troops from Calais to Dover, is certainly a remarkable illustration of the impregnability of effective naval defence. But his proposals obtained very half-hearted encouragement from the Russians, who had some useful acquaintance with the difficulties of Asiatic campaigning, and a wholesome distrust of the associate in whose company they were invited to set out. They were by no means eager to embark on distant Eastern adventures, or to lock up their troops in the heart of Asia, upon the advice and for the advantage of the restless and powerful autocrat whose armies still hovered about their western frontier. They stipulated for a partition of the Turkish Empire as a preliminary dividend upon the joint-stock enterprise and as a strategic base for any further advance eastward. To this condition, however, Napoleon refused his assent, alleging, reasonably enough, that it would be playing into the hands of England, since if the Russians were to take Constantinople, the English would at once retaliate by seizing Egypt. An imposing French mission was, nevertheless, sent to Persia, and the Anglo-Indian governments were much startled by the activity of the French agents at Teheran and other Asiatic courts.

It is from this period that we must date the embarcation of Anglo-Indian diplomacy upon a much wider sphere of action than heretofore. The English ministers soon discovered Napoleon's plan of an Asiatic campaign, and all his secret negotiations were thoroughly known to them. For the purpose of counteracting the French demonstrations and of throwing up barrier after barrier against the threatened expedition from the Black Sea and the Caspian, the Indian Governor-General, Lord Minto, sent missions to all the rulers of states on and beyond his northwestern border —to Ranjit Singh at Lahore, to the Afghan Amir, to

RANJIT SINGH'S SAMADH AT LAHORE.

Sind, and to the Shah of Persia, who was just then overawed by the combined preponderance of France and Russia.

Now that Napoleon had become Alexander's intimate friend and ally, the Persian king knew what to expect from French mediation, so he turned for protection to the English. At Teheran a treaty was settled, after much dispute and various misunderstandings (for the English envoy from Calcutta was superseded by another envoy from London), engaging England to subsidize Persia in the event of unprovoked aggression upon her. From Lahore the mission withdrew when, after some negotiations, it was discovered that Ranjit Singh claimed recognition of his sovereignty over territory south of the Sutlaj River. At Peshawar Mountstuart Elphinstone, the envoy to Afghanistan, found the whole country distracted by civil war. The Afghan king, Shah Shuja', was barely holding on to the skirts of his kingdom; the Durrani monarchy, attacked on the west by Persia and hard pushed on the east by the Sikhs, was already breaking up again into separate chiefships. Elphinstone's negotiations were cut short by the defeat of Shah Shuja', who fled into exile, to be restored thirty years later by an ill-fated expedition that eventually cost the English an army and the king his life.

But all these schemes for establishing close alliances and barrier treaties with Afghanistan, the Panjab, and Sind were dropped or postponed as the tide of events again began to turn westward. The Spanish insurrection and the preparations for invading Russia soon provided Napoleon with such ample occupation in Europe that he abandoned his schemes of Asiatic adventure. Russia was now England's ally in a grand coalition against France; she made peace with Persia, and our apprehensions of danger from that quarter subsided when the long war which ended with Napoleon's overthrow left us in undisturbed possession of India. The sea-roads were guarded by an irresistible navy; the total collapse of the French Empire, the exhaustion of all the great European states, the manifest decay and immobility that were spreading through Central Asia—all these circumstances united to secure us fourteen years of comparative freedom from movements or demonstrations affecting our immunity from molestation by land, and ending only in 1826, when Russia attacked Persia, thus inaugurating a long stride eastward in 1828, which revived British anxieties.

The sole result of all the missions sent from India was, indirectly, the ratification of a substantial frontier settlement, in 1809, with Ranjit Singh, who, under pressure, renounced his pretensions to sovereignty over certain Sikh chiefships south of the Sutlaj. From that time forward his friendly relations with the English on his southeastern frontier, combined with the civil strife within Afghanistan on the northwest, afforded him the means and opportunity of extending his territory across the Indus, of annexing Kashmir, and of building up the Sikh power with a solidity that kept it standing in alliance with the English for nearly forty years.

On the other hand, the eventual consequences of all this premature diplomatic agitation were by no means unimportant or transitory. We have seen how French rivalry accelerated the earlier British conquests; and how at a later time the correspondence of native princes with France and the presence of French officers in the Indian armies aroused English susceptibility. It has

SITE OF RANJIT SINGH'S ENCAMPMENT NEAR RUPUR, ON THE SUTLAJ.

been shown how this furnished Lord Wellesley with the necessary leverage for advancing his policy of bringing into subjection or subordinate alliance every Mohammedan or Maratha state that might cross England's path toward undisputed predominance in the interior of India. In the same manner the intelligence of Napoleon's projects first diverted Great Britain's attention from the seaboard to her land frontiers, and first launched the British government upon that much larger expanse of Asiatic war and diplomacy in which it has continued to be almost unremittingly engaged ever since.

Up to the end of the eighteenth century the field of Anglo-Indian politics had been circumscribed within the limits of India, being confined to relations with the Indian states over which England was asserting an easy mastery by the natural and necessary growth of her ascendency. Now she entered for the first time upon that range of diplomatic observation in which all the countries of Western Asia, from Kabul to Constantinople, are surveyed as interposing barriers between Europe and the Anglo-Indian possessions. The independence and integrity of these foreign and comparatively distant states are henceforward essential for the balance of Asiatic power and for the security of the frontiers of British India. Before this epoch the jar and collision of European contests had been felt only in England's dealings with the inland powers of India; she struck down or disarmed every native ruler who attempted to communicate with her European enemies.

But from the beginning of the nineteenth century we have had little or nothing to fear from Indian rivals, and we have gradually taken rank as a first-class Asiatic sovereignty. The vast weight of our Indian interests has ever since weighed decisively in the balance of our relations, not only with all Asia, but with any European state whose views or dispositions might in any degree affect our position in the East. We have thus become intimately concerned in the political vicissitudes of every important state on the Asiatic continent. The chronic disquietude which began at this period has been the source of some hazardous military projects and premature diplomatic schemes, of two expeditions into Afghanistan, of a war with Persia, and of a policy that is constantly extending the British protectorate far beyond the natural limits of India.

From the opening of the nineteenth century, then, may be dated the establishment of England's undisputed ascendency within India. From the same period also may be reckoned the appearance of that susceptibility regarding the possible approach of European rivals by land, which led first to negotiations and treaties, and eventually to wars, between England and the foreign states adjoining or approaching her Indian dominion.

So long as the European conflict lasted, the Anglo-Indian government had continued to survey all Western Asia watchfully, and to stand on its guard against any movement by land that might seem to affect or endanger its position. In the meantime, England's naval superiority enabled her to sweep all enemies out of the Eastern waters and to occupy any point from which the coasts or commerce of India might be exposed to molestation. The Cape of Good Hope, that important naval station half-way to India, had been finally occupied in 1806; and in 1810 Lord Minto's expedition ejected the French from Java and Abercrombie captured Mauritius; so that the sea-routes, the ports of shelter and supply, and the harbours were all in British hands.

At the beginning of the long peace which followed the termination of the great war in 1815 England had secured undisturbed possession of her enormously valuable conquests in the southern seas—of the Cape, of Ceylon, and of Mauritius. All the foreign settlements on the Indian seaboard were disarmed, and not one of the states within India could now measure its strength against her power and resources. Six of the chief principalities were now bound to the English system by subsidiary treaties. In Western and Central India, Baroda, Poona, and Haidarabad, in South India, Mysore and Travancore, and, toward the northwest, Oudh with a large number of minor chieftainships were all under British suzerainty and protection. Beyond the English frontiers were the growing kingdom of Ranjit Singh in the Panjab, and the Gurkha state of Nepal along the southern slopes of the Himalayas. Only in Central India there remained three principalities, surrounded by British territory, that had not yet come formally within the circle of English dominion. They belonged to the three families who still represented the fighting and predatory traditions of the Maratha confederacy, Sindhia at Gwalior, Holkar at Indore, and the Bhonsla at Nagpur. To these may be added, though the status was different, the ruling house of the Gaikwar at Baroda.

From the cessation of the great war that determined in England's favour the contest with the native states for ascendency in India we may also reckon the introduction of orderly administration within her territories, and of a systematic policy in regard to her neighbours, the recognition, in fact, of her imperial duties and obligations. The Mohammedan states of Haidarabad and

A TEMPLE AT GWALIOR.

Oudh were indebted for their survival to British protection; they would have been destroyed, but for England's intervention, by fiercer and more vigorous rivals in the general scramble for dominion. Nevertheless, it must be admitted that at times they had paid heavy salvage to the British for their rescue. In some of England's earlier transactions with them she had used the rough thoroughgoing methods of a stormy and dissolute period; and on emergencies their lands and revenues had been laid under severe contributions to her military expenditure. The time had now come when the British government, no longer driven to these summary expedients by the struggle for existence, but drawing from an ample and secure revenue, its own possessions, could regulate its dealings in civilized fashion by settled treaties, and could begin to adjust all its dealings with native states on the fair and equitable basis of their subordinate relationship.

So also England now had some leisure for looking into the condition of her domestic administration and bringing the great provinces which had been recently acquired into some kind of order. The investigation of land-tenures, the institution of an elementary police, the first serious attempts to check the brigandage prevailing in English districts, and the arrangement and supervision of the local courts of justice took substantial form at the beginning of the nineteenth century; the roots of that immense system of organized government which has since spread over all India were planted at this season of comparative tranquillity. The first five years of the nineteenth century were occupied with continuous wars, with great territorial changes, with the removal of landmarks, and with the rearrangement of rulerships. But from that time forward the country has experienced immunity under British jurisdiction from foreign invasion or serious violation of its frontier, and even (except in 1857) from internal commotions. It may be questioned whether any state in Asia, or even in Europe, has enjoyed such complete political tranquillity during the same period.

CHAPTER XVI

THE GOVERNOR-GENERALSHIP OF LORD HASTINGS

1813-1823

SOME attempt has already been made to explain the views and circumstances under which, after Lord Wellesley's departure, the British government determined to retire within its own administrative borders, to transact its political affairs in future upon the principle of limited liability, and to maintain, outside its actual obligations, the attitude of a placid spectator, unconcerned with the quarrels or misfortunes of his neighbours. It is a policy which a strong European state, placed in the midst of uncivilized rulers or races, has vainly endeavoured to uphold from time immemorial. It appears at first to be simple and prudent, and to be dictated by enlightened self-interest and by public morality. Unfortunately, it has hitherto invariably failed to do more than check or postpone for an interval the really inevitable tendency of an organized power to override, if not to absorb, loose tribal rulerships and ephemeral despotisms, which spring up and survive merely because more durable institutions are wanting and until they are supplied. Not only, indeed, is the check temporary, the reaction is apt to produce a rebound; a halt is followed by a great stride forward, a few steps taken backward look like preparation for a longer leap; so that masterly inactivity is attributed to astute calculation, and we are often unjustly accused in India of allowing the pear to rot that it may drop the easier into our hands.

It is usual to lay the blame of this invariable expansion upon those who direct imperial affairs on the frontier or in the outlying provinces, but the true impulse comes quite as often from the metropolis, where the accumulation of capital, or the pressure of national interests, drives war and enterprise forward along the line of least resistance. This onward movement may be temporarily arrested by such physical obstacles as mountains or deserts, but it comes to a standstill only when the way is at last blocked by a rival power of equal calibre, or when the central forces begin to decline. The truth is that in the art of political engineering solid construction depends on the material available and on the proper adaptation of resistance to natural pressure. It is as impossible to lay down a frontier on an untenable line as to throw a dam across a river on bad foundations. The dam is carried away at the next flood; nor will the strictest prudence long maintain a frontier or a system that does not run upon the natural lines of political or territorial permanency.

When, therefore, at the beginning of the nineteenth century we drew back from what seemed to Lord Cornwallis a network of embarrassing ties and compromising guarantees, we retained, as has been said, certain great states within the sphere of our surveillance; but we left almost all Central India, including Rajputana, to take care of itself. All round our own territories we drew a cordon of rigid irresistible order; while outside this ring-fence, in the great interior region that

BAKHLAWAR SINGH'S CENOTAPH AT ULWAR IN RAJPUTANA.

contained the principalities of the Maratha families and of the ancient Rajput chiefs, we allowed a free hand to Sindhia, Holkar, and the predatory leaders. Scattered among the Maratha territories were a crowd of tribal chiefships and petty feudatories in various stages of dependence. Beyond the Maratha border, toward the great western desert, lay the Rajput states, too weak and disunited to oppose the exactions and dilapidations of great predatory armies.

This group of primitive tribal chiefships, the last surviving relics of mediæval India, had outlasted the Afghan and the Moghul empires, and had weathered the tumultuous anarchy of the eighteenth century. But they were rent by intestine feuds, and the militia of the Rajput clans was quite incapable of resisting the trained bands of the Marathas or the Afghan mercenaries of Amir Khan. Some of these states were now remonstrating earnestly with the British government for refusing to admit them within its protectorate, which they claimed as a matter of right; so that, as Sir Charles Metcalfe, the Resident for Rajputana, wrote in June, 1816, "They said that some power in India had always existed to which peaceable states submitted, and in return obtained its protection against the invasions of upstart chiefs and the armies of lawless banditti; that the British government now occupied the place of that protecting power, and was the natural guardian of weak states which were continually exposed to the cruelties and oppression of robbers and plunderers, owing to the refusal of the British government to protect them."

Lord Minto, who had gone out to India with the intention of maintaining what was called the defensive policy, changed his views materially before 1813, when he made over the Governor-Generalship to Lord Moira, afterwards Marquis of Hastings. He had found himself compelled to interpose with an armed force for the protection of Holkar's government against a captain of banditti, and to place an army in the field to overawe the freebooter Amir Khan, who was about to overrun the Nagpur country. From 1811 to 1813 the Pindaris increased rapidly in numbers. The origin of these famous bands is to be found in the scouts and foragers who had always formed the loose fringe, so to speak, of every Indian army, receiving no pay, and subsisting by pillage, but generally submitting to the orders of the commander of the whole force.

As the regular armies of the native states were reduced, and as the governments lost strength, these bands detached themselves from all military or civil subordination and set up as hordes of free lances under their own leaders. By this time they had invaded, plundered, and ransomed the territories of the Nizam and the Peshwa, the allies of the British, and now they were threatening with fire and sword the rich English province of Behar. The principle of non-interference seems to have been defended upon the ground that all these jarring and complicated elements of disorder would gradually settle down and become fused into strong and solidly constituted states. But it soon became manifest that an attempt to confine epidemic disease within fixed areas in the midst of some populous country would be not much more unreasonable than the plan of allowing political disorders to breed and multiply in the centre of India.

In the first place the Maratha chiefs were sullen, discontented, naturally ill-disposed toward the government which had recently overthrown their predominance, and seeking by all means to repair and augment their military forces. Secondly, the enforcement of systematic order all round them, and of restriction within fixed boundaries, was irreconcilable with the conditions that had engendered their power and that were still necessary to its existence; for the Maratha princes could maintain large armies only by levying exactions from their neighbours and by constantly taking the field upon marauding excursions. And, thirdly, it was evident that the cessation of irregular warfare and the establishment of a steady protectorate over the greater portion of India must inevitably aggravate the sufferings and intensify the confusion in those parts where the supreme pacifying authority disclaimed jurisdiction and formally abdicated every right of interference. Large bodies of troops were disbanded by the British government and by its allies. But as all this multitude of men who lived by the sword and the free lance found their occupation gone within the pale of orderly government, they poured out of the pacified districts into the kingdoms of misrule like water draining from a cultivated upland into the low-lying marshes.

It was indeed impossible that a kind of political Alsatia, full of brigands and roving banditti, could long be tolerated in the midst of a country just settling down into the peaceful and industrious stage. Such a situation, nevertheless, necessarily followed upon the introduction of the new principle by a sharp turn of policy. The British government could not now stay at home or stand aloof without stopping half-way in the pacification of India and leaving one great homogeneous population under two different and entirely incompatible political systems. For although the Indian people are broken up into diversities of race and language, they are, as a whole, not less distinctly marked off from the rest of Asia by certain material and moral characteristics than is their country by the mountains and the sea. The component parts of that great country hang together, physically and politically; there is no

RUINS OF TYRE, THE ANCIENT PHŒNICIAN CITY ON THE MEDITERRANEAN.

more room for two irreconcilable systems of government than in Persia, China, or Asiatic Turkey.

The attitude of insulation might not have been inconsistent in the infancy of the English dominion, when the forces of the native states were better divided and more equally balanced, and when we might have confined our enterprise to the establishment of a great maritime and commercial power on the shores of the Indian and Arabian seas, like the Phœnicians or the Venetians in the Mediterranean. But it has been seen that, during the second half of the eighteenth century, England penetrated inland, striking in among the local wars and seizing territory, in order to protect herself and forestall the French. Then, before the last apprehensions of French rivalry had vanished, she had been confronted by the Marathas and the Mysore rulers, whose natural jealousy of her rising power was abetted by the French, and whose well-appointed armies directly threatened her position.

To meet this danger Lord Wellesley had organized subsidiary forces on a large scale, undertaking on the part of the British government the general defence of all states that submitted to England's political influence, and confining within fixed boundaries all those that held aloof. Lastly, when Mysore and the Maratha confederacy — the two powers that made head against the British—had been the one destroyed and the other disabled, England's ascendency so overshadowed all India that it was too late to descend from the height she had attained or to stand still abruptly on the road to universal dictatorship. She had now become a conquering power; she had assumed a continental sovereignty; and upon her the duty of providing the police of India had manifestly fallen. When the British attempted to disclaim this responsibility, no one else could undertake the business; and the smaller chiefships, who saw themselves spoiled and devoured, protested against a government that had pre-occupied the imperial place, but nevertheless evaded the imperial obligation.

In the meantime the condition of the whole central region was sinking from bad to worse. It has been seen that India was crowded in the eighteenth century with mercenary soldiers who followed the trade of war; and an incredibly large proportion of the population subsisted by freebooting, a flourishing profession that had now openly been practised in India for several generations. The annexations and conquests of Lord Wellesley's era and the enlargement of the British borders and of the British protectorate had led to an extensive disbandment of troops. It was reckoned by a competent authority that, at a moderate computation, this wide pacification of the country had turned loose half a million professional soldiers.

Many of these men, with most of the freebooting class, whose occupation was disappearing with the contraction of that field of private enterprise, had collected in Central India, where, instead of diminishing and settling down as had been expected, they increased to an alarming degree. Some of the native rulers encouraged them secretly, they intimidated the rest, and no power was strong enough to suppress them. The swarming of these predatory bands, which had been a comparatively transient and occasional evil when they could range over the whole Indian continent, became a mortal plague when it was hemmed in within set bounds, for the inland countries were exhausted by endemic brigandage. While the lesser principalities were thus being systematically bled to death, the great military chiefs were recruiting their forces, replenishing their treasuries, and enlarging the range of their operations, not without some prospect of recovering the formidable military footing which they had lost in the previous war.

The subsidiary system, moreover, had other consequences besides those of causing the disbanding of the loose mercenary militia and the condensation of the freebooting plague. As the military power of the states which contracted these treaties was conveyed into British hands, the result was to weaken the internal authority of their rulers, by diminishing their feeling of responsibility for governing well and moderately, because they were sure of English protection in the event of attack or revolt. Undoubtedly the sense of dependence upon a higher power relaxed the energies of a native prince, who knew that in the last resort he could always call in the British government to save him from utter destruction.

Against these disadvantages of the subsidiary alliances must, however, be set the consideration that without British protection most of the allied states would certainly have been dismembered in the incessant warfare that prevailed wherever they were left to themselves. The effect of English alliances upon the majority of these states was, therefore, to arrest the natural process of their disruption, but not to strengthen the internal authority of their rulers. In this manner the burden of repressing disorder within the territory of England's allies followed the transfer of the duty of external defence and gradually became shifted to the shoulders of the British government. Her policy might vary, backward or forward, but England still found herself mounting step by step up to the high office of ultimate arbiter in every dispute and supreme custodian of the peace of all India.

Under the circumstances that have just been described, the marauding bands of Central India, like the Free Companies of mediæval Europe, had prospered and multiplied; until in 1814 Amir Khan, a notable military adventurer, was living upon Rajputana with a compact army of at least thirty thousand men and a strong artillery. That a regular army of this calibre should have been moving at large about Central India, entirely unconnected with any recognizable government or fixed territory, and acknowledging no political or civil responsibility, is decisive evidence of the prevailing disorganization. But Amir Khan's troops were under some kind of discipline and were employed upon a system in some degree resembling regular warfare, their commander's aim being to carve out a dominion for himself.

The true Pindari hordes had no other object but general rapine; they were immense bands of mounted robbers; their most popular leader, Chitu, could number no less than ten thousand horsemen; they could subsist only by irruptions into rich and fertile districts; and they were a perpetual menace to the country possessed or protected by the British power. It cannot be doubted that they maintained a secret understanding with the independent Maratha rulers at Poona, Nagpur, and Gwalior, who were not particularly anxious to join in the suppression of armed bodies that spared Maratha districts while they harried British lands and the Nizam's country, and who probably remembered that the Pindaris might prove very serviceable auxiliaries in any future attempt to make head against British domination.

The war that broke out with Nepal in 1814 had inspired the Marathas with some hope of finding their opportunity in England's difficulty. About 1768 a chief of the Gurkhalis or Gurkhas, a race springing from the intermixture of Hindus with the hill tribes, had subdued all the highlands and valleys on the southern slopes of the Himalayas overlooking Bengal. His successors had carried their arms northwestwards along the mountain ranges above Oudh, Rohilkhand, and the provinces watered by the Ganges and the Jumna, up to the confines of the Panjab. This difficult tract of hill and forest, into which the Moghuls had never cared to penetrate, had previously been possessed by a number of petty Hindu rajas, who subsisted to a large extent by making occasional forays into the plain country below.

The Gurkha chief, taking his lesson from what was going on in Bengal, had set up a disciplined force with which he easily exterminated the local rajas, and his dynasty ruled, with the usual contests upon each succession, until his grandson was assassinated by conspirators in 1805. After that date the kingdom was no longer governed by a single ruler; it fell into the hands of a group of high military officers belonging to the dominant clan, who kept the hereditary king in subjection and governed Nepal in his name. As their soldiery were drilled and equipped in European fashion —for in military matters the Gurkhas have always been skilful copyists from the English model—they rapidly pushed their conquests westward over the petty hill states, and soon began to make encroachments upon the sub-Himalayan lowlands within the English border. Between the minor chiefs who lived on the skirts of the mountains and the great proprietors in Bengal there had been chronic fighting from time immemorial, for all these Nepalese border chiefs had annexed strips of land in the plains immediately below them; but now the Gurkhas had subdued all the highlands and the English had brought the low country under their authority.

It followed that the constant quarrels over this debatable border soon embroiled the two governments. The Nepalese officers on the frontier encroached audaciously upon the lands of British subjects, occupied tracts belonging to Bengal, and refused to retire. At last, when they seized two small districts in 1814, Lord Hastings sent to their government a peremptory demand that they should evacuate, and on receiving merely evasive replies, he re-occupied these districts by a detachment of troops, before whom the Gurkha officers quietly retired. But so soon as the troops had been withdrawn, the Gurkhas made a sudden attack upon the British police stations and massacred some twenty men. Their government, after holding a formal council, had resolved upon war, being persuaded that the English could never penetrate into the mountains of Nepal.

Then ensued the first of those numerous expeditions into the interior of the great hill-ranges surrounding India, in which the Anglo-Indian government has ever

A NEPALESE SHIELD.

since been at intervals engaged. The frontier which was to be the scene of war stretched for a distance of about six hundred miles, and the enemy had the command of all the passes leading up into the highlands. The attack was made by the English at three separate points; and although General Gillespie was repulsed and killed in attempting to storm a fort, yet in spite of a brave and obstinate resistance, the British troops gained their footing within the hills and drove the

Gurkhas out of all their positions on the west. The Nepalese government was compelled to sign a treaty ceding a long strip of the lower Himalayas, with most of the adjacent forest lands, extending from the present western frontier of the Nepal state northwestward as far as the Sutlaj River. All the hill-country that now overhangs Rohilkhand and the Northwest Provinces up to the Jumna River, with the valuable belt of low-lying forest that skirts the base of the outer ranges toward India, thus fell into English hands.

By this cession of a Himalayan province the Anglo-Indian frontier was carried up to and beyond the watershed of the highest mountains separating India from Tibet or from Cathay; and the English dominion thenceforward became conterminous for the first time with the Chinese empire, whose government has ever since observed British proceedings with marked and intelligible solicitude. The Gurkha chiefs of Nepal, having thus been confined within a narrow belt of highland territory immediately overlooking England's most valuable province, have nevertheless maintained their system of military domination through several internal revolutions, and have sedulously pursued a policy of training their troops upon the European model by discipline and the importation of arms.

In the meantime the freebooting bands of Central India were increasing in numbers and audacity. The Pindaris, who were openly disowned and secretly encouraged by the Maratha chiefs, had made an inroad into certain districts of the Madras Presidency, carrying off great booty, and had also plundered on the frontier of Bengal. Amir Khan, the Pathan leader, was besieging Jaipur, whose raja applied to the English for succour. After much negotiation Lord Hastings succeeded not only in bringing the Rajput state of Jaipur within the English protectorate, but also in concluding a subsidiary treaty with the Bhonsla Raja of Nagpur, whereby an important member was detached from the Maratha confederation. But this raja soon repented an engagement which affected his complete independence; and under the influence of a party at his capital hostile to the English, he began to correspond secretly with the Peshwa at Poona, who had become restless, disaffected, and exceedingly impatient of British mediation in his dealings with feudatories or neighbouring states.

The war in Nepal, which seemed likely to be long and troublesome, encouraged an inclination among the Marathas to try conclusions again with the English. The Peshwa began to assemble his troops and collect military stores; the British Resident replied by calling in the subsidiary force; and a kind of sporadic insurrection, privily fomented by the Poona authorities, was breaking out in the country. All these threatening symptoms reached a crisis when the Gaikwar's envoy, who had been sent to Poona on a special mission under British guarantee, was assassinated, with the Peshwa's connivance, by one of his confidential favourites. The murderer's surrender was extorted from the Peshwa, with the greatest difficulty, by the British Resident, but he escaped from prison, and the Peshwa, who seemed about to take up arms in his defence, only lost courage and made terms just as an open rupture was becoming imminent. In 1817 he signed a treaty making cessions of territory in exchange for an increased subsidiary force, and virtually renouncing all his previous pretensions to supremacy in the Maratha confederation.

Lord Hastings now decided that the time had come when he could begin his combined operations for the suppression of the freebooting hordes, and for such a general reformation of the condition of Central India as might eradicate the predatory system. The policy of isolation had, he found, completely failed; its effect was not only to foster the spread of confusion and disorder outside the Anglo-Indian frontiers, but also to endanger the main position of the British government. His remedy was to step forward as the arbitrator and authoritative peacemaker, to dissolve the plundering bands, and to mark out the whole of the vast inland region into recognized rulerships, so that no part of it should be left outside the jurisdiction of some responsible authority. He relied on the supreme influence and paramount power of the British government in arms to insist, when this had been done, upon the pacification of the whole country through the chiefs to whom it should have been assigned in severalty. He projected, in short, the consummation of the work that had been begun by Lord Cornwallis, and carried very far by Lord Wellesley—the extension of British supremacy and protectorate over every native state in the interior of India.

In such a cause, however, the hearty co-operation of the Maratha princes could not reasonably be expected. Amir Khan, the Pathan leader, was persuaded or intimidated into disbanding his army and settling down on the lands guaranteed to him. But Sindhia reluctantly agreed to associate himself with the campaign against the Pindaris; he delayed the departure of his troops with the manifest purpose of watching events, and was overawed into signing a treaty of co-operation only by the display of force. The Peshwa, galled by the yoke which the recent treaty had fixed upon him, collected his forces and broke out into open hostility, attacking the British troops at Poona in November, 1817; while at Nagpur the raja declared for him as the head of the Maratha nation and sent his own troops against the British Residency. On both occasions the Marathas were repulsed, though not without stout fighting at Nagpur; and as Holkar's army, which attempted to join the Peshwa, had been defeated at Mehidpur in December of the previous year, the opposition of the Maratha powers to the Governor-General's policy of pacification soon came to an end.

The Peshwa, pursued by the British flying columns, fought one or two sharp actions; but his troops were at last scattered, his forts were taken, and he himself was pursued until he finally surrendered in June, 1818, upon an assurance of suitable provision. Lord Hastings had determined to exclude him and his family from any further share of influence or dominion in the Deccan; and the greater part of his territories passed under British sovereignty. The State of Satara was reconstituted out of the Peshwa's domains and placed under the descendant of Sivaji, the original founder of the

PEASANTS OF MAHABLESHWAR, NEAR SATARA, IN THE BOMBAY PRESIDENCY.

Maratha empire, whose dynasty had been supplanted by the Peshwas, a line of hereditary prime ministers. The Nagpur State had also to cede several important districts, and its military establishments passed under British control. The group of ancient Rajput chiefships which had been spoiled and ransomed for years by the Marathas and Amir Khan, with a number of minor principalities, were placed under the immediate protection and guarantee of the British government.

The tributes claimed from the lesser states by the Maratha rulers were fixed and confirmed, upon conditions that payment should be made through the British treasury.

By these measures the Maratha rulership of the Peshwa was now finally extinguished, and the three leading families that had so often opposed the British, Sindhia, Holkar, and the Bhonsla of Nagpur, were definitely bound over to keep the peace of India. The Pindaris, who were merely the remnants of the once flourishing predatory system, the dregs of the roving bands that had harried India during a century of anarchy, were dispersed or exterminated. The Maratha states were restricted to carefully demarcated limits; the trades of marauding conquest and of mere brigandage on a large scale alike disappeared; the whole species vanished with the change of those conditions of government and society by which it had been engendered.

The result was to secure for the British provinces unbroken immunity from the hostile attacks or plundering inroads to which they were always exposed so long as rapine and violence thrived in the centre of India. But it would have been useless to put down these enormous evils unless precautions had also been taken against their revival. Henceforward it became the universal principle of public policy that every state in India (outside the Panjab and Sind) should make over the control of its foreign relations to the British government, should submit all external disputes to British arbitration, and should defer to British advice regarding internal management so far as might be necessary to cure disorders or scandalous misrule. A British Resident was appointed to the courts of all the greater princes as the agency for the exercise of these high functions; while the subsidiary forces and the contingents furnished by the states placed the supreme military command everywhere under British direction.

This great political settlement of Central India—the disarmament and pacification of the military chiefships, and the adjustment of distinct relations of supremacy and subordination—established universal recognition of the cardinal principle upon which the fabric of British dominion in India has been built up. It completed and consolidated the policy of Lord Wellesley. The last shadow of interference by any European rival had now for the time faded away. The contest with the native states for ascendency was finally decided, and not only the right but the duty of intervention for the security and tranquillity of the Indian people was now everywhere acknowledged, from the two seas northward up to Sind and the Sutlaj River. From the Sind frontier at the mouths of the Indus River, down the west coast of the peninsula to Cape Comorin, and thence northeastward again along the Bay of Bengal to the frontier of Burma, the whole sea-line of India was under the authority of England. On the north she held a long belt of the Himalayan highlands, and her political jurisdiction extended to the western edge of the deserts bordering on upper Sind and the Panjab.

The largest, most important, and by far the most valuable portion of this region was now under the direct administration of the British; the rest was under their sovereign influence. Taking the natural boundaries of India to be the ocean and the mountains, it may be said that the Anglo-Indian Empire now commanded the whole circuit of its sea frontier, that it was securely settled upon a base in the Himalayas, and that its western flank was covered to a great extent by the cis-Indus desert. On two sections, and two only, the frontier was still unstable and liable to disturbance—on the northeast, where the Burmese were advancing into Assam, and on the northwest, where the Sikh kingdom beyond the Sutlaj had acquired formidable fighting strength under Ranjit Singh.

AN INDIAN RUPEE OF QUEEN VICTORIA'S REIGN.

CHAPTER XVII

COMPLETION OF DOMINION

1823 - 1858

UP to this epoch the scene of all the East India Company's wars had been within India; and for the last fifty years—from the withdrawal of the French in 1763 to the end of the Pindari war in 1818—the antagonists of the British had been the native Indian powers. As the expansion of England's dominion carried her so much nearer to foreign Asiatic countries, her rapid approach to the geographical limits of India proper discovered fresh complications for her, and she was now on the brink of collision with new races. The first non-Indian power that provoked her to actual hostility had been the Gurkha chiefship; but as Nepal lies on the southern slopes of the Himalayas, its population belongs, by blood and religion, for the most part to Hinduism. The second non-Indian state that challenged the British from beyond the Indian frontier was the kingdom of a people differing entirely from Indian races, the Burmese.

It is a remarkable coincidence that during the first fifty years occupied by the rise of England's dominion in India, other rulerships were being founded simultaneously, by a not dissimilar process, around her. In the course of that period (1757 - 1805) the tribes of Afghanistan had been collected into subjection to one kingdom under the dynasty of Ahmad Shah; the petty Hindu and Mohammedan chiefships of the Panjab had been welded into a military despotism by the strong hand of Ranjit Singh; and the rajas on the lower highlands of the Himalayas had submitted to the domination of Nepal. Lastly, about the time when Clive was subduing Bengal, a Burmese military leader had established by conquest a rulership which had its capital in the plains traversed by the Irawadi River and its principal affluents, from the upper waters of those rivers down to the sea.

The kingdom of Burma, founded in 1757 by Alompra's subjugation of Pegu, now included not only the open tracts about the Irawadi and the Salwin, extending from the hills out of which these rivers issue to the low-lying seacoast at their mouths, and stretching far southward down the eastern shores of the Bay of Bengal. It was absorbing all the mountainous region overhanging the eastern land frontier of India; and the Burmese armies were pressing westward across the watershed of those mountains through the upland country about the Brahmaputra toward the great alluvial plains of eastern Bengal. There had, consequently, been frequent disputes on that border between the

Anglo-Indian and the Burmese authorities, for the dividing-line was unsettled and variable, and on both sides the landmarks had been unavoidably set forward in pioneering fashion, until they were separated only by strips of semi-dependent tribal lands and spheres of influence, from which each party desired to exclude the other. It will be remembered that along all the

BURMESE WARRIORS.

ranges of the mountains that cut off the Indian plains from the rest of the Asiatic continent, there runs an unbroken fringe of rugged highlands, inhabited by tribes of mixed origin who are more or less warlike and independent.

On the northeast of Bengal lay the kingdom of Assam, with a territory, now part of the British province which bears that name, interposed between the English districts or protectorates and the Burmese dominion. There had been some sanguinary contests for power among princes of the reigning house, and among powerful ministers who aspired to rule absolutely in the name of one Assamese prince or another, with the inevitable result that the defeated party called in the Burmese from across the mountains eastward. Fresh troubles soon followed, for the king who had been reinstated by the Burmese troops soon quarrelled with them, finding, as usual, that a foreign army of occupation is an exceedingly dangerous remedy for civil war; and the Burmese, after putting several puppets up and down, brought matters to the ordinary conclusion by placing Assam under a governor of their own.

That a feeble and distracted semi-Hindu state on the Anglo-Indian frontier should thus be converted into a province of a warlike and aggressive Indo-Chinese kingdom was by no means to the advantage of the English, with whom it is always a first principle of politics to shut out all strange intruders into India from beyond the mountains or the sea. The Burmese now held the upper waters of that great navigable river, the Brahmaputra, and of other streams flowing from the Assam hills into the sea through Eastern Bengal; they were on the crests of the mountain passes leading into the lowlands, and they were subduing or intimidating all the petty chiefs along our frontier.

It has always been the practice of the English in India, as of other civilized empires in contact with barbarism, to maintain a zone of tribal lands and chiefships as a barrier or quickset hedge against trespassers upon their actual frontier by taking these chiefships or little border principalities under their protection. The Burmese were now violating this protectorate in a very menacing fashion. They were engaged in subduing all the northeast corner of India; they had taken Manipur, were making inroads into Cachar, then under British protection, and they had even claimed the British district of Sylhet. In fact they were breaking through all the natural barriers that fence off India by land from Eastern Asia, and were evidently seizing the issues or sally-ports available for sudden descent, whenever and however they might choose, upon the level plains of Bengal. They had seized, not without bloodshed, an island on the British side of the estuary which separated English territory from Arakan.

To be thus openly defied and attacked was a novelty for the English in India, but the Burmese, like the Gurkhas, having never measured themselves hitherto against civilized forces, saw no reason why they should not go on extending their dominion until they had palpably tested a neighbour's capacity to resist them. When regular hostilities began, there was some very sharp skirmishing on the Assam border, in which the British troops did not always come off victorious; but the despatch of a small army across the Bay of Bengal to attack Rangoon made an effective diversion, for, to a maritime enemy, this was the vulnerable side of the Burmese kingdom. The expedition sent by Lord Amherst, then Governor-General, to Pegu represents the first campaign undertaken by Anglo-Indian troops on the Asiatic continent beyond India. It ascended the course of the Irawadi; and the Burmese, after an obstinate defence, were compelled to submit to England's terms. This was a war that produced important and far-reaching consequences for Great Britain, because it carried our arms for the first time beyond the Indian frontier, extended our dominion into a totally different country, and subjected new Asiatic races to our sovereignty. The annexation of Arakan and the Tenasserim provinces placed in English hands almost all that part of the coast which fronts India across the Bay of Bengal, except the maritime province of Pegu, which includes the mouths of the Irawadi River, and which was not annexed until after the war of 1852; and it also threw Burma back over the watershed of the mountain range that runs parallel to this part of the sea-line.

We had now brought a large population, different from the Indians in origin, manners, language, and religion, within the jurisdiction of the Indian empire, and the expansive and levelling forces of European power had been set travelling in a fresh direction upon another line where we were destined to encounter just so much resistance as would compel us to advance by the mere act of overcoming it. A secondary but important consequence of the defeat of the Burmese was their recognition of our protectorate over upper Assam, Cachar, and Manipur, the tract beyond Bengal and along the Brahmaputra River which is now incorporated within the great northeastern Chief-Commissionership of Assam.

The acquisitions made by the Burmese war had thus effectually sealed up and secured the eastern Anglo-Indian frontier, as the Gurkha war had quieted the only state that could molest the British along the line of the northeastern Himalayas. When a usurper seized the Bhartpur chiefship in 1826, Lord Combermere took by assault the strong fortress of Bhartpur, before which Lord Lake had failed in 1805. Within India there were now actually only two sovereign powers, the English and the Sikhs; for the Amirs of Sind scarcely fell within the category of Indian rulers. Ranjit Singh, under whom the Sikh domination in the Panjab reached its climax early in the nineteenth century, had acquiesced, after some indications of hostility, in the policy of maintaining friendly relations with the British government. In 1809 he had consequently signed a treaty that confined his territory to the north and west of the Sutlaj River, with the exception of a strip of country on the south bank, in which he was bound not to place troops. This exception had important consequences later; but the broad line of demarcation between the two states

THE GOLDEN THRONE OF RANJIT SINGH.

was the river, and this arrangement preserved unbroken for nearly forty years the peace of the northern Anglo-Indian frontier.

The Governor-Generalship of Lord William Bentinck has the distinctive characteristic of representing a period of brief and rare tranquillity in Anglo-Indian history; it was an era of liberal and civilizing administration, of quiet material progress, and of some important moral and educational reforms. Lord Amherst, whom Lord Bentinck succeeded, had just closed a costly and troublesome Burmese war; and with Lord Auckland, who followed him, began the disastrous British campaigns in Afghanistan. Between Amherst and Auckland came an interval of calm rulership that was well employed in the work of domestic improvements and internal organization, favoured by the current of public opinion and political discussion in England. The liberal spirit which had accomplished the enfranchisement of Roman Catholics at home, and which was insisting on Parliamentary Reform, had to some extent influenced the views of Englishmen toward India. The expiration of the term of the East India Company's charter and the debate over its renewal had drawn attention to Indian affairs; and the act which was passed in 1833 to prolong the charter removed the last vestige of the Company's commercial monopoly, and finally completed the transformation of the old trading corporation into a special agency for the government of a vast Asiatic dependency.

It was Lord William Bentinck who issued, a few

months before his term of office expired, the resolution which finally decreed that English should be the official language of India. This important state paper is based on Macaulay's famous minute, in which he utterly routed the party that still held to the system of promoting learning and literature in India through the

LORD WILLIAM BENTINCK.

medium of Oriental languages. The controversy arose out of a question as to the distribution of educational grants from the public purse; and Macaulay argued victoriously in favour of English as the language which gives the key to all true knowledge, and as the only proper means of pursuing the higher studies. Lord William Bentinck thereupon issued orders, in accordance with Macaulay's view, that were received with some doubt and demur on their arrival in England.

It seems to have been James Mill, then an influential officer at the India House, who drafted a formidable censure upon Bentinck's proceedings, laying stress upon the impolicy of forcing upon the natives of India, by an abrupt reversal of educational policy, a superficial kind of English culture that would be used as a passport to public employ rather than as a channel for the acquisition of solid knowledge. Mill and Macaulay were old antagonists, and Macaulay evidently thought the Orientalists talked insufferable nonsense; nevertheless, it can hardly be said, on retrospection, that the weight of argument was altogether on his side. The letter appears never to have been issued; the higher education became almost exclusively English; and as all restrictive press laws were abolished very soon afterwards, the new policy soon produced important and far-reaching consequences.

But the chief title of this Governor-General to posthumous fame rests on the act which he had the courage to pass for putting an end to the burning of Indian widows.[1] In these days such a measure may appear obviously just and necessary; but in 1829 it was not adopted without much hesitation and many misgivings, for the real nature of public opinion on such subjects among the natives of India was then very imperfectly understood. The point at which law will be supported by natural morality in overruling superstitious sanctions is always difficult to discover; but we know that law and morality have a very complex interaction upon

[1] See the second chapter of the next volume.

each other, so that what the positive law refuses to tolerate often becomes immoral, and what morality condemns the law has to denounce. It may be guessed that inhuman or scandalous rites are never really popular, while it is certain that whenever a civil ordinance takes its stand upon an indisputable ethical basis, religion has to give way. The crime was prevalent chiefly among the docile and habitually submissive races of Lower Bengal, and the Governor-General rightly inferred that its peremptory suppression, far from involving political danger, would be accepted as a welcome liberation.

Of Lord William Bentinck's foreign policy there is not much to be said. He was the first—indeed, he has been the last—Governor-General in whose time unbroken peace has been given to British India, if we exclude the despatch of troops to put down local insurrections in Mysore and in Coorg. In the management of some troublesome business with Haidarabad and the Rajput states he could rely on the skill and experience of Sir Charles Metcalfe; and he adjusted with success the much more important question of English diplomatic relations with Ranjit Singh, the ruler of the Panjab. But his commercial treaty with Ranjit Singh and his convention with the Amirs of Sind for opening the Indus River to British commerce were, in point of fact, the preliminary steps that led the British, a few years later, out upon the wide and perilous field of Afghan politics. The possibility of the overland invasion of India and the question of the measures necessary for the security of the northwestern frontier were now occupying the minds of India's rulers; and the discussion was beginning that has never ended since.

Beyond the Panjab, on the farther side of the Afghan mountains, there were movements that were reviving the ever sensitive apprehensions of insecurity in India. The march of Russia across Asia, suspended by the Napoleonic wars, had latterly been resumed; her pressure was felt throughout all the central regions from the Caspian Sea to the Oxus; and by the treaty of Turkmantchai in 1828 she had established a preponderant influence over Persia. From that time forward our whole policy and all our strategic dispositions upon the northwest frontier have been directed toward anticipating or counteracting the movements or supposed intentions of Russia. To the English diplomatists of that day it seemed as if our original line of confederate defence had been drawn too widely, because Persia's discomfiture had proved that we had no means of upholding her integrity against Russian attack. So we negotiated in 1828 a release from our treaty obligations to aid Persia in resisting aggression, and we fell

ON THE NORTHERN INDIAN BORDER.

back upon Afghanistan as our defensible barrier. It followed that, as England receded, Russia pressed on, occupied the diplomatic ground that we had vacated, and converted the Persian power into an instrument for the furtherance of her own interests, which were not ours.

As Persia had just ceded to Russia some districts in the northwest, she was encouraged, by way of compensation, to revive a long-standing claim upon territory belonging to Afghanistan across her northeastern borders. In 1837, therefore, the Shah of Persia, who claimed Western Afghanistan as belonging of right to his crown, was preparing for an attack upon Herat, the chief frontier city of the Afghans on that side, and the key to all routes leading from Persia into India. Some of the leading Afghan Sirdars were in correspondence with the Persian king; and Shah Shuja', the hereditary prince, who had been driven out by a new Afghan dynasty, was an exile in the Panjab, whence he made unsuccessful attempts to recover his throne, soliciting aid both from the Sikhs and the English.

Shah Shuja' represented the legitimate line of descent from Ahmad Shah Abdali, who had created the Afghan kingdom, but a few years before this time his family had been supplanted by the sons of a powerful minister. This is a well-known form of dynastic changes in Asia, produced by the natural tendency of rulership to fall out of the hands of those who cannot keep it into the grasp of those who can. It will be remembered that the royal house of the Maratha empire had been evicted in the eighteenth century by a ministerial dynasty, the Peshwas; and in the nineteenth century a precisely similar revolution took place in Nepal.

The cardinal point of the whole Asiatic question was now becoming fixed in Afghanistan. From its situation, its natural strength, and its high strategic value, this country has been always a position of the greatest importance to the rulers of India, and the claims of Persia brought it prominently into the political foreground. The British government at home laid down the principle, big with momentous consequence, that the independence and integrity of Afghanistan were essential to the security of India; and missions from India had already explored the Indus and been received by the Amir Dost Mohammad at Kabul. When, therefore, the Shah of Persia in person, attended by some Russian officers, led an army against Herat in 1837, and when the Afghan Amir, disappointed in his hopes of an English alliance, was negotiating with a Russian agent, it will be easily understood that all the elements of alarm and mistrust drew speedily to a head. An English expedition to the Persian Gulf occupied the island of Kharak and made a demonstration against Southern Persia that was quite sufficient to provide the Shah with a good excuse for retiring from Herat, where his assault on the town had failed and where his supplies were scanty.

But the withdrawal from Herat by no means fulfilled views, now prevalent both in England and India, with regard to the British system of precautionary defence. In London the ministers had declared that " the welfare of our Eastern possessions require that we shall have on our western frontier an ally interested in resisting aggression, in the place of chiefs ranging themselves in subservience to a hostile power "; and they had pressed Lord Auckland to take decisive measures in Afghanistan. The Governor-General proceeded to conclude, with the full approbation of the English ministry, a tripartite treaty, by which the British government and Ranjit Singh covenanted with Shah Shuja‘ to reinstate him in Afghanistan by force of arms. Lord Auckland declared that the unsettled state of that country had produced " a crisis which imperiously demands the interference of the British government," and that he would continue to prosecute with vigour his measures for the substitution of a friendly for a hostile power in the eastern Afghan provinces, and for " the establishment of a permanent barrier against schemes of aggression on our northwest frontier." In 1838 a British army marched through Sind up to the Baluch passes to Kandahar, with the avowed object of expelling Dost Mohammad, the ruling Amir, and of restoring Shah Shuja‘ to his throne at Kabul.

This, then, was the position of the English dominion in India at the opening of Queen Victoria's memorable reign. The names of our earlier allies and enemies—the Nizam, Oudh, the Maratha princes, and the Mysore State—were still writ large on the map, but they had fallen far into the rear of our onward march; while in front of us were only Ranjit Singh, ruling the Panjab up to the Afghan hills, and the Sind Amirs in the Indus valley. The curtain was just rising upon the first act of the long drama of Central Asian politics,

THE RELIEF OF LUCKNOW BY SIR HENRY HAVELOCK.

not yet ended in our own time. What did this new departure imply? Not that we had any quarrel with the Afghans, from whom we were separated by the five rivers whose floods unite in the Indus. It meant that, after half a century's respite, the English believed themselves to be again in danger of contact with a rival European influence on Asiatic ground; and that, whereas in the previous century they had to fear such rivalry only on the seacoast, they now had certain notice of its gradual approach overland, from beyond the Oxus and the Paropamisus.

The story of the first British campaign in Afghanistan is well known. Shah Shuja' was easily replaced on the throne, and the English remained in military occupation of the country round Kabul and Kandahar for about two years. But the whole plan had been ill-conceived politically, and from a strategic point of view the expedition had been rash and dangerous. The base of British operations for this invasion of Afghanistan lay in Sind, a foreign state under rulers not well affected toward the English; while on our flank, commanding all the communications with India, lay the Panjab, another foreign state with a numerous army, watching our proceedings with vigilant jealousy. Such a position was in every way so untenable, and the advance movement was so obviously premature, that no one need wonder at the lamentable failure of our first attempt to extend the British protectorate beyond the limits of India.

The occupation of their country by a foreign army was profoundly resented by the free tribes of Afghanistan, whose patriotism equals their fanaticism, and who have always fought resolutely for their national independence. On his first reappearance among his countrymen Shah Shuja' was welcomed to some extent, but it was quite certain that whatever popularity might accrue to him as their ruler by birthright would rapidly decrease if his throne continued to be surrounded and supported by English troops; for the aphorism that one can do anything with bayonets except sit upon them has much truth even in Asia.

Probably the best course that could have been taken would have been to withdraw the British army, leaving Shah Shuja‘ to rely upon his personal influence, on the fact that he held possession, and on the disciplined local regiments that had been raised for his service. But Lord Auckland had proclaimed, as one main object of his expedition, the establishment of the integrity and independence of Afghanistan; and it was obvious that this was not to be made very sure by leaving Shah Shuja‘ in charge of the country. Yet this chance of success, though precarious, was really the only one, for the alternative was to prolong the military occupation of a mountainous region with a severe winter climate, where supplies are scarce and communications so difficult that combined operations from one centre are constantly interrupted, among a people who pass their lives in guerilla warfare.

This alternative, however, was unluckily adopted. Sir William Macnaghten, the chief political authority, had heard that the Russians were marching from Orenburg or Khiva, and that Dost Mohammad, the Amir whom the British had expelled, was hovering about the northern provinces, while the outlying districts were still unruly. Macnaghten accordingly determined to consolidate the Shah's government before he retired.

But the attempt to raise a kind of standing army for the Amir stirred up fatal jealousies among all the powerful chiefs of the Afghan clans, who, like feudal nobles and free folk everywhere, defer to a king, but detest a master. Disaffection grew and spread, until, in 1841, partial revolts and local risings culminated in universal insurrection. The supplies of the English troops ran short; they had been wearied out by incessant skirmishing; they were under an incapable commander; their outposts were besieged or cut off; and Macnaghten, hoping vainly for a turn of fortune, delayed evacuation of Kabul until the winter had set in. Then, when retreat became inevitable, a series of inconceivable blunders led to the destruction of the whole British force in their passage through the defiles between Kabul and Jalalabad. Nevertheless, the fort at the latter place was gallantly held until it was relieved, in the autumn of 1842, by General Pollock, who marched up to Kabul and re-occupied the city; while at Kandahar General Nott baffled all the attempts of the Afghans to dislodge him.

But in 1841 the Whig ministry, who were the authors of the policy of intervention in Afghanistan, had been displaced, and early in 1842 Lord Ellenborough succeeded Lord Auckland as Governor-General. He issued orders at once for the withdrawal of all British troops from Kandahar and Jalalabad; nor would the British government have escaped the discredit of a hasty and somewhat dishonourable retirement if the military commanders had not taken upon themselves the responsibility of bolder measures. By the end of 1842, nevertheless, all the English forces had been quietly brought away. Dost Mohammad had been restored to power in Kabul, the country had been evacuated, and the policy of bringing Afghanistan within the sphere of British influence, which was now definitely abandoned, lay dormant until it was successfully revived, under very different conditions, nearly forty years afterward.

In 1839 the territory of the Amirs of Sind, in the valley of the Indus, had been brought within the political control of the British by Lord Auckland, who needed it as a stepping-stone and as a basis for his operations toward South Afghanistan. The port of Karachi, near the Indus mouth, had been seized, and the river had been thrown open to British commerce. When Lord Ellenborough determined to retire from Afghanistan, he was very reluctant to give up the valuable position that we had taken up in Sind; he desired, on the contrary, to acquire permanent possession of the stations that our troops had occupied temporarily, and he took advantage of delay in the payment of tribute to press for territorial cessions. Sir Charles Napier, who had been sent to Sind as a congenial representative of demands that were likely to produce war, submitted to the Governor-General a memorandum arguing that, while we were bound to insist on the rigid observance of treaties, yet such strict punctilio would confine us permanently within the limits of the stations which the treaty assigned to us, and would thus prevent us from interposing for the general good of the Sind people. "Is it possible," he asked, "that such a state of things can long continue?" and "if this reasoning is correct, would it not be better to come to results at once," by annexing the places which we now hold temporarily? Proceeding to consider "how we might go to work in a matter so critical," he enclosed a memorandum of five cases in which the Amirs "seemed to have departed from the terms or spirit of their engagements," and he urged that it would not be harsh, but on the contrary humane, to coerce them into ceding the places required.

SIR CHARLES NAPIER.

Accordingly, Sir Charles Napier was empowered by Lord Ellenborough to press upon the Sind rulers a new treaty, framed on the basis of exchanging tribute for territory. The Amirs signed it, but mustered their troops and attacked the British Residency at their capital; whereupon Sir Charles Napier marched into their country and gained a decisive victory over their army at Miani in February, 1843. The results were the deposition of the Sind Amirs, and the transfer of the lower Indus valley to the British dominion, whereby we obtained possession of Karachi and the Indus estuary and brought the whole unbroken circuit of the Indian seacoast within our control. In 1844, however, Lord Ellenborough's administration was terminated by his recall, and he was succeeded by Sir Henry Hardinge.

In the meantime, from the date of Ranjit Singh's death in 1839, the Sikh government of the Panjab, which had lasted barely thirty years, had been rapidly falling into dilapidation. One chief after another had assumed the administration and had been overthrown or assassinated. In Asia a new kingdom is almost always founded by some able leader with a genius for military organization, who can raise and command an effective army, which he employs not only to beat rivals in the field but also to break down all minor chiefships, to disarm every kind of possible opposition within his borders, and generally to level every barrier that might limit his personal authority. But he who thus sweeps away all means of resistance leaves himself no supports, for support implies the capacity to resist; and the very strength and keenness of the military instrument that he has forged renders it doubly dangerous to his successors. If the next ruler's heart or hand fail him, there is no longer any counterpoise to the overpowering weight of the sword in the political balance, and the state of the dynasty is upset.

The Sikh dominion had been established in the spirit of religious brotherhood and revolt against Mohammedan oppression; and while such popular, almost democratic forces were immensely strong when condensed

THE BATTLE OF MIANI, AT WHICH NAPIER DEFEATED THE AMIRS (FEB. 17, 1843).

into driving power for a well-handled military despotism, they were certain to become ungovernable and to explode if any error or weakness were shown in guiding the machine. None of Ranjit Singh's sons, real or reputed, had inherited his talents, nor could they manage the fierce soldiery with whom he had conquered the Panjab, driven the Afghans back across the Indus into their mountains, and annexed Kashmir. His eldest and authentic son, Kharrak Singh, died within a year; his reputed son, Sher Singh, the last who endeavoured to maintain his father's policy of friendship with the British, was soon murdered with his son and the prime minister. The chiefs and ministers who endeavoured to govern after Sher Singh's death were removed by internecine strife, mutinous outbreaks, and assassinations.

The Sikh state was on the verge of dissolution by anarchy, for all power had passed into the hands of committees of regimental officers appointed by an army that was wild with religious ardour, and furiously suspicious of its own government. The queen-mother, Ranjit Singh's widow, and her infant son Dhulip Singh were recognized as nominal representatives of the reigning house; but they were liable at any moment to be consumed by the next eruption of sanguinary caprice, and their only hope of preservation lay in finding some outlet abroad for the forces which had reduced the Sikh state to violent internal anarchy. For this purpose it was manifestly their interest to launch their turbulent army across the Sutlaj against the English, and thus provoke a collision that would certainly weaken and probably destroy it. The military leaders were not blind to the motives with which they were encouraged to march upon the English frontier; but their patriotism had been excited by rumours of the advance of the British army, for Sir Henry Hardinge, the Governor-General, fearing some disorderly inroad, was bringing up troops to reinforce his outposts. There had also been some inopportune frontier disputes, which had embittered the Lahore government, not altogether unreasonably, against the English.

When, therefore, the Sikh soldiers were taunted with questions whether they would tamely submit to European domination, they answered by crossing the Sutlaj River, which was the strategical frontier, and intrenched themselves on the southeastern bank, in territory, which, though it belonged to Lahore, the Lahore government was bound by treaty not to enter with any considerable armed force. This was taken to be an act of war, and in December, 1845, the Sikhs were met by the British army. On our side the preparations were incomplete; for we had undervalued both the strength and the activity of the enemy; and we had been so long accustomed to easy victories on the open plains of India that the resolute defence of their field-intrenchments made by the Sikhs, and their well-served artillery, took us by surprise.

In the first battle, at Mudki on December 18, 1845, we paid dearly for our success; and three days later, at Firozshah, began the most bloody and obstinate con-

THE BATTLE OF MUDKI, AT WHICH HARDINGE DEFEATED THE SIKHS (DEC. 18, 1845).

test ever fought by Anglo-Indian troops, at the end of which the English army was left in bare possession of its camping-ground, and in a situation of imminent peril from the approach of the Sikh reserves under Tej Singh. But the English maintained a bold front; Tej Singh retired; and in the two battles that followed at Aliwal and Sobraon—the latter fought on February 10, 1846 — the Sikhs, fighting hardily and fiercely, were driven back across the Sutlaj and compelled to abandon further resistance in the field. The Governor-General occupied Lahore in February, 1846, with twenty thousand men; Ranjit Singh's infant son was placed on the throne under English tutelage; some cessions of territory were exacted; the Sikh army was reduced; and for two years the Panjab was administered as a state under the general superintendence and protection of the British government.

But the expedient of placing the machinery of native government under temporary European superintendence can succeed only when the irresistible authority of the superintending power is universally felt and recognized. The system is unstable because it does not pretend to permanence; it lacks the direct and weighty pressure required to keep down the smouldering elements of military revolt. Although the Sikhs numbered not more than one-sixth of the population of the Panjab, they were united by the recollection of rulership; and the fighting men, who were justly proud of having played an even match against the English, were not yet inclined to settle down again to peaceful agriculture. At the Lahore court intrigue and jealousies prevailed; and in the outlying districts there was more than one focus of discontent.

The assassination of two British officers at Multan in April, 1848, was the signal for an insurrection that led to a general rising of the military classes, a reassemblage of the old *Khālsa* Sikh army, and a second trial of strength with the British troops. In January, 1849, the English general, who displayed very little tactical skill, lost twenty-four hundred men and officers before he won the day at Chilianwala; but in the following month the Sikh army, after a stubborn combat, was at last overthrown by so shattering a defeat at Gujarat that the English were left undisputed masters of the whole country.

These transactions followed the natural course of events and consequences. Contact had produced collision, and collision had terminated in the overthrow of an unstable and distracted government. The English had thus been compelled to break down with their own hands the very serviceable barrier against inroads from Central Asia that had been set up for them by the Sikhs fifty years earlier in North India. It was impossible for the British to leave the country vacant and exposed to an influx of foreign Mohammedans; and it had become a matter of growing importance that England should have the gates of India in her own custody; for the line of Russian advance toward the Oxus, though distant, was declared; and in the last war the Afghans had joined the Sikhs as auxiliaries.

THE BATTLE OF ALIWAL, IN WHICH SMITH WAS VICTORIOUS OVER THE SIKHS (JAN. 28, 1846)

That Lord Dalhousie, who was Governor-General from 1848 to 1856, determined, after mature deliberation, against renewing the precarious experiment of a protected native rulership in the Panjab, must now be acknowledged to have been fortunate; for if there had been a great independent state across the Sutlaj when the Anglo-Indian sepoys revolted, eight years later, the Sikhs might have found the opportunity difficult to resist. Before the commencement of hostilities with the British in 1845 they had made several attempts to shake the loyalty of the native army; nor had the spectacle of the Sikh soldiery overawing their government and dictating their own rate of pay been absolutely lost upon all the British sepoy regiments. The Governor-General's proclamation of 1849, annexing the Panjab to the British crown, carried England's territorial frontier across the Indus right up to the base of the Afghan hills, finally extinguished the long rivalship of the native Indian powers, and absorbed under British sovereignty the last kingdom that remained outside the pale of the Anglo-Indian empire.

After this manner, therefore, and with the full concurrence of the English nation as expressed through its Parliament, successive Governors-General have pushed on during the nineteenth century by forced marches to complete dominion in India, fulfilling Lord Clive's prophecy and disproving his forebodings. The long resistance to universal British supremacy culminated and ended in the bloody but decisive campaigns against the Sikh army. Henceforward all English campaigns against Asiatic powers were to be outside and around India; for the consolidation of the British empire as a state of first-class magnitude, extending from the sea to the mountains, disturbed all neighbouring rulerships

FINDING THE COLOURS OF THE 24TH REGIMENT AFTER THE BATTLE OF CHILIANWALA (JAN. 13, 1849).

within the wide orbit of its attraction, and affected the whole political system of Asia.

Lord Dalhousie had scarcely reduced the Panjab and planted the British standard at Peshawar, when he became involved in disputes with the Burmese kingdom which led to an important annexation of territory in the southeast. The government of Burma, which has always been as obstinate and foolhardy in its dealings with foreigners as the Chinese have been far-seeing and comparatively temperate, refused either apology or indemnity for the injurious treatment of British subjects by its officers. Yet the Burmese war of 1826 ought to have convinced less intelligent rulers that they were at the mercy of a strong maritime power in the Bay of Bengal, which could occupy their whole seaboard, blockade their only outlets, and penetrate inland up the Irawadi River. These steps, in fact, the Governor-General found himself compelled to take, with the result that Pegu, a country inhabited by a race that the Burmese had subdued, easily fell into British hands, and was retained when the Burmese armies had been defeated and driven out, its annexation being officially proclaimed December 20, 1852.

This conquest made the British possessions continuous along the eastern shores of the Bay of Bengal, and once more placed the English in a position of the kind which seems to have been peculiarly favourable everywhere to the expansion of dominion. The possession of a flat and fertile deltaic province at the outflow of a great river, whether in Asia or in Africa, enables a maritime power to settle itself securely on the land with a base on the sea; it gives control of a great artery of commerce, and provides an easy waterway inland. With these advantages, especially as the people of such a province are usually industrious and unwarlike, an enterprising intruder is easily carried up-stream by the course of events, and to this general rule British progress in Burma certainly affords no exception. As the

English settlement at Calcutta, upon the Ganges estuary, led to the conquest of Bengal; as the occupation of Karachi near the Indus was followed by the taking of Sind; and as the British position at Cairo necessitates a frontier in Upper Egypt, so the planting of a new British capital at Rangoon, near the mouth of

THE FORT AND HARBOUR OF KARACHI.

the Irawadi, was a first step toward a march up the river to Mandalay.

Having conquered two provinces on two diametrically opposite frontiers of the empire, Lord Dalhousie turned his attention to the interior. When the power of the Maratha Peshwas was extinguished in 1818, the titular Maratha king, Sivaji's descendant, had been released from his state prison, and the principality of Satara had been conferred on him by Lord Hastings. In 1848, on the death of his successor without heirs, Lord Dalhousie refused to sanction the adoption of an heir. He laid down the principle that the British government is bound in duty as well as in policy to take possession of a subordinate state that has clearly and indubitably lapsed to the sovereignty by total failure of heirs natural, unless there should be some strong reason to the contrary. Satara was accordingly absorbed; Jhansi followed in 1853; and in 1854 came the lapse of Nagpur, when Lord Dalhousie emphatically declared that "unless I believed the prosperity and the happiness of its inhabitants would be promoted by their being placed permanently under British rule, no other advantage which could arise out of the measure would move me to propose it."

There has never been any doubt about the recognized principle of public policy, based on long usage and tradition, that no Indian principality can pass to an adopted heir without the assent and confirmation of the paramount English government. Lord Dalhousie did not deny that succession might pass by adoption, but he claimed and exercised the prerogative of refusing assent, on grounds of political expediency, in the case of states which, either as the virtual creation of the British government, or from their former position, stood to that government in the relation of subordinate or dependent principalities. And if he withheld assent, the state underwent incorporation into British territory by lapse. Nothing, thought the Governor-General, could be more fortunate for the subjects of a native dynasty than its extinction by this kind of political euthanasia.

It may be worth while to add here that this doctrine of lapse is now practically obsolete, having been superseded by the formal recognition, in Lord Canning's Governor-Generalship, of the right of ruling chiefs to adopt successors, on the failure of heirs natural, according to the laws or customs of their religion, their race, or their family, so long as they are loyal to the crown and faithful to their engagements. The extent to which confidence has been restored by this edict is shown by the curious fact that since its promulgation a childless ruler very rarely adopts in his own lifetime. An heir presumptive, who knows that he is to succeed and may possibly grow impatient if his inheritance is delayed, is not desired by politic princes for various obscure reasons; so that the duty of nominating a successor is often left to the widows, who know their husband's mind and have every reason for wishing him long life.

The Panjab and Pegu were conquests of war; the states of Satara, Jhansi, and Nagpur had fallen in by lapse. The kingdom of Oudh is the only great Indian state of which its ruler has been dispossessed upon the ground of intolerable misgovernment. At the beginning of the nineteenth century the vizir pledged himself by a treaty made with Lord Wellesley to establish such a system of administration as would be conducive to the prosperity of his subjects; and it was also agreed that the vizir would always advise with and act in conformity with the counsel of the Company's officers. These pledges had been so entirely and continuously neglected that the whole of Oudh had fallen into constantly increasing confusion, until it subsided into violent disorder, tumults, brigandage, and widespread oppression of the people.

In fact, the kingdom was sustained artificially under a series of incapable rulers only by the external pressure of the British dominions surrounding it, and by the presence of a subsidiary British force at the capital. The formal and even menacing warnings sent from time to time by the Governors-General to the Oudh government were as ineffectual as such intimations usually are when addressed to persons without strength or inclination to profit by them. It was impossible that the support of British troops stationed within the country could continue to be given to such a régime, while to withdraw those troops and disown all responsibility would only have let loose anarchy. And as the alternative of the temporary sequestration of the king's authority was rejected, on deliberation, as a dangerous half-measure, the British government determined to assume the administration and to vest the territories of Oudh in the East India Company. This was done by proclamation in February, 1856; and before the end of that month Lord Dalhousie made over the Governor-Generalship to Lord Canning.

The British empire seemed now to have reached its zenith of peace, power, and prosperity, for the territory under its direct government had been very greatly enlarged, its frontier line had crossed the Indus on the northwest and the Irawadi on the southeast, and throughout all this vast dominion law and order appeared to prevail. But those peculiar symptoms of unrest, which Shakespeare calls the cankers of a calm world, are still in Asia (as formerly in Europe) the natural sequel of a protracted war time, when the total cessation of fighting and the general pacification of the whole country leave an insubordinate mercenary army idle and restless.

From 1838 to 1848 hostilities had been intermittent

THE CHARGE OF THE HIGHLANDERS BEFORE CAWNPUR, UNDER GENERAL HAVELOCK.

but incessantly recurring; the sepoys had been in the field against the Afghans, the Baluchis of Sind, the Maratha insurgents of Gwalior, and the Sikhs of the Panjab; and in 1852 they were engaged in the second expedition against the Burmese. Except in the calamitous retreat from Kabul in 1841 - 1842, where a whole division was lost, the Anglo-Indian troops had been constantly victorious; but in Asia a triumphant army, like the Janissaries or the Mamluks, almost always becomes ungovernable so soon as it becomes stationary.

The sepoys of the Bengal army imagined that all India was at their feet, while in 1856 the annexation of Oudh, which was the province that furnished that army with most of its high caste recruits, touched their pride and affected their interests. When, therefore, the greased cartridges roused their caste prejudices, they turned savagely against their English officers and broke out into murderous mutiny.

In suppressing the wild fanatic outbreak of 1857 the British were compelled to sweep away the last shadows, that had long lost substance, of names and figures once illustrious and formidable in India. The phantom of a Moghul emperor and his court vanished from Delhi; the last pretender to the honours of the Maratha Peshwa disappeared from Cawnpur; and the direct government of all Anglo-Indian territory passed from the Company to the crown in 1858. The supremacy of that government now stands uncontested, in opinion and sentiment as well as in fact, throughout the whole dominion. The extinction of the last vestige of dynastic opposition or rivalry has been the signal for the beginning of a modern phase of political life, for the complete recognition of the British dominion in India, and for the formation within the state of parties which, however they may differ in administrative views, aspirations, and aims, are agreed in the principle of loyalty to the English crown.

CHAPTER XVIII

INDIA UNDER THE CROWN

1858 - 1907

IN the foregoing chapters an attempt has been made to sketch in outline the gradual expansion of our territorial possessions in India, from the time when the rapid disintegration of the Moghul empire had left the whole country in political confusion, up to the complete establishment over it of the British dominion. During about one hundred years, from the middle of the eighteenth century, the English had been occupied in subduing rivals for power, in pacifying and reuniting the scattered provinces under their sovereignty. Whatever may be, in the western world, the proper division between ancient and modern history, it is safe to affirm that the dividing line between ancient and modern India is marked everywhere by the date at which each province or kingdom fell under British dominion. But if it were necessary to draw a single line for India as a whole, the epoch that might be taken would be the assumption by Queen Victoria of the direct government of India under the Crown, in 1858. The vibration caused by the shock of the mutiny of the Bengal sepoys had not entirely ceased before 1860, but the heat of that violent conflagration fused all the elements of further disaffection and welded together the different parts of the empire into compact unity. Its extinction terminated the long series of wars within India, and has been followed by fifty years of internal tranquillity.

The Queen's Proclamation, announcing that the administration of India had passed from the East India Company to the Crown, confirmed all the treaties and engagements made with the native princes, strictly prohibited interference with the religious beliefs of her Majesty's Indian subjects, and desired that, so far as might be, all her subjects should be freely and impartially admitted to offices in her service. Under such auspices the work of pacification and reform went on rapidly. Oudh, annexed in 1856, quieted down after two years of agitation; the great landholders were disarmed and conciliated by a favourable revenue settlement. In the Panjab, where the Sikhs in large numbers had taken service in the British army and had fought with great spirit against the mutineers, Sir John Lawrence's energetic and sagacious administration had reconciled all classes to the new rulership. The last titular representative of the old dynasty had scarcely disappeared

SIR JOHN LAWRENCE.

from his palace at Delhi when a new monarchy was inaugurated, and the political reconstruction of the fragments of the Moghul empire was consolidated by a series of edicts and statutes. For British India, the territory under our immediate government, the narrative of this period is comparatively uneventful – it records internal affairs and administrative progress. But some account of external affairs must be given; first, in regard to the native chiefships whose lands, though not British territory, are enclosed within British India, and secondly, in regard to events and transactions, some of them of great importance, in the adjacent countries outside the external limits of our territorial jurisdiction.

The policy, inaugurated by Lord Wellesley's subsidiary treaties, and continued by his successors, of bringing all the native states of India into subordinate relation with the British sovereignty, has already been briefly described. Under this system the supreme government has undertaken their protection and defence, arbitrates in any disputes among them, determines all claims to succeed to the rulership, maintains the chief's legitimate authority against revolt, and interferes with their internal affairs in cases of serious abuse of power or grave disorder. In 1860 Lord Canning conveyed to all these chiefs the assurance of the Queen's desire that their rulership should be perpetuated, and that, accordingly, adoption of successors made in accordance with the law and custom of their families would be recognized and confirmed. The effect of this declaration was to regulate and define the succession upon a fixed principle of public policy, and above all to convince the ruling chiefs that in future no annexation, upon default of heirs, of their territories was to be feared.

The area occupied, in the aggregate, by these states is at present about 650,000 square miles, with a population of some 66 millions. They vary in size from Haidarabad, with a population of 11½ millions, to petty chiefships containing less than 1000 inhabitants; they represent for the most part, as has been said, the territorial possessions or estates acquired by force and the fortune of war after the dilapidation of the Moghul empire, or the hereditary possessions of chiefs who survived that period of general confusion, and were preserved by the establishment of British supremacy.

The internal tranquillity of these chiefships, from 1860 up to the present time, has left few events worthy of record. The British government has indeed been obliged to interpose occasionally to punish the serious or criminal misconduct of individual chiefs and to determine authoritatively on the conflicting claims to succession. The presence, at the capitals of the larger protected states, of subsidiary British troops is not only a guarantee of a ruler's rights, but also of his duties toward his subjects. Where succession to the chiefship has been disputed or doubtful, the British government has been frequently required to arbitrate between conflicting claims; occasionally to put down revolt; and in rare instances to punish acts of excessive or criminal misconduct committed by a chief or his ministers. In illustration of the use made of this prerogative of interposition, two cases of unusual gravity may be noticed. In 1876 the Gaikwar of Baroda, who had been tried before a Commission for complicity in an attempt against the life of the British Resident, and who was convicted of gross maladministration, was formally deposed and removed to a place of detention. And in 1891, the Maharaja of Manipur, a small state on the eastern frontier of Bengal, took refuge in British India from a military revolt, headed by his brothers. When the Chief Commissioner of Assam proceeded to make an inquiry into the affair, and to take measures for suppressing the disorder, he was enticed to a conference and treacherously murdered, with some of his officers, within the town of Manipur. A British force was despatched, which occupied the state for a time, until those concerned in the assassination had been punished. The Maharaja had abdicated; and since his incapacity was proved beyond doubt, he was replaced by another representative of the reigning family.

An important addition has been made to the list of these self-governing principalities by the revival of the State of Mysore, in southern India. In the fourteenth chapter[1] brief reference has been made to its previous history. The territory had been forcibly seized by Hyder Ali, and reconquered from Tippu Sultan by Lord Wellesley,[2] when part of it was restored to the old

[1] See pages 309–310. [2] At that time known as Lord Mornington.

Hindu dynasty. But in 1831 the Indian government had been obliged to assume the administration, and retained it for fifty years. In 1881, however, the state was reconstituted under the rule of the descendant of the ancient Hindu family from whom it had been taken nearly a century earlier, under conditions that provided for the acknowledgment of the British sovereignty, and for the welfare of the Mysore people. These conditions have been faithfully observed, and this just and politic action of the British government was appreciated by all the native chiefs throughout India as a confirmation of the declared intention to uphold their territorial independence.

But while our relations with the feudatory states lying inside the external frontiers of India have been successfully maintained and strengthened, the course of affairs beyond those frontiers has been complicated by important events and their consequences. Our annexation of the Panjab in 1849 had extended the dominion up to the skirts of the Afghan mountains, and had thereby brought our border into immediate contact with the highlands inhabited by warlike tribes, who had been accustomed for ages to make plundering raids upon the plains below. For the protection of our own districts, and for the punishment of intolerable brigandage, many expeditions into these highlands had been made, but with little or no permanent effect upon intractable barbarians. In 1863 it became necessary to dispatch a strong force into the hills overhanging the Peshawar valley against a settlement of fanatic Mohammedans who had been keeping the whole border-side in alarm by their plundering incursions, which the adjoining tribes were encouraged by their example to join. At the Umbeyla Pass the British commander, finding himself confronted by a combination of all the neighbouring clans, was obliged to take up a defensive position, where he was fiercely assailed, and the force was for a short time in considerable jeopardy. The predicament was serious, for a reverse might have been followed by a general rising of the tribes to break in over the frontier into British territory. Some hard fighting ensued, until reinforcements came up, when, after the enemy had suffered severe loss, their leaders submitted to terms, the stronghold of the fanatics was demolished, and their gathering effectively dispersed.

This expedition, known as the Umbeyla campaign, was one of the most hazardous and difficult of the forays and petty wars provoked by the tribes on the northwestern frontier; and the brief notice of it that has been here given may serve to illustrate the state of unrest and insecurity that has ensued whenever the British Government has resolved to set bounds to its territorial expansion, to stop short, draw a line, and abstain from all interference with the affairs of the country beyond it. Just as, in many parts of Asia, cultivation ceases abruptly at the farthest point reached by artificial irrigation in a desert tract, so primitive barbarism may exist just outside the edge of settled civilization; and the situation on the northwest frontier of India exhibits this sharp contrast of social and political conditions. It would be a costly and difficult operation to extend administrative control over this tribal zone, yet no other effective remedy of chronic disorder has hitherto been discovered, and the problem still awaits solution.

The war with Bhotan, in 1864, was forced upon the British government by similar causes and circumstances. Bhotan is a small state within the exterior ranges of the Himalayan mountains, lying east of Nepal, inhabited by a poor and ignorant people, accustomed to make predatory incursions into the province of Bengal. In one of these raids some British subjects had been carried off into captivity by the Bhotias, and a mission had been dispatched to the capital of the state with instructions to demand their release; but the request was contemptuously rejected, and the envoy was treated with gross insolence and threats of personal violence. It became necessary to send an armed force into the country to exact reparation and to rescue the captives. The troops, at first unskilfully handled in a region of hills and jungles, suffered a reverse which compelled them to retreat in some confusion; but the Bhotias anticipated a fresh advance in greater strength by submitting to terms which imposed upon them the penalty of ceding a strip of lands along the base of the Himalayas; and they have since given no further provocation. As Bhotan is under a ruler with some general authority recognized over a definite area, it was easier to effect some durable settlement with him than in the case of the ungovernable tribes in the Northwest.

Baluchistan, the country of the Baluch clans, lies along the western border of the Panjab and Sind, extending down to the Arabian Sea; it is under the nominal authority or hegemony of a chief, whose headquarters are at Kelat; but his power was insufficient to restrain the turbulent leaders of the rival clans, who were in constant rebellion against him, and the British border was continually troubled by their brigandage. In 1876, when Lord Lytton was Viceroy, Major Sandeman was deputed to mediate between the Khan and the chiefs, and to arrange for the freedom of trade routes and the general pacification of the border. He succeeded in negotiating a treaty by which the Khan acknowledged the influence and paramount overlordship of the British government in Baluchistan, in exchange for protection and support. The subordinate chiefs willingly accepted a settlement that put an end to incessant civil war, faction fighting, and misrule; and from that time the country has rapidly quieted down, until at the present moment the authority of the British representative is virtually exercised in Baluchistan up to the confines of Persia on the west, and the administration is conducted under his direction and guidance. The passes leading up from India were opened and guarded, and a garrison of native troops was posted at Quetta, not far from the frontier that divides the Baluch territory from southern Afghanistan, on the road toward Kandahar. The importance of this advanced position and of opening the communication in its rear through the Bolan Pass into India, was almost immediately demonstrated.

MOUNTAIN PASSES NEAR QUETTA IN BALUCHISTAN.

It is impossible, within the limits of this chapter, to recount in detail the incidents and transactions that preceded and led up to the Afghan war of 1878 - 1881. They were intimately connected with the larger spheres of war and diplomacy in Europe, and with the attitude of Russia in Central Asia.

When British India had expanded to its geographical limits, from the sea-shore to the mountains, it might have been expected that our record of warfare in Asia was closing. Our command of the sea was unchallenged, and landward no country has stronger natural fortifications. But in the history of Asia during the latter half of the nineteenth century, the dominant element has been the increasing spread of European ascendency, creating a general sense of political instability. For all the kingdoms of Asia felt the growing pressure of formidable neighbours, while the European powers were striving to hold each other at arm's length, and watching with jealous apprehension the gradual approximation of their respective frontiers. On the Asiatic continent the British dominion seemed at last to have reached its appointed limits at the base of the Afghan mountains; but Russia's advance through Central Asia was acquiring increased momentum in proportion to the mass of her conquests, and she was rapidly increasing her dominion. For manifest reasons of policy and strategy the English, who desire to keep other European powers at a distance, insist on reserving a preponderating influence in the countries marching with their own territory, and allow no foreign interference with them. Toward the end of the nineteenth century, therefore, the British government was watching, with redoubled attention, the approach of Russia in the direction of the Oxus River and the northwestern provinces of the Afghan kingdom.

By the subjugation of Khiva the Russian outposts had been brought much nearer to the Afghan frontier, and the attempt of the English Cabinet to check this movement by negotiations had elicited little more than vague assurances from St. Petersburg. In 1873, however, the Russian emperor declared Afghanistan to be completely outside the sphere within which Russian influence might be exercised; and the boundary-line of that kingdom had been partially defined by diplomatic agreement. The whole policy, therefore, of British statesmen at this time was directed upon the object of securing the independence and integrity of Afghanistan. And the record of Indian foreign affairs during the period with which we are now concerned exhibits a series of discussions and ineffectual negotiations, until out of the gathering cloud of misunderstandings and the pressure of events, an Afghan war was suddenly precipitated in 1878. When, in 1868, the Amir of Afghanistan, Sher Ali, had mastered the whole of this country after a long and fiercely contested war for succession to the throne, the situation of his state between two powerful European empires filled him with anxiety, and he turned to India for alliance and material support. In 1869 he paid a visit to Lord Mayo, then Viceroy, at Umballa, where he was received with much ceremony, with large presents of arms and money, and with many friendly assurances. But the Amir desired a formal treaty and a fixed subsidy, which Lord Mayo was not authorized to grant, so that the conference ended without any settlement on the substantial basis of an alliance. In 1873, when negotiations were renewed, Lord Northbrook proposed to accord to Sher Ali a guarantee against foreign aggression, but sanction was refused by the ministry at home, and to this disappointment, with other grievances, may be ascribed the distrust and resentment which Sher Ali displayed in his subsequent dealings with the British government.

In 1876, however, the English ministry had become convinced that it was necessary to secure closer and more definite relations with the Amir; and Lord Lytton, on his appointment to the Viceroyalty, took out with him to India instructions to carry out this policy. His first step was to propose sending a mission to Kabul, but this overture was so unfavourably received by the Amir that, after some abortive negotiations, it was abandoned, not without friction and estrangement on both sides. In 1877 came the war between Russia and Turkey, and in 1878, when the Russian army was before Constantinople, the British government prepared for armed intervention by sending Indian troops to Malta. The Russians replied by a counter-move; they pushed forward a detachment from their army in Central Asia towards the Afghan frontier; and a Russian envoy arrived at Kabul, who proceeded to draw up a treaty of alliance with the Amir. The Viceroy of India retaliated by a demand for the immediate admission of a British envoy at Kabul; but Sir Neville Chamberlain's mission was forcibly turned back at the Afghan outposts, whereupon an ultimatum, insisting upon the reception of a British envoy, and requiring a reply by a fixed date, was dispatched to the Amir. By that date no reply came, so war was declared in November, 1878, and three columns of troops entered Afghanistan from different points. The column which advanced from the south by Quetta occupied Kandahar almost without opposition; the two northern columns threatened Kabul from Kuram and Jalalabad; and when General Roberts had dispersed the Afghan troops at the Peiwar Kotal, the Amir, leaving Kabul, took refuge in his upper provinces near the Oxus, whence he appealed for succour to the Russian authorities in Transcaspia. But the interest of Russia in his affairs had ceased with the signature of the Berlin treaty; he was advised to make peace with the British government, and early in 1879 he died in great distress. His son, Yakub Khan, offered to negotiate for the cessation of hostilities, conditionally upon his own recognition, with British support, as successor to the Amirship. After considerable discussion, the treaty of Gandamak was concluded with him, whereby he ceded certain outlying tracts that would facilitate our command of the routes leading into Afghanistan, and agreed to receive a British envoy at Kabul. To this post Sir Louis Cavagnari was deputed in July, 1879.

But the whole country had been thrown into confusion by the war, and the death of the Amir Sher Ali had left it without a ruler. Yakub Khan had neither the experience nor the strength of character required for the mastery of such a situation; his troops were unpaid and mutinous; and his influence was slight over a fierce, indomitable people, whose inveterate hatred of foreigners was intensified by the presence of a British officer at Kabul. The whole fabric of our arrangements with Afghanistan, as it had been built up on the treaty of Gandamak, depended on the envoy's personal safety. Within three months his assassination brought it down with a terrible crash; and thus, while during the first period of the war we had been engaged in fighting the Amir Sher Ali, in the second we found ourselves involved in the much more arduous task of fighting the Afghan people. Immediately upon receipt of the news that Cavagnari, with all his escort, had been murdered, the war was renewed. Kabul was captured by a rapid and daring march of Sir Frederick Roberts upon the capital; Kandahar, which Sir Donald Stewart had just evacuated, was reoccupied; but although we managed to retain a firm military hold on these two important points, the Indian government was now confronted by a most awkward dilemma. The attempt to subdue and pacify the whole country was beyond our power, and had never been contemplated by our policy, while, if we withdrew our garrisons, Afghanistan would have been left to masterless anarchy, and the war would have been waged to no purpose. The armed tribes, believing that the subjugation of

Afghanistan was intended, broke out into insurrection around Kabul, and in December, 1879, they combined for a resolute assault upon the British intrenchments outside the city. Their defeat, after some very sharp fighting, quieted the surrounding districts for the time, and communications with India were reopened; but the manifest interest of the British government was to make over Afghanistan to some capable and not unfriendly ruler; and, indeed, the war had been undertaken with this sole object.

ABD-AR-RAHMAN, AMIR OF AFGHANISTAN, FROM A PHOTOGRAPH MADE BETWEEN 1870 AND 1880.
From The Life of Abdur Rahman.

From this dilemma we were extricated by the appearance in the northern province of Abd-ar-Rahman, the nephew of the Amir Sher Ali's predecessor, who had been driven out of the country when Sher Ali won his throne in the civil war for succession, and had been living under Russian protection beyond the Oxus River. The Viceroy of India (Lord Lytton) made amicable overtures to him, with assurances that his accession to the vacant rulership would not be opposed, and he received an invitation to the British headquarters at Kabul, for the purpose of discussing terms upon which he might be recognized as Amir, and the rulership of the country might be made over to him. In June, 1880, Lord Lytton resigned his Governor-Generalship of India to Lord Ripon, by whom this arrangement was, not without difficulty, concluded. Abd-ar-Rahman's accession was proclaimed in the British camp at Kabul; he was strengthened by grants of arms and money, and by a formal promise of support against foreign aggression; and the British troops were just starting on their return to India, when news came that Ayub Khan, Sher Ali's younger son, had marched with an army from Herat upon Kandahar. In July he routed a British force at Maiwand, not far from Kandahar, and was beleaguering the garrison within the walls of that city. A strong expedition was immediately dispatched from Kabul, under the command of Sir Frederick Roberts, who reached Kandahar by forced marches at the end of August, attacked and completely defeated Ayub Khan, relieved the garrison, and drew off his troops into India by the Bolan Pass. Simultaneously the British army at Kabul had withdrawn from Afghanistan by the direct northern route; and in 1881 the evacuation of Kandahar left the Amir free to enforce his authority over the southern province. Abd-ar-Rahman, thus left to his own resources, drove Ayub Khan (who had returned) out of the country, and rapidly extended his power everywhere, until in a few years all Afghanistan was, for the first time in its history, amalgamated into a strong independent kingdom under a ruler of singular ability and merciless severity. During the following years the frontiers of this kingdom were laid down. The demarcation of its northwestern boundary, from the Oxus River to the confines of Persia, was undertaken by a joint commission of Russian and English officers; but a dispute over one section of the line caused a collision between Russian and Afghan troops at Panjdah, which brought England and Russia to the verge of a rupture in 1885, at a moment when the Amir was a guest of the Viceroy (Lord Dufferin) in his camp in North India. When that peril had been averted, the whole northwest frontier adjoining Russian possessions was settled by an international convention; and the next measure was to define the Afghan frontier on its eastern side, where a belt of tribal highlands is interposed between the Amir's territory and British India.

The general effect of all these measures has been of the highest importance to our dominion in India. During the nineteenth century Afghanistan has been a foreign kingdom which the English, who have no desire to possess, are nevertheless imperatively compelled to protect, and which must be retained at all risks and costs within the orbit of British influence, since its independence is essential to the security of any rule or dynasty in India. Under the Moghuls this country was a province of their empire; under the British system it is a protectorate; the Afghan mountains are still the necessary barrier against irruptions into the Indian plains. Since 1880, when the formal promise to defend

Afghanistan from foreign aggression was given to the Amir, the condition of his kingdom has steadily improved; it is no longer distracted by chronic civil wars and intestine revolts; it has been comparatively quiet and prosperous for twenty-seven years; and the present reigning Amir succeeded to the throne, on his father's death, without opposition; whereas all previous successions had been contested, or had been followed by rebellions. This transformation of the internal condition of the country may be ascribed, primarily, to the aid and support received by its rulers from the British government; and secondly to the delimitation of the Afghan frontiers, which has been ratified by a public convention between the two European powers.

In order to complete the narrative of events on the northern frontiers of India, it may be here mentioned that in 1896 - 1897 the petty chiefships on the southern slopes of the Hindu Kush mountains beyond Kashmir, were included within the range of the British protectorate. This extension of our political control was not accomplished without some resistance by the tribes of that wild and hitherto inaccessible region. They beleaguered and brought into some peril a British garrison in Chitral, until it was relieved by an expedition that made a difficult and hazardous march to its assistance. Our sphere of influence has thus been extended up to the borders of the Chinese empire in Kashgar; and its landmarks have been permanently set up in those remote highlands. The general result of all these operations, military and diplomatic, has been to lay out along the northern and northwestern frontiers of India a broad zone of protected states, which separate China, Russia, and Persia from the territories under our direct administration.

In the meantime, however, while we were engaged in clearing and strengthening the strategic position

THE GOLDEN MONASTERY, MANDALAY, BURMA.

beyond Northern India, on our southeast frontier new and grave complications had arisen. Since 1853, when the lower provinces of Burma had been conquered and annexed, the attitude of the Burmese rulers toward the British government had been resentful and vindictive. In 1885 the Burmese king persisted in rejecting reasonable demands made for reparation of injuries to British subjects, and what was much more serious, it was discovered that he was secretly negotiating a treaty with France, so framed as to give French interests a predominant influence in his country. When remonstrance and warning had proved entirely ineffectual, an ultimatum, backed by the assembling of an army on his frontier, was dispatched to him by the Indian government. The reply was by a proclamation in a tone of hostility, whereupon, in November, 1885, the troops advanced up Mandalay. The Burmese army made no serious resistance, the capital was occupied, the king was captured, and the annexation of Upper Burma was announced by the Queen's government. After nearly two years of internal disorder, for the conquered provinces were infested by marauding bands and disbanded soldiery, the work of pacification was accomplished, and the civil administration organized. Beyond the north-eastern districts of Upper Burma the petty chiefships in the wild tracts up to the Mekong river became our tributaries, and the tribes in the scarcely explored hills in the north have partially submitted to our control. The ruler of Siam, a kingdom that lies east of Burma, separating it from the French possessions in Cochin China, had become involved in disputes with the French authorities, and since the situation of Siam renders its independence of substantial concern to India, the British government interfered diplomatically in 1896, to prevent the kingdom's dismemberment, and to obtain recognition of the British protectorate over the Siamese provinces nearest to our own border.

This, the latest, expansion of British dominion by the

incorporation of Upper Burma has made a considerable addition to the weight of our political responsibilities. Between the populations of India and of the countries known as Indo-Chinese, there is little or no affinity. Here we have broken fresh ground in Asia, we have come into contact on our advanced position with strange races and languages: we are exploring a region hitherto almost unknown to Europeans, we have to demarcate the outlines and fill in the detail of our ever-widening territorial map. Our policy, on this side as on the Afghan border, is to maintain friendly relations with the Chinese officials, who are very sensitive to our proceedings, and to establish over the barbarous folk in the tracts intervening between the two empires a protectorate sufficient to reclaim them gradually from turbulence, to convert them from plundering borderers into border police, and to exclude foreign influence or encroachments.

Except by the annexation of Burma, the area under the direct and regular administration of the Indian Government has undergone little change since 1856. On the other hand, the external frontier of the empire, if the line is drawn, as it must be, to include the outlying regions that have been brought within the sphere of British influence or superior control, has been very materially widened in the course of the last fifty years. This frontier is now conterminous with the Russian possessions in Central Asia on the northwest, it marches for several thousand miles with the empire of China; and on the southeast it touches the Asiatic colonies of

France. By a recent expedition to Lhasa, the capital of Tibet, we have emphasized our determination to permit no encroachment of another European power upon the vast tracts of mountains and deserts that stretch from the Himalayas northward to the confines of Mongolia. Our policy is to keep clear of intrusion all the approaches to India, and to hold in our hands the keys of all its gates. Upon this system we have been obliged to multiply and throw forward our military outposts, and accept a great augmentation of sundry and manifold political responsibilities. The outer frontier of the British dominion that our policy now requires us to defend, has an immense circumference. Its southeastern extremity rests on the Gulf of Siam, whence it sweeps round Tibet on the north; it touches the Hindu Kush range of mountains and the Oxus; on the northwest it covers Afghanistan and Baluchistan, until it terminates at its western extremity on the shores of the Arabian sea. The consequence of this expansion of our spheres of political influence far beyond the area of our actual dominion is that the frontiers of the British empire are changing their character. The boundaries of India proper are naturally defined on three sides by an almost unbroken wall of mountains or by desert tracts and on the fourth side by the sea. But the political circumscription of our exterior frontier has now been formed by tracing artificial lines, settled by international agreements, across the slopes and valleys of the Central Asian highlands, and across desolate plains or rugged half-explored hill-tracts. These fixed lines of frontier represent the out-works of our strategical position; and from the northwest to the southeast they adjoin the dominions of two other great Asiatic empires, Russia and China. The political situation in Asia is now closely dependent upon any entanglement of the network of international relations throughout the world, so that any serious strain or rupture would be felt not only in India, but in all the adjacent countries under European influence; nor is it too much to say that the destiny of the greater part of Asia depends on the balance of power and the adjustment of forces in Europe.

The history of British dominion in India has been written, up to this point in the narrative, with little or no reference to matters of interior administration. It has described, in broad outline, the origin and expansion of British rule by territorial conquest and cessions, the gradual rise of its supremacy over all rival Indian powers, and the external policy adopted for the defence and security of our possessions. But during the latter half of the nineteenth century great internal changes have supervened; the enlargement of territory has increased the number and diversity of the population; the moral and material condition of the people has made important advances. It has, therefore, been thought expedient to complete this volume by adding some brief account of the progress of civil government, and of the reforming measures from time to time introduced, in the course of the period to which this section relates.

The Sepoy Mutiny of 1857 was reactionary in its causes and revolutionary in its effects; it shook for a moment the empire's foundations, but it cleared the area for reconstruction and improvement. In a previous chapter it has been said that for the twenty years immediately preceding, from 1837 to 1857, there had been only short intervals of peace between recurrent wars, and that British territory had been greatly extended

THE MASSACRE AT CAWNPUR, JUNE 26, 1857.

by successive annexations. When, in 1849, the Panjab had been subdued and pacified after two hard-fought campaigns, and when Oudh, the last and largest kingdom in northern India, had been incorporated by Lord Dalhousie in 1856, it might have been plausibly anticipated that the rough war-time had ended, and that the whole country could settle down in tranquillity under our dominion.

In reality we were only just turning the first leaf of a new chapter, which opens with the outbreak of a fierce civil war. The thunderstorm of revolt broke in upon these visions of repose, and on the prospects of unclouded calm; the native army, which for a hundred years had shared all our triumphs and reverses in war, rose against us, and was overpowered after a desperate struggle. In Oudh the great landholders set up the standard of rebellion; and throughout the northern provinces British authority was for some time either swept away, or sustained only by the force of arms and the resolution of those who confronted a tremendous crisis with courageous energy. Thus in 1860, when order had been at last restored, the older provinces were recovering from a dangerous insurrection, which had seriously disturbed the adjoining native States; while in the territories that had been recently acquired the fabric of government had been merely provisional, suited to the immediate needs and emergencies of their occupation. With the complete pacification of the country came leisure for organization, for placing the executive authority of the various local governments on a definite footing, and substituting laws properly framed for unmethodical procedure and discretionary ordinances. The moment was opportune for undertaking this work, as the constitution of the Indian government, after passing through various stages of transition, had now reached a condition that rendered comprehensive alterations urgently necessary, in order to adapt it to civilized uses and to the needs of a changing society.

The administration of the Moghul empire had been to some degree systematic; and its scheme of distribution into districts and provinces, with the methods of assessing the local revenue, still survived in outline. But the native rulerships immediately preceding the British dominion had neither system nor stability, since the incessant warfare and scramble for territory during the eighteenth century had left even able chiefs without time or means for administrative settlement. Yet even the Moghul emperors, in the plenitude of their power, had never promulgated general civil or criminal laws backed by state sanction, in the European sense of these terms; nor had they at any time pretended to regulate authoritatively the customs and domestic relations of the people, being content to levy revenue and do rough justice according to the arbitrary will of the sovereign or of his deputies. The multifarious groups that make up the population of India had lived under their personal institutions and rules of conduct, mainly religious; for it may be said that in Asia law and religion are almost universally regarded as two sides of the same subject. Under the earlier regimen of the East India Company the practice had been to issue provincial Regulations of an old-fashioned type framed to suit the requirements and circumstances of sundry times and divers places, loosely drawn and intermixed with instructions and explanations, and further complicated by empirical decisions of the local courts. Latterly some Acts, of importance and value, passed by the supreme legislature, were put in force throughout the older provinces. But the new territories, as they were annexed to the dominion, were placed by the Governor-General provisionally under his direct control by what was called the Non-Regulation system, reserving his power of extending discretionally the regular laws and procedure, with directions that their spirit

THE "SLAUGHTER-HOUSE," WHERE THE CAWNPUR MASSACRE TOOK PLACE.

rather than their letter should be followed, to be supplemented in doubtful cases by the guidance of equity and good conscience.

When, therefore, after the final suppression of the mutiny and of the agitation that it had spread throughout the northern provinces, the permanent reconstitution of government became practicable and necessary, the task of the British authorities was to deduce order out of this confusion, and to lay the foundations of a new and uniform polity. The country had been the scene of more rapid and abrupt transitions, political and economical, than had ever, perhaps, been recorded in the history of nations. For in India old and new forms of civilization had become intermixed, not only by the influx of European ideas upon an Asiatic society, but because it contained an immense population in different stages of material and intellectual progress. The English had originally taken over an empire in a state of political dilapidation; and they had now to complete its administration on a scientific plan, with a solicitous regard for the inveterate prejudices of many races and religions.

Previously to the mutiny of 1857, this process of reformation had been going on slowly; but from that time forward it acquired great momentum. By an Act of Parliament passed in 1858, the supreme powers of control over Indian affairs, which had been hitherto divided between the Court of Directors and the ministers of the Crown, were vested in a Secretary of State in Council; and all the naval and military forces of the East India Company were transferred to the imperial service. Then, in 1861, the India Councils Act modified the constitution of the Governor-General's Executive Council in India, and remodelled the legislature by establishing a Council, presided over by the Governor-General, to make laws for the whole of India, with subordinate legislative Councils at Madras, Bombay, and Calcutta. Another statute instituted High Courts of Judicature under royal charter, at these three capitals;

and in 1860 - 1861 the enactment of the Penal Code and the Code of Criminal Procedure assimilated throughout the country the general system of criminal law. By these measures the executive and judicial administration was systematically re-arranged; so that, when Lord Canning, the first Viceroy of India, left Calcutta in 1862, he made over to his successor a government very different in organization and character from that which had been transmitted to him, six years earlier, by Lord Dalhousie. The royal supremacy, proclaimed in 1858, became the actual and visible sign of substantial incorporation into the British Empire in all parts of the world, at a time when India had received large accretions of territory; while the sense of unity created by the Queen's assumption of direct government restored confidence, and gave a powerful impulse to the moral and material advancement of the Indian people.

The administrative history of India during the next fifty years may be described as a development upon the lines that were laid down by these fundamental executive and legislative reforms. It records the methodical prosecution of the work of adjusting the mechanism of a modern state to the circumstances and customs of a most heterogeneous population. On the one hand, personal laws, precepts of caste and creed, and prescriptive rights had to be respected. On the other hand, the effect upon many of these rules and usages made by the introduction of a strong and systematic administration was to derange and modify them, because the needs and circumstances under which they had grown up were passing away. In this manner the vague and elastic ordinances of primitive societies were naturally falling into disuse, with a tendency toward dissolution. But the operation of the British courts of justice, which had been established in the older provinces, was to arrest this spontaneous decomposition. To these tribunals every question of right, every dispute over matters of inheritance, property, and customary law generally, was necessarily referred, and the result was commonly to fix by the judicial decisions, and thus to stereotype an order of things that was by its nature elastic, that had taken its shape from the rude exigencies of lawless times, and was becoming inconsistent with the new social and economical environment, with peace, with the growth of wealth, security of property, and the spread of education. The effect was to give inflexible precision and rigidity to loose undefined usages, for, while a self-regulating community can amend or abandon an inconvenient precept of caste or creed, in the hands of an English judge the rule becomes immutable, and the bonds are tightened. But the conditions of life, for all classes of the population, had been so profoundly affected by the advent of British dominion, that nothing but our own positive and inflexible law could have prevented a corresponding modification of archaic ideas and institutions.

It had thus come to pass that while the general civil law of India was to a great extent intricate and uncertain, varying from province to province, with multifarious distinctions and exceptions created by religious singularities and local traditions, its complexity was further increased by the importation of an exotic legal procedure. Yet government by a clear and scientific body of laws, binding upon the authorities and appropriate to the circumstances of the people, is the only real security for the progress and prosperity of a country; so that it was essential to mould this mass of heterogeneous sections and rulings into some compact and intelligible shape. The problem was to simplify and generalize the civil law and procedure, and to enact large principles of equity and morality, with the least possible disturbance of the practices, prejudices, and organic institutions of Indian society.

Under the direction of Sir Henry Maine, a jurist whose insight into the forms and ideas of early civilizations admirably fitted him for the task, the solution of this problem was initiated. When, in 1862, he assumed charge of the legislative department of the Indian government, the two great Acts codifying the Penal Law and procedure had already been passed; but the subject of civil or domestic legislation was much more complicated. It is obvious, for example, that questions touching marriage and inheritance lie at the base of every society, being related to fundamental interests and affecting very delicate susceptibilities; so that any interposition by foreign legislators must be exercised with the utmost caution. In India the rules which preside over family life and the distribution of property are intermixed with and dependent upon religious ritual, worships, and beliefs; their diversity and multiplicity preclude any attempt to comprehend them within a uniform Civil Code. The only practicable course, therefore, was to frame Acts embodying broad principles of jurisprudence, providing, so to speak, the lines upon which social evolution might be assisted. The precise scope and operation of these emancipating Acts cannot be here explained; though the Indian Succession Act may be taken as an illustration of the process. It codified the law relating to the effect of death or marriage upon successors to property, and to testamentary bequest; but it does not apply to Hindus, Mohammedans, or to others who are subject to their own personal laws; it provides a definite civil status for those classes of the population whom the novel rites and peculiar doctrines, which are continually disintegrating orthodox Hinduism, or the softening of manners and intellectual elevation, may have separated from their original sects or communities.

Other Acts, such as that for the remarriage of converts to Christianity, embodied the principle that change of religion involved no loss of ordinary civil rights. The Acts dealing with Evidence and Contract reduced to concise and explicit form a mass of law that the courts had previously been obliged to extract from text-books, reports, and conflicting rulings, and the procedure of all courts of civil jurisdiction was determined by comprehensive enactments. In short, the aim and outcome of the legislation during this period was to simplify and summarize the administration of justice, and to promote by successive measures the general principle of civil and religious liberty, taking power to extend them as their expediency and moral superiority should be gradually recognized by the people; and slowly moulding their habits to the conception of government by laws.

The policy of reform and consolidation pursued during this period in one great department of administration is of such importance, and to some extent of such general interest from the standpoint of comparative legislation, that some brief explanation of it may not be here out of place. In India, where the public income from land has always been the chief mainstay of the state's finances, and where the population in a very great majority subsist by agriculture, the just and skilful management of this source of revenue has always been of vital importance to the welfare of every government and of the people. From the beginning of British rule the provincial authorities have been continually engaged in deciding questions of ownership and occupancy, in allocating the payments due to the treasury from every estate and sometimes from every field, in revising earlier systems of taxation, and in passing laws or framing executive rules to settle disputed proprietorship or to remedy agricultural distress. The fact that from time immemorial the State has invariably shared in the surplus profits of agriculture has provided every strong government in India with a direct and very substantial motive for protecting the actual cultivator; the liability of the country to periodical drought adds weight to this primary interest and obligation.

But many parts of India, when they first came under British sovereignty, had suffered from the passage of armies, from marauding bands, from the dispersion or impoverishment of the cultivators, and from all the calamities of war. In the violent contests for possession of territory and revenue the lands had been forcibly seized, and the strife had been incessant between the old and the new proprietors. In the outlying districts, during intervals of confusion, neither rent nor revenue could be regularly levied, as an intermittent struggle between those who strove to exact too much and those who would pay nothing at all was maintained among tenants, landlords, and official tax-gatherers. In this manner, by the swaying to and fro of the conflict, by local accidents, and by the vicissitudes of political power, was produced that intricate variety of proprietary and cultivating tenures, with an arbitrary and fluctuating assessment of revenue, which the English found in the different provinces that fell at different times under their administration.

The precarious nature of proprietary and occupancy rights, bearing traces of ruinous exaction or lawless resistance, left room for every kind of theory as to the basis upon which the relations between landlord and tenant, and between both classes and the state, should be permanently or temporarily determined. What meaning and what measure of legal recognition should be assigned to local usage and prescriptive claims, how far the law ought to interfere to modify the stringency of contracts imposed upon the tenantry, whether the

State's demand should be raised or lowered, to what extent double ownership of land should be subjected by statutory definition, all such questions had to be investigated and decided upon considerations of equity

DETAIL FROM THE HALL OF A HUNDRED COLUMNS AT CONJEVARAM.

and expediency. It was necessary to mediate between the two interests of ownership and occupancy in agriculture, interests which are so sensitive to economical changes, that the most skilful attempts to distribute them formally, and to provide by legislation, however elastic, for all the incidents of the connection, have hitherto failed to prevent severe recurrent strains upon it.

To give, even in outline, an intelligible account of the methods, legal and executive, by which they were determined in the various provinces, would be impracticable within the limits of this chapter. It must be sufficient to state that the determination of these questions in Northern India, especially in the Panjab and Oudh, engaged for several years the attention of the government. The subject holds a prominent place in the administrative history of this period, since the agrarian reforms and the fiscal regulations then settled, after long and accurate inquiries, have probably contributed more than any other measures to the confirmation and popularity of the British rule.

Among the most potent instruments of civilization in India have been the railways. Up to about 1850 the main roads were still unmetalled, and a few years later the first railways were just begun. Since that time, they have branched out over the whole country, disseminating everywhere the benefits of rapid intercourse and commercial interchange, and with great advantage to our strategical position. The external trade of India has increased with the multiplication of outlets to the seaports, and the productive powers of the soil have been augmented over a large area by the extension of artificial irrigation. By the diversion of the flow of the great rivers into canals, many hundred miles in their aggregate length, and by the storage of water in numerous reservoirs, the largest irrigation system in the world has been constructed in India. The effect of these great productive works has been to augment and distribute the national wealth; they have perceptibly modified the aspect of the country, and the habits of the people. The capital invested in these undertakings by the state has been, for the most part, obtained from loans, which were raised at low interest on the credit of the British government. The public debt of India to England has been sometimes represented as an intolerable burden, yet probably no incident of the connection between the two countries has been of greater advantage to India than this expenditure of many millions on the development of its natural resources.

In 1877, the assumption of Queen Victoria of the title of Empress of India, declared before a grand assemblage of chiefs and notables at Delhi, gave public form to the fact of sovereignty, and the magnificent durbar of King Edward in 1902, at which the king was represented by the Viceroy, and which was perhaps one of the most gorgeous Oriental pageants of all time, again attested the recognition of supremacy.

For India, therefore, the last fifty years have been pre-eminently an era of consolidation by laws and administrative reform. The British government may now be described as a highly organized machine, so powerful, and so complicated in its functions, that scientific management and control of them is indispensable, and accordingly their superior direction has been hitherto retained in English hands. Foreign dominion must

The Durbar of 1902

Never was there grander display of Oriental pomp and dazzling splendour than at the durbar in honour of King Edward, as Emperor of India, in 1902. Gorgeous fêtes, ceremonies, and processions lent magnificence to the celebration, and India rivalled England in doing homage to the new sovereign.

necessarily be more or less autocratic for some time after it has been acquired; and since the rulers are usually compelled to rely for its maintenance at first upon the strength and fidelity of their own countrymen, the chiefs of their civil and military government have almost invariably been imported from abroad. The Moghul emperors appointed men of their own race or creed to their military commands, and to most of their highest civil offices; the British nation has been forced, by similar conditions of political existence, to reserve the upper grades of their Indian administration for Englishmen. But the Moghul government was essentially personal and absolute; and, in fact, no other form of rulership has ever been attempted in a purely Asiatic state. The people have been used to concern themselves only with the question whether a despotism was strong or weak, tolerable or intolerable; for the expedient of improving a government by altering its form has not yet been discovered in Asia; the only remedy, if things went outrageously wrong, has been to change the person. The English rule, therefore, succeeded to an empire of this character, with a centralized authority presiding over different provinces recently conjoined, and a population in promiscuous ethnical variety. But the inhabitants of India have thereby become fellow-citizens with a European nation that has for centuries been working out popular institutions in a totally different atmosphere; in an island sheltered from invasion, in circumstances peculiarly favourable to the evolution of self-government, among a homogeneous people knit together by common interests and national sentiment. Whereas India has for ages been plagued with invasions; its vast territory has been incessantly split up and parcelled out among foreign conquerors and contending dynasties; the population is internally subdivided to a degree unparalleled elsewhere, even in Asia. Yet it has inevitably come to pass that the differences of wealth and learning, frequent intercourse with Europe, and the saturation of the educated classes with Western ideas and political axioms, have stimulated the desire for a larger share in the government of their country among the leaders of native public opinion. An efficient administration no longer satisfies them; on the contrary, it has created ulterior hopes and aspirations. We began with great organic reforms, with improving the police and the prisons, with codes of law, a hierarchy of courts of justice, a trained civil service, and all the apparatus of a modern executive. Latterly we have undertaken the gradual introduction of representative institutions, legislative councils in all the important provinces, and municipalities in every substantial town; we are seriously preparing for the slow devolution of self-governing principles.

But undoubtedly this is an operation of extraordinary difficulty, for we have no precedents to guide us in the experiment. It must certainly be conducted within the limitations necessary to preserve undisturbed and indisputable the fabric of British sovereignty, but some solution of this difficulty is demanded, for now that the English have accomplished the building up, after the high Roman fashion, of an immense polyglot empire, the stability of the structure must depend upon a skilful distribution of weight, because excessive centralization is radically insecure, and supports are useless without some capacity to resist pressure. The solution of these problems requires the sympathetic insight as well as the scientific methods of statesmanship, supplemented by the good will and the growing intelligence of the Indian people.

Education, scientific and literary culture, better acquaintance with public affairs, and an enlarged understanding of the conditions of practical politics, may be expected to produce among the foremost advocates of constitutional reform views and proposals moderated by a clearer appreciation of inherent difficulties. Nor is there, so far as can be discerned, any revolutionary element in the ideas now current among serious thinkers in India, where modern thought seems to be taking a strong utilitarian colour in morals, mundane affairs, and even in religious movements. The two countries, England and India, are at any rate associated in a community of moral and material interests, that has already lasted, throughout most of the dominion, for several generations, has exercised a powerful influence over the history of each people, in Europe and Asia, and must affect, to no small degree, their future destiny. It may be confidently affirmed that this alliance cannot now be impaired or interrupted without incalculable injury to both nations.

CHAPTER XIX

THE BRITISH DOMINION IN ASIA

AT the present time, therefore, his Majesty the king-emperor surveys all India united under his sovereignty, whether directly administered, or through allied and friendly princes. And since upper Burma came under British rule in 1886, an Indo-Chinese dependency, side by side with the Indian empire, has been formed by the incorporation of a wide region that extends along the Irawadi and Salwin Rivers, and touches at certain points the western bank of the upper Mekong, the stream which was taken by the French in 1896 as the present boundary of their advance upward from the southeast.

But it must always be remembered that in India the political jurisdiction of the English has at no time been commensurate with the districts under their administration. From the beginning of the nineteenth century, at any rate, the empire has been composed partly of provinces and partly of states under British protection and paramount influence. With this composite formation its position and character have latterly been undergoing an extensive and significant development. And

H. R. H. George Frederick, Prince of Wales

One of the most interesting events in the life of the Prince of Wales is his tour through India in 1905, when he visited all of the principal cities of India and some of the seats of the native princes. This tour was intended to promote good feeling and loyalty toward the English Government, which had discredited itself with the Bengalese by the division of the Province of Bengal.

Published by The Grolier Soc. London & N.Y.

since this remarkable change of situation must be ascribed largely to the consistent operation of the policy of protectorates, some account of the origin and effects of that policy may serve to explain the expansion of the British dominion in Asia.

The system of protectorates has been practised from time immemorial as a method whereby the great conquering and commercial peoples have masked, so to speak, their irresistible advance, and have regulated the centripetal attraction of greater over lesser masses of territory. It was much used by the Romans, whose earlier relations with Asia and Africa were not unlike the British attitude, in that they acknowledged no frontier power with equal rights. The motives have been different, sometimes political, sometimes military, sometimes commercial; the consequences have been invariably the same. It is used politically as a convenient method of extending various degrees of power and of appropriating certain attributes of sovereignty without affirming full jurisdiction. It has become the particular device whereby one powerful state forestalls another in the occupation of some position, or scientific frontier line, or intermediate tract that has a strategical and particularly a defensive value. It is employed to secure command of routes, coaling stations, or trading posts whenever one nation desires to be beforehand with an enterprising competitor. Under this system, applied in these various manners, the extra-territorial liabilities of England all over the world are rapidly increasing, and our frontiers are rapidly expanding.

Now, the origin and extension of British protectorates on the Asiatic mainland follow a clear and almost uniform process of development. Just as a fortress or a line of entrenchments requires an open

SUBMISSION OF THE MAHARAJA DHULIP SINGH TO SIR HENRY HARDINGE, AT KANHA CUSHWA, FEB. 19, 1846.

space around or in front of it, so it is manifestly advantageous for the security of an outlying frontier province to keep the foreign territory adjoining it free from the intrusion or occupation of powerful neighbours. There is no great objection to neighbours who are merely troublesome, such as tribes who may be turbulent and predatory, or even petty states that may be occasionally unfriendly, if they are not strong enough to be seriously dangerous.

It is always a question whether the most unruly barbarian is not, on the whole, a much better neighbour than a highly civilized but heavily armed state of equal calibre. In the case of the free tribe or the petty despot, although the tranquillity of the common border may suffer, it is possible to bring them gradually into pacific habits and closer subordination. In the case of the civilized state, its neighbour undoubtedly obtains a well-defined and properly controlled frontier on both sides of it; but it will be also a frontier that needs a vigilant patrol, and that will probably require fortifications, garrisons, and constant watching of all movements, diplomatic and military, beyond the exact line that divides the contiguous territories.

It is probably due to England's insular traditions that in Asia we are very susceptible to the distrust and danger inseparable from a frontier that is a mere geographical line across which a man may step. Having no such border-line in Europe, except perhaps at Gibraltar, England has always been naturally reluctant to come to such close quarters with any formidable Asiatic rival. Upon this principle it has long been the policy of the Anglo-Indian government to bring under its protective influence, whether they desired it or not, the native states, or chiefships, or tribes, whose territory has marched with its own boundaries; the reciprocal understanding being that the British undertake to safeguard them from foreign aggression on condition that they shall have no dealings with any foreign power other than the English. England surrounds herself, in this manner, with a zone of land, sometimes narrow, sometimes very broad, which is placed under political taboo so far as concerns rival powers whose hostility may be serious; and thus her political influence radiates beyond the line of her actual possession, spreading its skirts widely and loosely over the adjacent country.

The particular point, therefore, that is here to be emphasized is that the true frontier of the British dominion in Asia, the line which we are more or less pledged to guard, and from which we have warned off trespassers, does not tally by any means with the outer edge of the immense territory over which we exercise administrative jurisdiction, and in which all the people are British subjects for whom the Anglo-Indian governments make laws. The true frontier includes not only this territory, but also large regions over which the English crown has established protectorates of different kinds and grades, varying according to circumstances and specific conditions. This protectorate may involve the maintenance of internal order, or it may amount only to a vague sovereignty, or it may rest on a bare promise to ward off unprovoked foreign aggression. But, whatever may be the particular class to which the protectorate belongs, and however faint may be the shadow of authority that the British choose to throw over the land, its object is to affirm the right of excluding a rival influence, and the right of exclusion carries with it the duty of defence. The outer limits of the country which we are prepared to defend is what must be called our frontier.

In order to apply this principle to England's Asiatic frontiers, and to explain why they have been so movable, we must now run rapidly along the line which demarcates them at this moment. Passing over the very complicated case of Egypt, we may begin the British Asiatic protectorates with Aden, at the mouth of the Red Sea. From time immemorial the movement of the sea-borne trade between India and Egypt has pivoted, so to speak, upon Aden. It is now the first stepping-stone across the Asiatic waters toward the Anglo-Indian Empire and the westernmost point of English occupation on the Asiatic mainland; and it furnishes a good example in miniature of the manner in which protectorates are formed. We have taken and fortified Aden for the command of the water-passage into the Red Sea; but our actual possession is only a projecting rock like Gibraltar, and so we have established a protective border all round it, within which the Arab tribes are bound by engagements to accept English political ascendency and to admit no other. Not far from Aden lies the protected island of Sokotra, a name in which one can barely recognize the old Greek Dioskorides; and from Aden eastward, round Arabia by Oman to Muscat and the Persian Gulf, the whole coast-line is under British protectorate; the policing of these waters is done by British vessels, and the Arab chiefships along the seaboard defer to England's arbitration in their disputes and acquiesce in her external supremacy.

But these scattered protectorates in Western Asia are merely isolated points of vantage or long strips of seashore; they depend entirely on Britain's naval superiority in those waters; they are all subordinate and supplementary to her main position in Asia, by which, of course, India is meant. It is there that we

VIEW OF MUSCAT FROM THE HOUSETOPS.
From Edwin Lord Weeks's Through Persia and India.
(Copyright, 1895, by Harper and Brothers.)

can study with the greatest diversity of illustration, and on the largest scale, the curious political situations presented by the system of maintaining a double line of frontiers; the inner line marking the limits of British territory, the outer line marking the extent of the foreign territory that the English undertake to protect, to the exclusion, at any rate, of foreign aggression.

The long maritime frontiers of India furnish a kind of analogy between the principle upon which a seashore is defended and the system of protectorates as applied to the defence of a land frontier. In both cases the main object is to keep clear an open space beyond and in front of the actual border-line. England does this for the land frontier by a belt of protected land which she throws forward in front of a weak border; and her assertion of exclusive jurisdiction over the belt of waters immediately surrounding her seacoasts is founded upon the same principle. We English are accustomed to consider ourselves secure under the guardianship of the sea; although, in fact, the safety comes not from the broad girdle of blue water, but from the strength and skill of the English navy that rides upon it. And for a nation that has not learnt the noble art of seamanship, no frontier is more exposed to attack, or harder to defend, than the seashore.

The principle of defence, therefore, for both land and sea frontiers, is to stave off an enemy's advance by interposing a protected zone. If a stranger enters that zone he is at once challenged. If he persists, it is a hostile demonstration.

It would thus be a mistake to suppose that England's Asiatic land frontier is conterminous with her Asiatic possessions, that is, with the limits of the territory which she administers, and which is within the range of her Acts of Parliament. It is not, like the Canadian border, or the boundary between France and Germany, a mere geographical line over which an Englishman can step at once out of his own country into the jurisdiction of another sovereign state. The frontier of the British Asiatic dominion is the outmost political boundary projected, as one might say, beyond the administrative border; and it must be particularly observed that the outmost boundary is here specified, because British India—the territory under the government of India—has interior as well as exterior boundaries. In such countries as France or Spain, and indeed in almost all modern kingdoms, the government exercises a level and consolidated rulership over a compact national estate, with a frontier surrounding it like a ring fence.

But the Indian Empire sweeps within the circle of its dominion a number of native states, which are enclosed and landlocked in the midst of British territory. We have seen that many of these states were built up out of the dilapidated provinces of the Moghul Empire by rebellious governors or military leaders, who began by pretending to rule as delegates or representatives of the emperor, and ended by openly assuming independence, as soon as the paralysis of central government permitted them to throw aside the pretext. With the fall of the Moghul Empire came the rise of the British dominion, and in the course of a century some of the imperial provinces were again absorbed by conquest or cession into British India; while others were left as self-governing states under the English protectorate. There is also an important group of Rajput chiefships which have always been independent under the suzerainty of the paramount power.

In all these states the rulers are debarred from making war and peace; but they make their own laws and levy their own taxes; and the British treat their territory as foreign, although the dividing border-line can hardly be called a frontier, since most of these states are entirely surrounded and shut in by British India. Nevertheless, their history serves to illustrate at every turn the bearing of this system of protectorates on the Anglo-Indian frontier; and what is now going on is chiefly the continuation of what went on from the beginning.

It will be found that from the time when the English became a power on the mainland of India, that is, from their acquisition of Bengal in 1765, they have constantly adopted the policy of interposing a border of protected country between their actual possessions and the possessions of formidable neighbours whom they desire to keep at arm's length. In the eighteenth century we supported and protected Oudh as a barrier against the Marathas; and early in the nineteenth century we preserved the Rajput states in Central India for the same reason. The feudatory states on the Sutlaj were originally maintained and strengthened by us, before we took the Panjab, as outworks and barricades against the formidable power of the Sikhs. The device has been likened to the invention of buffers; for a buffer is a mechanical contrivance for breaking or graduating the force of impact between two heavy bodies; and in the same way the political buffer checked the violence of political collisions, though it rarely prevented them altogether.

It may even be suspected that the system rather accelerated than retarded the rapid extension of the English frontier; because, whereas we annexed fresh territory after each collision with our rivals, so we constantly advanced their protective border beyond the

RECEPTION OF GENERAL OUTRAM AND STAFF AT THE DURBAR OF THE RAJA OF TRAVANCORE.

actual line of annexation, and thus have always made a double step forward, keeping the strategic or political boundary well in advance of the limit of our administrative occupation. The lines of earlier British frontiers, now left far behind in the interior of India, may often be traced by the survival of some petty principalities, that escaped being swallowed up by a powerful neighbour because it was originally the English policy to protect them.

Upon this system of pushing forward protective outworks until the British were ready to march beyond them, the Anglo-Indian dominion advanced across India. But as soon as we had reached the geographical limits of India—the range of mountains which separate it from Central Asia, and which form, perhaps, the strongest natural barriers in the world — one might have thought that the protectorates, which are artificial fortifications of an exposed border, would no longer be needed. On the contrary, they have grown with the expansion and rounding off of Anglo-Indian dominion; and the empire in its plenitude seems to find them more necessary than ever.

We have run our administrative border up to the slopes of the hills that fringe the great Indian plains; but on the northwest we are not content with the guardianship of a mountain wall. We look over and beyond it to the Oxus, and we see Russia advancing across the Central Asian steppes by a process very like our own. She conquers and consolidates, she absorbs and annexes, up to an inner line; and beyond that line, in the direction of India, she maintains a protected state. The Oxus divides Bokhara from Afghanistan, the Russian from the English protectorate. Here is a rival and possible enemy far more formidable than any of those whom we have hitherto discerned on our political horizon; and consequently our protective border has taken a wider cast than ever. Two countries whose broad extent and physical conformations adapt them admirably to be strong natural outworks, Baluchistan and Afghanistan, lie beyond her western border, full of deserts and mountains, hard to traverse and easy to defend, inhabited by free and warlike races, to whom liberty is, as to ourselves, the noblest of possessions. Both these countries have been brought by England within the range of our political ascendency, and thus we have assumed a virtual protectorate over that vast tract of country which stretches from the confines of India to Persia and the Oxus River.

Taking as the central point of departure the Victoria Lake, whose shores are the high mountain cradle of the Oxus, the line separating Russian from English spheres of influence runs eastward to the Chinese frontier, and westward along the course of the river. Turning southward from the Oxus to the Indian Ocean, the whole western boundary-line which separates Afghanistan and Baluchistan from Russia and Persia has been marked out under English supervision, and secured by treaty or agreement. It must not be supposed that this line is secured upon any formal international compact with the states inside it, although their rulers have agreed to the arrangement which it represents; it has been fixed by negotiations with the states beyond, with Russia and Persia, who have promised and are pledged to respect it.

Here, then, beyond the extreme northwest of India, we may survey the system of protectorates operating on a grand scale; and we may find the strongest illustration of the principle that the true frontier delineates not only the land that is administered, but the lands that are protected. On that side we are not content with fencing ourselves round by a belt of free tribal lands or a row of petty chiefships; we have barricaded the roads leading from Central Asia into India by two huge blocks of independent territory, Afghanistan and Baluchistan. Up to the end of the seventeenth century the kingdom of Persia and the Moghul Empire of India were nominally conterminous; for Kabul and Kandahar were held by the Moghul. But in the great political convulsions of the eighteenth century the highland country interposed between Persia and India was rent away and formed into the separate chiefships which we now uphold as our barriers; they are the boulders or isolated masses that remain to attest the latest period of territorial disruption.

MAJOR-GENERAL SIR HENRY HAVELOCK.

Now, as both Russia and England have been employing the same political tactics in their advance toward each other, throwing forward protectorates, and occupying points of vantage, it has long been certain that Afghanistan, which lies right between the two camps, must fall into one or another of these spheres of influence. If England did not protect Afghanistan, that country would undoubtedly be brought under the wardship of Russia, which has already taken under strict tutelage Bokhara, just across the Oxus. For the Afghan mountains dominate the Indian plains and command the roads from the Oxus to the Indus; and a country of such natural strength, a weak and barbarous kingdom overhanging the frontiers of two powerful military states, must always fall, by the law of political gravitation, on one side or the other.

It may perhaps be asked why this must be—why England does not adopt the European method of dealing with a country that is too weak to stand by itself—why she does not neutralize Afghanistan, as Belgium and Switzerland are neutralized, by a joint agreement to respect its integrity and independence. The answer is that neutralization has never been a practical method of statecraft in Asia. An ill-governed Oriental kingdom left as neutral ground between two European powers, neither of which could interfere with its internal affairs, would rapidly fall into intolerable disorder, and probably into dilapidation. The native ruler would be distracted by the conflicting demands and admonitions of two formidable and jealous neighbours; he would listen alternately to one or the other, and would be constantly giving cause of offence to both; he would find himself between the upper and nether millstone; and his end would probably be as the end of Poland, which became a focus of intrigue and anarchy, and was finally broken up by partition.

A very curious historic parallel might be drawn, if space allowed, by comparing the existing position of Afghanistan between the Anglo-Indian and the Russian empires with the position of Armenia between the Roman and the Parthian empires during the first two centuries of the Christian era. The Armenian ruler held the mountainous country and the passes between Europe and Asia; his kingdom was the barrier between the territories of two great military states; it was an essential point in the frontier policy of Rome to maintain her influence over the ruler, and her protection over his country. The Armenian chiefs leant alternately toward Rome and toward Parthia; they tried to save their independence by maintaining the balance; but whenever they allied themselves with Parthia, they were attacked by Rome, precisely as the Afghan Amir was attacked by England in 1879, when he made a treaty with Russia. Armenia, like Afghanistan, owed all its importance, not to its intrinsic strength, for it was weak and barbarous, but to its geographical situation; and the history of its relations with Rome — of the setting up and pulling down of client kings, and of the efforts of the Romans to maintain exclusive control over its government without occupying its territory — must remind one very forcibly of the English connection with Afghanistan.

That connection represents the broadest development of the protectorate system; and its efficacy may before long be brought to a decisive test. The demarcation of the western Afghan frontier by a joint commission of Russians and English in 1886 is plain evidence that the spheres of Russian and English influence, which have long been approaching, have at last touched each other. It will be recollected, as an example of the delicate handling required by modern political machinery, that the first contact very nearly produced a collision and was felt in a vibration that reverberated through all the Cabinets of Europe. A slight difference in regard to the laying down of the boundary across the slopes of the Hindu Kush brought on a skirmish between Afghans and Russians at Panjah in 1885 and filled all Europe with rumours of war between England and Russia. Lord Dufferin, a diplomatist of great skill and invaluable experience, was then Viceroy of India, and the affair was compromised; but it showed the English, as by a sudden flash, where their true frontier lay, and what kind of possibilities were involved by its demarcation. The fact that for a breadth of some hundred miles between the disputed

A PILLAR AT TIRUMALA NAYAKA, MADURA.

boundary-line and the border of India proper the territory is ruled by the Afghan Amir, went for nothing; the Anglo-Indian frontier is always commensurate with its responsibilities for protection.

Taking, therefore, this view of the operation of the British system of protectorates, it is worth while to survey the immense sweep of the radius which describes the outer circumference of England's Asiatic frontier. For those who may apprehend that it has been pushed too far and too fast, there is, at any rate, the reassuring condition that it can hardly go farther; after more than a century's continuous expansion it must now come to a standstill, because it has at last struck westward and eastward against hard ground; that is, it has met in both directions the solid resistance of another well-organized state. When this point is reached, the moving and fluctuating border-lines at once begin to fix and harden; the protectorates settle down into orderly dependencies; disputes fall under the cognizance of regular diplomacy; and questions of war or peace become the concern of civilized governments.

The Indian Empire and its allies or feudatories now occupy virtually the whole area of southern Asia that lies between Russia and China, on a line drawn from the Oxus in the northwest down to the Mekong River in the southeast. On the northwest, where the proximity of Russia inevitably suggests special precautions, the line of advance from Central Asia into India is barricaded by protectorates, Baluchistan, Afghanistan, Kashmir, and the petty states beyond Kashmir up to the skirts of the Hindu Kush. Along the main northern line of the Himalayas we have few protectorates because we have no need of them; we have there a triple chain of almost impassable mountains, backed by the high table-land of Central Asia; and on the other side is the Mongolian desert. But it is only upon this section of England's outer line—between Kashmir and Nepal—that she is satisfied even with the stupendous mountain barriers of the Himalayas. She can allow no interference with Nepal from the north, and further eastward the encroachment of the Tibetans upon the protected state of Sikkim produced a little war of recent memory.

As on our northwestern frontier the British are very sensitive to the vicinity of Russia, so on our border-line in the northeast of Burma we begin to feel distinctly, beyond the mountains and untravelled highlands, the presence of that great organized state, the most ancient upon earth, which has so long dominated the eastern side of Asia—the Chinese Empire. Here, as toward the northwest, England is filling up the vacant spaces on the map; she is enlarging her dominion and setting forward landmarks. And here, also, her method of political exploration and reconnaissance is the protectorate in advance of the administrative boundary. In 1885 she made a great and important stride eastward when she was compelled to annex Burma, whose ruler not only showed symptoms of open hostility, but was bargaining for the protectorate of France.

Here, again, the acquisition of that kingdom carried

us far beyond its limits, for at once the double line began to form; and our real eastward frontier has been thrown forward up to the Mekong River, enclosing a line of semi-independent chieftainships, which serve as buffers between Burma proper and China. At this moment we are engaged in framing our relations with

THE TILO-MILO PAGODA AT PAGAN, BURMA.

these chieftainships, and in extending our influence over the border tribes; we are, in fact, planning out and consolidating the intermediate zone, which, as has been said, is invariably left between the two lines, the inner limit of actual jurisdiction and the outer political line of protection and defence.

And thus, on the east as on the west, England is slowly drawing into contact with rival powers of equal political magnitude; her extreme boundary-line reaches up to China and Siam; and at one point the political outposts of English exploration from Burma and of French pioneers from Tonkin are almost within hail. When all these boundaries are finally determined and ratified by the conventions of civilized diplomacy, the ground-plan of the future political settlement of Asia will have been laid out; and it is hardly too much to say that the whole of the Asiatic continent, outside the Chinese Empire, may eventually be either in the possession or under the protectorate of some European state.

It has been thought possible that this brief account of the manner in which the Anglo-Indian Empire has spread and been shaped out might be made interesting, because no process of the kind is now observable in Western Europe, although the same principles, with the same practical result, are plainly discernible in the gradual growth of the Roman Empire, and especially in the formation of that power's political and military frontier. The European continent has long ago been parcelled out into compact nationalities which afford no room for the system of intermediate protectorates, so that here the political and administrative frontiers always coincide. And where, as in the case of Belgium or Switzerland, a small country holds an important position on the political chess-board because it covers the vulnerable frontier of powerful neighbouring states, such a country is kept clear of intruders, not by a protectorate, but by neutralization.

With regard to the future of the British protectorates in Asia, one thing seems to be abundantly clear, that the system of protectorates—the practice of throwing out a line of frontier round a wide tract of unsettled country in order to exclude rivals — which was mainly invented in modern times by England for the building up of her Asiatic empire, is no longer her monopoly. So long as the English, like their predecessors the Romans, had the continent of Asia before them and had come into contact with no other substantial rivals, the expansion of their dominion went on as steadily and easily as the Asiatic extension of the Roman Empire, which was rapidly pushed eastward until it met the Parthians, by whom it was fiercely resisted and finally driven back. Britain's great naval superiority enabled her to beat off rivals in the distant seas, and on land she had only ill-organized native states to deal with. But in the latter half of the nineteenth century, and particularly during the last twenty years of unbroken peace in Western Europe, there has sprung up a keen competition for territory and trade in Asia and in Africa, which has led to the wholesale imitation of the English system of protectorates, either direct or through chartered companies.

Under the pressure and competition of France, Italy, Germany, and Russia, protectorates are rapidly multiplying in all the outlying quarters of the old world—over Tunis, Egypt, Abyssinia, Zanzibar, and countless tribes and chiefships in the interior of the African continent; and in Asia over Cochin China, the Annamite kingdom, Tonkin, and various half-explored borderlands.

What is the chief and manifest consequence of this renewed approximation of the European powers in Asia? The effect has been to demonstrate more clearly than ever the revival of an intimate connection between European and Asiatic affairs. The points of contact are multiplying with the different points of view, and with the recurrence of international apprehensions and rivalries. Political and commercial interests again begin to act and react upon each other; the expansion of Europe presses upon Asia by land and sea, from the Mediterranean to the Caspian Sea, from the Persian Gulf to the seaboard of China; and the antique kingdoms and societies are sustaining with difficulty the inroad of European arms and enterprise. The old conquering races of Asia, the Turkish dynasties at Stamboul and Teheran, the Uzbek of Bokhara, the Afghan of Kabul, and the rulers of Annam and Siam, are recognizing in different forms and degrees the predominant influence of the Western nations.

And since England still plays the leading part upon this vast stage of action and holds India as the central position, it is manifest that the isolation of India from the winds and currents of European politics must soon cease altogether and finally. She is rapidly drifting within the recognized sphere of European diplomacy; the enlargement of her borders has become a matter of European concern; and henceforward her external policy and her military establishment must necessarily be regulated upon European rather than upon Asiatic considerations. In the place of the jealousies of commercial companies, and instead of desultory wars between rival settlements or against native princes, we have the greatest military powers of the world—Russia, France, and England—feeling their way toward each other across wide deserts, difficult mountain ranges, and the debatable lands that skirt the Oxus

A SACRED POOL AT TIRUPARANKUNDRAM NEAR MADURA.

in the north or the Mekong River on the far southeast of the Anglo-Indian Empire.

To those, indeed, who demand permanency for territorial borders in Asia, it may have been instructive to follow, throughout the events and transactions rapidly sketched in the foregoing pages, the adventures of successive Anglo-Indian governments in search of a stable and scientifically defensible land frontier. The English have usually begun by projecting a political border-line, that is, by interposing some protected state between real territories and the power beyond them whose approach seemed to threaten our security. But the result of this manœuvre has too often been to accelerate our own extension, because we have eventually found ourselves forced to advance up to any line that rivals could not be permitted to overstep. Nor can anything illustrate more signally the radical and inherent mutability, and the accidental and elastic character of all territorial and political settlements in Asia, than the fact that at this moment England's statesmen are still in quest of that promised borderland whose margin seems to fade for ever as we follow it.

The object of this short and inadequate survey of the steps by which the English have mounted to ascendency in India has been to explain the combination of determining causes and events, in Europe as well as in Asia, that have placed England in possession of her Asiatic dominion. The explanation is, in the present writer's opinion, not difficult; it can be elicited from an attentive comparative study of the course of history in Asia and Europe during the last three centuries. The dominant fact as regards England may be said to be this—that as she has been preserved by the surrounding sea from the invasions, foreign wars, and revolutions that have interrupted the commercial and colonial enterprises of the Continental nations, she has been able to develop a vast mercantile system and to maintain a preponderance of naval power.

Yet although we can trace backward the sequence

of events and influences, their result is none the less singular. One remarkable characteristic of the history of the British dominion in Asia is that it affords an entire and connected view of the germination, growth, and expansion of a first-class territorial sovereignty. The ancient world has left us an unbroken record of the life of the Roman state, from its birth to its full strength and stature; but the phenomenon of an empire's complete evolution is most rare in modern times, and it may be said that India is the only example now existing. The Spanish dominion in America grew to vast dimensions out of the conquest of Hispaniola by Columbus, but the nineteenth century witnessed its disintegration, until at the present day Spain retains only a fragment of her former possessions.

The situation of the Indian Empire is thus unique in many respects; the annals of modern sovereignties show no parallel; and people still ask whether good or ill will come of it. When Sir James Mackintosh remarked that England had lost a great dominion in North America in 1783 and had won another in India by 1805, he added that it was still uncertain whether the former was any real loss, or the latter any permanent gain. Mr. Spencer Walpole, a much later authority, inclines toward the view that in the end nothing will have been gained. "Centuries hence," he writes in his "History of England," "some philosophic historian . . . will relate the history of the British in India as a romantic episode which has had no appreciable effect upon the progress of the human family."

Upon this it may be observed that, whatever may be the eventual advantage to England from her possession of India (for of the immediate advantage there can be little doubt), it already seems plain that the effect upon man's general progress must be very great.

That one of the foremost nations of Western Europe —foremost as a harbinger of light and liberty—should have established a vast empire in Asia is an accomplished fact which must necessarily give an enormous impulse and a totally new direction to the civilization of that continent. It will be remembered that since the Roman Empire began to decline, civilization has not been spreading eastward; on the contrary, it has distinctly receded in Asia; it was driven out and so fundamentally uprooted by the Turkish Sultans that the long dominion of Rome in Egypt, Syria, and Asia Minor has left very little beyond names and ruins. On the other hand, the exceedingly slow advance of new ideas and social changes among the Oriental races proves the strength of resistance possessed by barbarism entrenched behind the unchanging conditions of Asiatic existence. The only important ground in Asia recovered for centuries by civilization has been won in India by the English.

But although civilization has hitherto gone forward very slowly in Asia, the spread of European power is now clearing the ground for rapid movement upon a very extensive line of advance. Notwithstanding all risks and obstacles, the process of sweeping wide territories within new border-lines, under the form of protecting them, for reasons political, strategical, and commercial, is in constant use; the English, in particular, make almost annual additions to the ethnology of their empire. Undoubtedly an increasing border of territorial responsibilities must weigh on the minds of reflect-

THE GANESA TEMPLE AT TIRUVENAMALAI IN SOUTH ARKOT.

ive men in all times and countries. St. Augustine, looking out from his City of God over the still vast domain of Rome, debates the question whether it is fitting for good men to rejoice in the expansion of empires, even when the victors are more civilized than the vanquished, and the wars just and unprovoked. His conclusion is that to carry on war and extend rulership over subdued nations seems to bad men felicity, but to good men a necessity.

It is doubtful whether Englishmen can adopt a better conclusion. Continual expansion seems to have become part of their national habits and modes of growth. For good or for ill, England has become what she is in the world by the result of adventurous pioneering, by seeking her fortunes in the outlying regions of the earth, and by taking a vigorous part in the unending struggle out of which the settlement of the political world is evolved, as the material world is shaped out of the jarring forces of nature. It is this incessant opening of new markets, exploration of further countries, organization of fresh enterprises, the alternate contest with and pacification of rude tribes and unstable rulers, and the necessity of guarding her possessions and staving off her rivals that has caused, and is still causing, the steady enlargement of her borders.

Against an advance of this strength and magnitude the Asiatic nations have at present little power of resistance. The forces which in earlier times broke up the higher political organizations, and which thrust back the higher religion, no longer exist; neither the fighting power of Asia, nor her fanatic enthusiasm, is now in the least formidable to Europe. Not only is it certain that much of Asia lies at the mercy of the military power and resources of Europe, but in all the departments of thought and action she is still inferior. In these circumstances European progress is never likely to suffer another great repulse at the hands of Oriental reaction; and the English dominion, once firmly planted in Asia, is not likely to be shaken unless it is supplanted by a stronger European rival.

Henceforward the struggle will be, not between the Eastern and Western races, but between the great commercial and conquering nations of the West for predominance in Asia. From this contest England has now little to fear; and in the meantime she has undertaken the intellectual emancipation of the Indian people; she is changing the habits of thought, the religious ideas, and the moral level of the whole country. No one can as yet venture upon any prognostic of the course which the subtle and searching mind of India will mark out for itself amid the cross-currents of Eastern and Western influences. But we may be sure that the diffusion of knowledge and the changes of material environment are acting steadily on mental habits, and that future historians will have a second remarkable illustration of the force with which a powerful and highly organized civilization can mould the character and shape the destinies of many millions of people. And whatever may be the ultimate destiny of our Indian Empire, England will have conferred upon the Indians great and permanent benefits, and will have left for herself a good name in history.

INDEX

INDEX

A

Abd-ar-Rahman becomes Amir of Afghanistan under British protection, 443-444
Acts, two, passed by Parliament in 1773, 229
Aden, an important trade centre, 2
  British protectorate of, 474
Afghan War, first, 441
  Second, 442-444
Afghanistan, first English campaign in, 401
  Delimitation of, 445
  Political importance of, to Great Britain, 445-446
  Russian intrigues against, 439
  British protectorate, 481
  Why necessarily protected by England, 482-483
Ahmad Shah Abdali, Afghan leader, 170
  Seizes the Panjab, 77
  Invades Northern India, 192, 194
  Contest of, with the Sikhs, 269
  Death of, 269
Aix-la-Chapelle, Peace of, and the restoration of Madras, 107
Alexander Borgia, Pope, Bull of, dividing the undiscovered non-Christian world, 5
Alexandria an important trade centre for nearly eighteen centuries, 1
Aligarh captured by the English, 327
Ali Vardi Khan, Nawab of Bengal, 164
  Death of, in 1656, 164
Aliwal, battle of, 413
Amboyna massacre, 22
America, effect of the discovery of, on commerce, 4-5
Amherst, Lord, Governor-General of India, 389
Amiens, Peace of, 319, 324
Amir Khan besieges Jaipur, 378
  Disbands his army, 380
Anglo-Dutch alliance to drive the Spanish and Portuguese from the coast of India, 13
  Joint Stock Company, proposal for a, rejected, 13
  Treaty of 1619, 22
  War in India in 1651-1654, 29
  Alliance against Spain and Portugal in the beginning of the seventeenth century, 33
  Alliance against France in 1678, 38
Anglo-French alliance against Holland in 1672, 37, 38
  War on the Coromandel coast, 104
  Rupture in 1756 regarding the American Colonies, 106
Anglo-Portuguese alliance negotiated, 31
Anglo-Russian coalition against France, 355
Anglo-Spanish war of 1739, effect of, on France, 103
Arakan, annexation of, 390
Argaum, battle of, 327
Arkot (Arcot) seized by Clive, 119-120
Armenia, position of, historically analogous with that of modern Afghanistan, 483
Arras, battle at, 245
Asaf Jah, the first Nizam, death of, 115
Asia, competition for the trade of the southeastern countries of, 1
  Political situation in, at the present time, 450
  Powerless to resist European expansion, 496
Assam, kingdom of, 387-388
Assaye, battle of, 327
Auckland, Lord, Governor-General of India, 392
Augustine, St., on the expansion of empires, 495
Aurangzib, Emperor, accession of, 30
  Wars of, in Southern India, 48-49
  Compared with Louis XIV, 52-53
  Death of, in 1707, 75
  Civil war breaks out on the death of, 75-76

Austria and France, alliance of, 136
Ayub Khan unsuccessfully attempts to become Amir of Afghanistan, 443

B

Babar, Emperor, founds the Moghul Empire, 46, 161
  Memoirs of, 160-161
  Victory of, at Panipat, 161
Balaji Bala Rao, prime minister of the Maratha king, 174
Baluchistan made a British protectorate, 436, 480
Bantam blockaded by the Dutch, 30
  In the possession of the English, 35
  Key to Dutch control of pepper trade, 65
Barker, Sir Robert, 241
Barlow, Sir George, succeeds Cornwallis as Governor-General, 345
  Reactionary policy of, 346
Barrier-treaty of August, 1765, 201-202
Bassein occupied by the English, 245
  Treaty of, 321, 323, 329
Batavia, headquarters of the Dutch in the East, 65
Baxar, defeat of the Oudh vizir at, 188
Benares, insurrection of, 254-255
  Acquired by the English, 266
Bengal, value of the imports from, during the twenty years after the Restoration, 41
  English masters of, in 1758, 141, 176
  Native government of, in the beginning of the eighteenth century, 163-164
  Harbours of, 177
  Commerce and position of, 178-180
  Disputes between the English Company and the Nawab of, 182-183, 184
  Period of misrule in, 183
  Revenue in, 186, 221
  Famine in, 223
  Naval engagements in the Bay of, 257
Bentinck, Lord William, Governor-General of India, 392
  Makes English the official language of India, 392-394
  Abolishes suttee, 394-395
  Foreign policy of, 395
Bernier, François, quotations from, regarding the military and official classes in India, 47-48
  Writes of the strength of India, 162
Bhartpur, unsuccessful siege of, 330
  Taken by assault, 391
Bhotan, war with, 433
Bijapur destroyed by Aurangzib, 44, 54
Bombay, ceded to England in 1661, 31
  The headquarters of the English Company in 1685, 41
Boughton, a surgeon in the East India Company, made physician to the Emperor of Delhi, 23
Breda, treaty of, adjusting commercial disputes in Asia, 38
Buonaparte, scheme of Asiatic conquest of, 300-301
  Letter of, to Tippu, 304
Burgoyne, surrender of, at Saratoga, 247
Burke defends the East India Company, 228
  Attacks the East India Company, 275-276, 277-278
Burma, the kingdom of, 386
  First war with, 389
Burma, Upper, annexed by the British, 447-448
  Results of the annexation of, 486-487
Bussy at Haidarabad, 120
  Character of, 124
  Ordered to Pondicherri, 138-139
  Returns to India with reinforcements in 1783, 257

C

Cachar, Burmese inroads into, 389
Calcutta, the chief agency of the English in Bengal in 1687, 41
  English driven from, in 1756, 140
  Transfer of the headquarters of the English Company to, 176
  Reorganization of government in, and problems relating thereto, 231-234
Canning, Lord, Governor-General of India, 423
Cape of Good Hope, rounding of, largely affects commerce, 4-5
Cavagnari, Sir Louis, British envoy at Kabul, assassination of, 441
Ceylon seized by the Dutch, 30
  Held by the Dutch at the beginning of the eighteenth century, 71
  Taken from the Dutch, 302
Chanda Sahib murdered by the Marathas, 120
Channing, Lord, rule of, for determining succession in the native states, 428-429
Charles II, restoration of, 30
Child, Sir John, sent to India, 57-58
  Death of, in 1690, 59
Chilianwala, battle of, 418
China, as a rival of England, 486

Civilization, Asiatic, England's influence on, 494
Clive seizes Arcot, the capital of the Karnatic, 119-120
Expedition of, to recover Fort William, 140, 141
Letter of, to Pitt, predicting Lally's downfall, 145
Recovers Calcutta, 166
Returns to England, 183, 184
On the political situation in Bengal, 183
Return of, to India, 185, 198-199
Assumes the title of Diwan, 187
Accepts the Diwani of Bengal for the English Company, 199
Quotations from, regarding the political situation, 199, 200-201, 203
Receives a grant of the Five Circars (Sirkars) from the Moghul emperor, 211-212
Leaves India finally, 216
Evil effects of the departure of, soon felt in India, 223, 226
Arraignment of, 228-229
Death of, 229
Companies, chartered, systems of, for commercial expansion, 17
Rivalry of old and new East India, 66-67
nion of old and new English East India, 67-68
French and English, financial transactions of, 95-96
French and English, condition of, 96, 99
Methods of the French and English, compared, 112
French and English, exchange bitter recriminations from Madras and Pondicherri, 118-119
French and English, peace between, 123
Company, a new English East India, formed, 66
Colbert's East India, established in 1664, 86, 88
Colbert's West India, established in 1664, 86
Colbert's West India, charter of, revoked in 1674, 89
Company, Danish East India, extinguished in 1728, 90
Company, Dutch East India, privileges and power granted to, 12
Capital of, in 1618, 18-19
Strongly supported by the home government, 25-26
Terms of the charter of 1600 of the, 86
Company, English East India, first charter of the, in 1600, 9-10
In the East, unsupported by the home government, 24-25
Made responsible for all depredations of independent traders, 25
Given a new charter by Charles II, 30-31
Power granted to the, by the terms of the new charter, 32
Assumption of independent jurisdiction by the, in 1687, 42
War of the, against Aurangzib, in 1687, 45, 57-58
Instructions to the, regarding revenue, 56-57
Position of the, in India, in the last years of the seventeenth century, 57-59
Sends home for help against the French, 118
The real ruler of Bengal in 1767, 216
Necessity for State interference with the, 220
Assets of, in Bengal, in 1765, 221
Insolvency of, 224
Provincial regulations of, 453
Company, French East India, founded by Louis XIV, 33, 36-37
Terms of charter of, 87
Vicissitudes of, 91
Finances of, from 1735 to 1740, 92-93
Growth of the financial embarrassments of, 111-112
On the verge of insolvency in 1754, 134
Company, Ostend East India, chartered by the Emperor of Austria in 1722, and later suppressed, 90
Company, Universal East India, founded in 1602, in Holland, 12
Constantinople an important trade centre, 3-4
Taken by the Latins in 1204, 4
Decline of, 4
Cornwallis reaches India in 1786, 272
Governor-General and Commander-in-Chief in India, 281
Settlement by, of the land revenue of Bengal, 283
League of, against Tippu, 286-287, 294
Leaves India, 298, 302
Second governor-generalship of, 344
Pacific principles of, 344-345
Death of, 345
Coromandel coast, French and English at war on the, 104
Cuddalore, French outwitted by Lawrence at, 107
Surrendered to Tippu in 1782, 256, 257

D

D'Aché, French Admiral, character of, 142
  Fails to co-operate with Lally, 142
  Withdraws to the Isle of France, 143
Dalhousie, Lord, Governor-General of India, 418
Daulat Rao Sindhia, influence of, 308-309
Davenant, Sir Charles, on the East India trade conditions, 60-62
Delhi taken by Lake, 327
Dost Mohammad restored to power in Kabul, 404
Dover, secret treaty of, between the English and the French king, 39
Dow, extract from the history of Hindustan by, 203-204
Duff, Grant, author of a "History of the Marathas," 193
Dumas, an early governor of Pondicherri, 93
Dunkirk sold to France, 33
Dupleix appointed to the Governorship of Pondicherri in 1741, 93
  Schemes of territorial extension of, 101
  Violates the terms of the surrender of Madras, 106
  Defeats the Nawab of the Karnatic, 106
  Policy of, 107-108
  Motives of, in interfering with native politics, 116-117
  Recalled to France, 121
  Failure of the policy of, 121
  Death of, 123
  Characterization of, 129-131
Dutch-Spanish negotiations in regard to the Eastern trade, 11-12
Dutch and English quarrel in the East while they preserve the strictest amity at home, 12
  Exclude the English from the Spice Islands trade, 15
  At bitter war in the East, 21-22, 24-25, 29, 30
  Drive the English from the coast of Eastern Asia, 30
  Eastern position of, at the beginning of the eighteenth century, 90
  Defeated in Bengal by the English, 183

E

East Indies, meaning of the term in the seventeenth century, 14-15
Edward VII, durbar of, 464
Ellenborough, Lord, Governor-General of India, 403
  Determines to retire from Afghanistan, 403-404
  Recalled, 406
Elphinstone criticizes Dupleix, 125
Empress of India, title of, assumed by Victoria, 464
England and Holland combine against the Portuguese Asiatic settlements under Spanish rule, 8
  France and Holland allied against, in 1665, 33
  Possessions of, in Asia, 35
  Political reasons leading to the success of, in Asia, 36, 38
  Complications of the foreign relations of, 37
  Second war of, with Holland, in 1665, 38
  Third war of, with Holland, in 1672, 39-40
  Successful Eastern trade of, at the end of the seventeenth century, 60
  War of, with France, in South India, 72
  Declares war in Europe against France 100, 101
  Strength of the navy of, in 1755, 135
  Carries out Col. James Mill's scheme for conquering Bengal ten years after its inception, 163
  At war with France, Spain, Holland, and the American colonies, 259
  Confirmation by treaty of conquests of, in the East, 359-360
  Territory ruled by, in India, 383-384
  Why supreme in India, 493
  Control and influence of, beneficial to India, 497
English, defeat the Spanish Armada in 1588, 8
  Commerce in the East advanced by the hostilities between Holland and France, 40, 41
  Dominion in the East, reasons leading to, and history of, 63-74
  Alliance of the, with Nasir Jang and Mohammad Ali, 118
  Army, strength of, in India, in 1754, 131
  Dethrone Siraj-ad-daulah and set up another Nawab, 141
  Expel the French from Bengal, 141
  Reasons for the triumph of the, in India, 150-151
  Obtain a *farmān* in 1716 from the Moghul Emperor, 163
  Occupy Bengal, 176
  Seize all French settlements in India, 248

Fortunes of the, in India, waning in 1780, 251
Mysore, war of the, with, 287
League of the, with the Nizam and Peshwa against Mysore, 309-310
Treaty of peace of the, with Sindhia and the Nagpur Raja, 329
Expedition of the, to Afghanistan, 399
European competition for trade in the East, 17-18

F

Fleury, ministry of, 91
Fort St. David, futile expedition of the French against, 106
Fort St. George in the possession of the English, 35
Fox, East India Bill of, 274, 275, 277-279
Firozshah, battle of, 410, 413
France, wars of, in Europe, from 1690 to 1713, 53
Policy of, under Richelieu, 80
Reasons for the failure of, in India, 126, 150-151
Strength of navy of, in 1755, 135
French, under De la Haye sail to Ceylon and occupy the harbour of Trincomali, 37
Take possession of St. Thomé, near Madras, 37
Alliance of, with the Dutch, against England in 1666, 37, 38
Colonization, history of, 79-80, 83-102
Active in North America, 94
Allied with Muzaffar Jang and Chanda Sahib, 118
Army, strength of, in India, in 1754, 131
Expelled from Northern Sirkars, 142
Company in India dissolved in 1770, 147
Position at the peace of 1763, 147-148
Final expedition of the, against the English on the Indian coast in 1781, 153-155
Embassy to Persia, 352
French-Spanish treaty of 1598, 16-17
Friedland, battle of, 350

G

Gaikwar of Baroda, deposition of the, 430
Gandamak, treaty of, between England and Afghanistan, 440
Gawilgarh, fort of, captured by General Arthur Wellesley, 327
Genoa, rise of, as a trade centre, 4
George II makes a treaty of alliance with Frederick of Prussia, 136
Germanic States, alliance of, in 1691, 53
Ghazipur acquired by the English, 266
Goa, Portuguese garrison removed to, 21
Godeheu succeeds Dupleix at Pondicherri, 123
Golkonda destroyed by Aurangzib, 44, 54
Gujarat, Sikh army overthrown at, 417
Gurkhas (Gurkhalis), war of, with the English, 374-377
Gwalior, fortress of, taken by Captain Popham, 254

H

Haidarabad, Muzaffar Jang established as Nizam of, by the French, 119
Hyder Ali invades, 212
Decline of the State of, 295
Nizam of, transfers large districts to the English, 317-318
Hamont, M. Tibulle, the French biographer of Lally, 137
Hardinge, Sir Henry, Governor-General of India, 410
Hastings, Marquis of, Governor-General of India, 366
War of, with the Gurkhas, 374-377
Plans of, for the suppression of the freebooting hordes, 379
Hastings, Warren, first Governor-General in India, 237
Disputes of, with his Council, 234
Transactions of, against the Rohillas, 240-243
Treaty of, with the Marathas, in 1782, 254
Financial embarrassments of, 252, 253, 254, 255, 263
Resignation of, 258
Political intrepidity of, 261
Impeachment and trial of, 263-264
Burke's charges against, 278
High Courts of Judicature, establishment of, 455
Hindu Kush tribes come under British control, 445
Holkar, Jaswant Rao, attacked by Colonel Monson, 329-330
Signs a treaty with the English, 330
Dispersion of the troops of, 330
Policy of, 330
Army of, defeated at Mehidpur, 380
Holland, commercial ascendency of, in the East, 14
Increasing strength and pre-eminence of the Republic of, in the seventeenth century, 28, 29, 30
Decline of the naval power of, 71
War declared against, in 1674, by Louis XIV, 89
Hughes, naval engagements of, 256-257

Hugli River, English factory on, 23
Hyder Ali of Mysore, 208, 209
  Master of Mysore, 211
  Sends a large force into Haidarabad, 212
  At war with the English, 213
  Treaty of, with the English, 213, 214
  Vindictive spirit of, 249
  Triple alliance of, 251
  Ravages the Karnatic, 251, 252
  Death of, 257

I

Imports, Indian, value of, in England, in 1622, 19
India, awarded to Portugal by Pope Alexander Borgia, 5
  Civil war in, 30
  Inherent weakness of, 125
  General peace in, in 1784, 257-258
  Double government of, 279
  Passes to the Crown, 425-426
  Effect of the direct government of, assumed by the Crown, 456
  Within the sphere of European diplomacy, 490-491
  The only modern example of the evolution of an empire, 493
India Councils Act, passage of the, 455
India troops, European training of, 126
  Army components of, 170-171
Indian Succession Act, provisions of the, 459
Indies, meaning of the term, 86
Indo-Chinese dependency of the Indian Empire, formation of the, 468
Irrigation, effect of, on India, 463-464
Italy, commercial decline of, 6

J

Java, reduction of, 358
Jhansi, annexation of, 421

K

Kabul occupied by the English, 401
  Disastrous retreat of the English from, 403
  Russian envoy at, 439
  Afghans defeated at, 442
Kandahar occupied by the English, 401
Karikal acquired for France, 100
Karnatic, the, invaded by the Maratha chief Sivaji, 42
  War of succession in the, 99-100, 115-117
  Maratha invasion of the, in 1740, 100
  Incorporation of the, 314
Kasimbazar, factory of, seized by Siraj-ad-daulah, 165
Kharak, island of, occupied by the English, 398
Khiva subjugated by Russia, 438

L

Labourdonnais, Governor of Mauritius, prepares to attack the English, 103
  Besieges Madras, 104
  Thrown into the Bastile, 107
Lake, General, success of, in the northwest of India, 327
Lally, Count, instructions to, 137
  Character of, 139-140
  Expedition of, reaches India in 1758, 141
  Takes Fort St. David, 142
  Unpopularity of, 142, 143
  Besieges Madras, 143
  Attempts to recover Vandewash, but is defeated, 145
  Retreats to Pondicherri in 1760, 146
Laswari, battle of, 327-328
Lavaur, a Jesuit, whose intrigues in India hastened the downfall of Lally, 152
Law, criminal, reorganized in India, 456
Legislation, agrarian, 460-463
Leibnitz, in his "Consilium Aegyptiacum" urges Louis XIV to seize Egypt, and so command the trade of the East, 62
Lenoir, an early governor of Pondicherri, 93
Lhasa, British expedition to, 449
Lisbon, rise of, as a trade centre, 6
London merchants demand redress from the Dutch in 1611, 12
  Directors, letter from the, 210
Louis XIV, compared with Aurangzib, 52-53
  Declares war against Holland in 1674, 89
Louis XV, shortsighted policy of, 95-96
Lytton, Lord, appointed Viceroy of India, 439

M

Macassar in the possession of the English, 35
Macnaghten attempts to raise a standing army for Shah Shuja', 402-403
Madagascar, French expedition for colonization of, ends in disaster, 89
Madras, English Company settles at, 23
  The central post of the English Company in Eastern India in 1687, 41

Headquarters of the English Company, strongly fortified, 99
Besieged by Labourdonnais, 104
Surrendered to the French, 104
Restored to England by the French in return for Louisburg, 107
Siege of, raised by Lally, 144
War of, against Hyder Ali, 212
Treaty of, with the Nizam of Haidarabad, 212, 214
Mahadaji Sindhia, increasing power and territories of, 289
Death of, 289
Mahé acquired for France, 100
Taken by the English, 250
Maine, Sir Henry, takes charge of the Indian legislative department, 458
Manipur, captured by the Burmese, 389
Temporarily occupied by the English, 430
Maratha power, rise of, under the chief Sivaji, in 1660-1680, 42-43
Invasion of 1740, 100
Marathas, strength of, on the western side of India, 99
Rising power of the, 173-175, 237-239
Invade Upper India in 1758, 191-193
In the Karnatic, 213
Overthrown in Panipat, 237
Tactics of the, 238
Menace Rohilkhand, 238, 241
Strength and position of the, 246
French overtures to the, 247
New system of war tactics of the, 290-292
Invade Haidarabad, 302
Internal contests of, and flight of the Peshwa, 320-321
Marion, M., on French finance, 134-135
Martin, François, founder of Pondicherri, 92
Masulipatam, English Company settles at, 23
Taken by the English, 142
Mauritius, island of, occupied by the French, 91, 103
Reduction of, 258
Mazarin, policy of the French under, 83
Mekong River, British influence advances to, 487
Mill, James, on the success of England, 124
Scheme of, for conquering Bengal submitted to the Austrian emperor, 162
Minto, Lord, Governor-General of India, 349
Embassies from, 353-354
Mir Jafir proclaimed Nawab in place of Siraj-ad-daulah, 168
Deposed, 186
Restored in 1763, 187
Death of, 187
Mir Kasim ascends the throne, 186
Moghul Empire, rapid decline of the, 75, 76-78
Administrative system of the, 453
Mohammad Ali tacitly recognized as Nawab of the Karnatic, 123
Monson, Colonel, defeated by Holkar, 330
Montesquieu declares against emigration, 151
Morellet, Abbé, report of, concerning the finances of the French Company, 147
Mudki, battle of, 410
Münster, treaty of, in 1648, 23
Murshid Kuli Khan, Governor of Bengal, 164
Mutiny, political and legal reorganization after the, 452
Muzaffar Jang, accession of, 118, 119
Death of, 120
Mysore, a Hindu principality, 211
Partition of, 310
Reconstitution of native government in, 431

N

Nadir Shah, invasion of India by, 77
Death of, 77
Nagpur, outbreak at, 380
Annexation of, 421
Napier, Sir Charles, 404-406
Defeats Amirs of Sind at Miani, 405
Napoleon plans a Franco-Russian expedition to India, 351
Overthrow of, 355
Nasir Jang murdered by his mercenaries, 118
Native States, area, population, and administration of, since 1860, 429-430
Relation of, to the Indian Empire, 476-477
Navigation Law of Cromwell adopted by Charles II, 32
Nepal, war with, 374-377
A British protectorate, 486
Neutralization, why impossible in Asiatic statecraft, 482
Nimeguen, peace ratified at, in 1678, 40
Nizam of Haidarabad surrenders at Kurdla, 302, 307
Non-Regulation system, methods of, 454
North, Lord, 228, 229
Provisions of the Regulating Act of, 229-231

Northern India, strategic geography of, 188-190
Nott, General, holds Kandahar, 403

O

Ormuz, Persians and English combine to drive Portuguese from the island of, 20-21
Oudh, Vizir of, allies himself with the English, 198
Clive makes an alliance with, 200-201
Decline of the State of, 295
Vizir of, cedes all his frontier provinces to the English, 318-319
Annexation of, 422-423, 425
A barrier against the Marathas, 477

P

Palmyra, reasons leading to the destruction of, 3
Panipat, overthrow of the Marathas at, 194-197
Panjab, annexation of the, 417
Panjah, collision of Afghans and Russians at, 484
Paris, Peace of, in 1763, terminates the French rivalry in India, 155
Parliament inquires into the affairs of the East India Company, 221-222, 226, 274, 275
Acts of, 297
Parliamentary campaigns of 1783-1784, 278-279
Patna, massacre of English prisoners at, 187
Pegu, Anglo-Indian campaign against, 390
Annexation of, 419
Persia, negotiations with the Shah of, 396
Shah of, attacks Herat, 397, 398
Persians, overtures of, to Napoleon, 349-350
Peshwa at Poona attacks the British Residency, 380
Annexations attendant on the surrender of the, 381
Pitt, first Ministry of, 279
India Act of, passed, 279
Plassy, rout of, 167, 168, 169
Pollock, General, recaptures Kabul, 403
Pondicherri recovered by the Dutch in 1697, 73
The seat of the Governor-General of all the French settlements, 91
Founded by François Martin in 1674, 91-92
Strongly fortified, 99
Shelters the Mohammedan princes in 1740, 100
Fortified by Dupleix, 101
Besieged by the English, 107
Surrendered to the English in 1761, 147
Porto Novo, battle of, 252
Defeat of Hyder Ali at, 256
Portugal, activity of, in establishing her power in India, 5
Commercial activity of, crushed by her annexation to Spain in 1580, 6-7
Monopolizes Indian trade for a short time, 6-7
Decline of, 23
Eastern position of, at the beginning of the eighteenth century, 90
Protectorates, theory of the system of, 469-471
System of, adopted by other European nations in Asia and Africa, 489

R

Raghunath Rao, treaty of the English with, 244
Railways, effect of, in India, 463
Rajput States a barrier against the Marathas, 477
Ranjit Singh, the Panjab temporarily consolidated under the kingdom of, 197
Ruler of the Panjab, 391
Death of, 406
Red Sea, commercial navigation of the, important to the Roman emperors, 1-2
Richelieu, French colonizing companies under, 80, 83-86
Ripon, Lord, Governor-General of India, 443
Roe, Sir Thomas, embassy of, to the Great Mogul, 23
Rohilkhand annexed to Oudh, 243
Rohilla War, 241-243
Roman Catholic faith established in France, 80, 83, 85
Roman Empire, command of, over the main channels of Asiatic trade, 3
Rousseau on the influence of priestly ambition, 152
Rumbold, Sir Thomas, Governor of Madras, 251
Russia, march of, across Asia and influence on Persia, 396
Central Asian policy of, 437-440
Rival of England, 480, 482-483, 484-485
Ryswick, peace of, 40, 53

S

Salsette, the English anxious to acquire, 244
  Occupied by the English, 245
Sambaji, son of Sivaji, continues his father's revolt, 43
  Execution of, 45
Sandeman, Major, negotiates a treaty with the Khan of Baluchistan, 436
Satara, reconstitution of the State of, 381
  Annexation of, 421
Secretary of State for India in Council, creation of the office of, 455
Sepoy army, British, recruitment of, 171-172
Shah Alam grants the Five Circars (Sirkars) to Clive, 211-212
Shah Shuja', 401
  Exiled, 397
Shah Zaman invades the Panjab, 304
Sher Ali, Amir of Afghanistan, negotiations of, with Lords Mayo and Northbrooke, 438-439
Shore, Sir John, Governor-General, 302
  Refused to aid the Nizam of Haidarabad, 302, 303
Siam, relation of, to the British, 447
Siddhis, an independent Abyssinian colony, the only naval force on the Indian coast, 51
Sikh War, the first, 410
Sikhs, rapid expansion of the, 206, 268
  History of the, 269
  Internal anarchy among the, 406, 409
  Collisions of the, with the English, 410
  Barrier states against the, 477
Sikkim, war with Tibet over, 486
Sind, extent of conquests of, 253
  Amirs, territory of the, brought under British control, 404
  Fall of the dynasty of, 405
Sindhia occupies Agra and Delhi, 272
  League of, with the Nagpur Raja, 323-324
Siraj-ad-daulah succeeds Ali Vardi Khan as Nawab of Bengal, 164
  Attacks Calcutta, 140
  Driven out of Calcutta by the English, 141
  Routed at Plassy, 141
  Takes Calcutta, 165
  Death of, 168
Sivaji, a Maratha chief, death of, in 1680, 43
Sobraon, battle of, 413
Spain prohibits the exportation of her precious metals, 7
  Claims a monopoly of the trade in the East, 10-11
  Decline of, 33, 35
Spanish-Dutch negotiations in regard to the Eastern trade, 11-12
Spanish Flanders invaded by Louis XIV, 38
St. Helena granted to England, 32
St. Thomé in the possession of the French, 37
  Captured from the French by the Dutch, 37
Suffren, French Admiral, 154
  Naval engagements of, 256-257
  Sails for Europe, 257
Surat, battle at, 13
  English settle at, in 1612, 23
  Chief establishment of the English East India Company in 1638, 23
  In the possession of the English, 35
  Pillaged by Sivaji in 1664, 42

T

Tanjore, the English intervene at the banishment of a prince of, 114-115
  Fruitlessly raided by the French, 142
Temple, Sir William, negotiator of the Triple Alliance, 39
Tenasserim provinces, annexation of, 390
Thirty Years' War, 28
Tippu of Mysore, treaty of peace with, 257
  Sends embassies to Constantinople and Paris, 285
  Attacks Travancore, 286
  Signs a treaty of peace ceding territory to the English, 287
  Allied with the French, 304, 307
  Return of, from the Isle of France, 307
  Besieged in Seringapatam, 310
  Death of, 310
  Character of, 311-312
Trade routes, 3
  Security of, menaced, 3
Trade, value of Oriental, in 1615, 13
Treaty of 1673 between France, England, and Portugal against Holland, 39
Trinchinopoli, English send reinforcements to, 119
  French retire from, 120
Trincomali, harbour of, occupied by the French, 37
  Captured from the French by the Dutch, 37
  Captured from the Dutch by the English, 154
  Retaken by Suffren, 154-155

Triple Alliance formed by England, Holland, and Sweden against France in 1668, 37-38
Turkmantchai, treaty of, 396-397
Turks dominate the Red Sea and the Persian Gulf in the early part of the sixteenth century, 5-6

U

Umbeyla campaign, 431-432
Utrecht, peace of, in 1713, 41

V

Vandewash, Fort of, taken by the English, 144-145
Venice, rise of, as a trade centre, 4
Verelst, on the commerce of Bengal, 178
  Succeeds Lord Clive, 219
Versailles, Peace of, 155
Voltaire, leader of the anti-colonial party in France, 151

W

Walpole, ministry of, 91
Walpole, Spencer, citation from, 493
Watson, Admiral, 166
Wellesley, Arthur, 310-311
  Maratha campaigns of, 327
Wellesley, Lord, Governor-General, lands at Madras, 306
  Treaty of, with the Nizam, 309
  Conquest of Mysore by, 310
  System of subsidiary treaties of, 316
  Political system of, 323
  Offers to resign, 324
  Policy of, 331-334, 428
  Result of the rule of, 334-336, 339-340
  Critical estimate of the administration of, 340-342
Whig Ministry displaced in 1841, 403

Y

Yakub Khan becomes Amir of Afghanistan, 440

Published by

Facsimile Publisher
Ashok Vihar, Delhi-110052 (India)
Website: www.facsimilepublisher.com

Distributed by

Gyan Books Pvt. Ltd.
5, Ansari Road, Daryaganj, New Delhi-110002 (India)
E-mail: books@gyanbooks.com, Website: www.gyanbooks.com

8 888000 714590